No Place for the Weary Kind:
WOMEN OF THE SMOKIES

Courtney Lix

With best Smoky Mountain wishes!

Courtney Lix

© 2016 Great Smoky Mountains Association

9 8 7 6 5 4 3 2 1

ISBN 978-0-937207-82-6

Published in the USA by Great Smoky Mountains Association,
a nonprofit organization. All purchases benefit the park.
Printed in Korea.
Great Smoky Mountains Association is a private, nonprofit organization which supports the
educational, scientific, and historical programs of Great Smoky Mountains National Park.
Our publications are an educational service intended to enhance the public's understanding
and enjoyment of the national park. If you would like to know more about
our publications, memberships, guided hikes and other projects, please contact:

Great Smoky Mountains Association
P. O. Box 130
Gatlinburg, TN 37738
(865) 436-7318
www.SmokiesInformation.org

Edited by Steve Kemp and Kent Cave
Book design by Lisa Horstman
Editorial assistance by Claire Ballentine and Julie Brown

Song lyric "No Place for the Weary Kind" used in the title of this book is by permission of Ryan
Bingham from his song "The Weary Kind" from the movie Crazy Heart.
Great Smoky Mountains Association is grateful to Mr. Bingham for his generosity
to the Smokies and enduring contributions to authentic American music.

Illustrations by Lisa Horstman

Photo credits:
Lydia Kear Whaley, p. 11: NPS
Lizzie Caldwell, p. 27: Caldwell family archives
Dora Cope, p 43: Florence Cope Bush
Ella Costner, pp. 60, 61: Costner family archives
Phyllis Higgenbotham, p 83: The University of Tennessee Libraries
Marjorie Chalmers, p. 83: The University of Tennessee Libraries
Ila Hatter, p. 105: Holly Kays, Smoky Mountain News
Maya Treanor Avent, pp. 120, 121: Walter Nance, Mayna Avent Nance
Olive Tilford Dargan, p. 135: North Carolina Collection,
Pack Memorial Library, Asheville, N. C.
Lottie Queen Stamper, p. 145: Museum of the Cherokee;
Hunter Library Digital Collections
Wilma Dykeman, p. 161: Jim Stokely III
Amanda Swimmer, p. 171: Elizabeth Deramus
Dolly Parton, pp. 188, 189: Dollywood; back cover: David McClister
Laura Thornburgh, pp. 206, 207: NPS
Anne Broome, p. 225: NPS, William H. Hart
Margaret Stevenson, p. 253: Margie Ribble
Gracie McNicol, p. 253: from Gracie and the Mountain by Emilie Powell, Overmountain Press
Karen Wade, p. 269: NPS

For my parents
who encouraged my love of words, and woods

Table of Contents

Preface

As a kid, I was a wild mountain girl. I liked to disappear into the woods around my house for hours. Sometimes I'd take a book and a snack, but usually I'd just wander, watching for birds, foxes, snakes, or fish. I'd study the paw prints left in the banks along the creek—muskrat? Raccoon? After a heart-pumping, pathless climb up to the high ridge, I could scramble over a sagging barbed wire fence and emerge into a field of grass and buttercups. To this day, there is no smell I love more than the earthy sweetness of fallen leaves, which stirs memories of wandering through the mountains.

I suffered for my adventures. It seemed I was constantly afflicted by poison ivy, chiggers, or ticks—and at the right (or wrong) time of year, some combination of all three. But it was always worth it—exploring the mountains was in my blood. To me, that's what it means to be a woman of the Smokies: to feel a kinship with the land, to draw inspiration, possibility, and purpose from the mountains.

Researching and writing this book sometimes felt like roaming those childhood forests, fields, and streams again. I was making a path where one didn't exist previously, weaving a narrative from myriad books, articles, conversations, and scraps of history. I originally wrote two of the chapters in this book, Laura Thornburgh and Mayna Avent, for *Smokies Life Magazine*. From those two loosely connected points, my editor, Steve Kemp, asked if I would write a book about "Women of the Smokies." When I agreed, I never dreamed that, years later, this book would contain profiles of 19 remarkable women.

Sometimes the going was easier than others. I owe a great debt to writers before me who interviewed, wrote about, and saved the stories of some of the women in this book, including Emilie Ervin Powell, who wrote *Gracie and the Mountain*, and Hattie Caldwell Davis, who has preserved much of Cataloochee's history in *Reflections of Cataloochee Valley*, and other books. Also, Florence Cope Bush, who wrote about her mother Dora in *Dorie: Woman of the Mountains*, and Anna Fariello, professor at Western Carolina University whose research informed much of my chapter on Lottie Stamper.

There are, of course, countless noteworthy women whose lives have been touched by the mountains. But a book is a finite thing, which necessitated making some choices. I worked with a few general criteria: first, I wanted to be able to write about each woman in substantial detail. This eliminated quite a few intriguing characters who have very little presence in the historical record, or whose descendants proved too difficult to find. Second, I focused on a narrow geographic range—women who lived as close to the land within or around Great Smoky Mountains National Park as possible. I attempted to balance profiles of North Carolina and Tennessee women, as the park itself encompasses both states. Finally, I wanted to write about a diverse group of women—farmers, writers, artists, hikers—to highlight just how different women of the mountains can be from each other. This gave rise to organizing the book into its three main parts: women whose livelihoods were tied to the resources provided directly by mountains, women who supported themselves as artists, drawing inspiration from the mountains for their work, and women whose connection to the mountains was brought about by the national park and fostered by its hiking trails and breathtaking scenery.

But in one very significant way, the women are all the same: I was constantly impressed by their independence, however different the rest of their lives might have been from each other. Some were independent in their self-sufficiency: everything from food to clothing to cabin made by hand. Others were independent in their pursuit of artistic goals: a painting career when everyone knew women couldn't be artists; becoming a singer-songwriter of unsurpassed success, despite an impoverished childhood. Others loved the mountains in a very simple, direct way: by spending time in them, hiking trails, often on their own, learning about the plants and animals that call the Smokies home.

The acknowledgments contain a much longer list of people who played a role in helping me with this book, but I want to mention a few outsized supporters here: my parents who have encouraged my writing ambitions for decades; my editor Steve, for the opportunity to get to know the amazing lives of these women, and for his patience with my glacial writing speed and perfectionistic tendencies; and Christopher, who met and fell in love with me over the years that it's taken to write this book, and whose comments vastly improved the manuscript.

And finally, for every woman profiled in this book, there are dozens more with exciting, fascinating life stories—if you know such a woman, I hope you are inspired to interview her, write about her, and share her story.

Introduction

Miles away from the crowds that swarm the parking lot at New-found Gap, The Boulevard Trail is sometimes only six inches wide, a ribbon of rocks hemmed in by wild grasses, moss, spruce, and mountain-ash trees. Here, so close to the top of Mount Le Conte, the third highest mountain in the Smokies, the air is perfumed by ever-greens. The shrill call of a red squirrel, which locals call a boomer, might pierce the silence as the rust-colored, black-eyed critter dances in the boughs above the trail.

On a clear day, The Boulevard revives the spirits of tired hikers with breathtaking views; blue silhouettes of mountains, too many to count, extend to the horizon. The distance conveys a sense of peace, and of stoicism. These mountains are some of the oldest on earth, silent witnesses to changes over thousands of years. Human history in the mountains is much shorter, but has still wrought significant change. The past 200 years have transformed the mountains them-selves, and the lives of people, native and newcomer, who call them home. This is the larger backdrop against which the nineteen women in this book lived (or live), searched for happiness, and left their leg-acies—the context for their individual stories.

The Great Smoky Mountains were once Cherokee hunting lands. Black bears rambled from groves of oak trees to patches of blue and raspberries. Brook trout crowded the deep pools of clear streams. The cry of a mountain lion would send shivers down even the bravest hunter's spine. The Cherokee lived on farms and in towns in the fertile lower valleys of the mountains they called simply "blue," and hunting parties occasionally ventured deep into the woods. Contrary to modern misconceptions, the Cherokee built log homes, not teepees. Men hunted and farmed; women helped with farming and largely took care of the rest: cooking, making clothes, raising children, cleaning, making bedding, and more. Women also became the weavers and potters of Cherokee culture, largely because the vessels were used for storing and cooking food. Designs and techniques for this craftwork were passed down through families, as reputations for artisanship developed.

The European-American settlers, who began arriving in the mountains during the late 1700s, lived much the same way the Cherokee had: clearing the forest for small farmsteads that produced food for their families and a little extra to sell, augmented with whatever wild plants and animals they could hunt or harvest.

The region was so isolated and sparsely populated that doctors were nearly nonexistent—there weren't enough patients to run a successful practice. Instead, people carefully cultivated herb gardens and used what was growing in the mountains around them for medicine. Particularly skilled women became known as midwives, called on at all hours to help birth babies and prepare the dead for burial.

Life was difficult in such wild country, forcing families to focus on the basic questions of survival: would the crops produce enough food for two parents, a grandparent, and eight children? Would the handmade quilts stuffed with rags and sleeping pallets filled with cornhusks keep everyone warm enough in winter? Would a hot onion poultice cure the baby's cough?

The middle decades of the 1800s would affect life in the mountains in sweeping ways. Congress passed the Indian Removal Act in 1830. Most of the Cherokee were forced West to Oklahoma on the Trail of Tears. Thousands died in the inhumane conditions of the relocation. In the Smokies, a few hundred Cherokee successfully remained in their homeland, now known as the Eastern Band of Cherokee Indians.

In the 1860s, the Civil War brought a second wave of terror and heartbreak. As with much of the country, middle-aged and young men joined the army—both Union and Confederate—and left women, children, and elders to maintain the farms. Being in the mountains was a blessing and a curse: hiking the mountains today—the heart-pumping steepness, the difficulty of navigating even on a well-maintained trail—brings an appreciation for the difficulties large armies would have faced. The slopes are too steep for hauling cannons or even riding horses in some places, which spared many mountain communities from witnessing battles. Instead, they lived in fear of being robbed or killed by deserters or vigilantes who also benefitted from the absence of soldiers. Stories of women's desperation and ingenuity during the war—hiding heirlooms in hollow logs; secreting jars of preserves and hams under floorboards; defending their farms with rifles—have become treasured family lore.

As survivors of the Civil War rebuilt slowly, refocusing on earning a living again from farming and hunting, another change was brewing: the logging industry had discovered the southern Appalachians. Advancements in railroad and train technology meant that the vibrant, primordial mountain forests were now ripe for harvesting. The peak of logging in the Smokies took place from the early 1900s until the Great Depression.

Logging work transformed the mountains, culturally and ecologically. Timber companies set up camps for their employees to be close to their work. These company-sponsored communities soon grew to include schools and churches to make the temporary towns more welcoming to families. While this new way of life came with certain advantages, like better access to education, it untethered many mountain families from their farms and traditionally self-sufficient lifestyles. Logging companies also paid in cash, adding to the importance of currency in what had previously been a largely barter economy. Women's roles in society began to shift: with no farmland, there were no farm chores to do. Instead, young women made clothes from store-bought cloth—sometimes using sewing machines. They could earn money by running boarding houses for loggers, cooking for them, and doing laundry.

Introduction

Most logging employment was seasonal, however, and some mountain families traveled to the Carolinas to work in the cotton mills, while others moved back in with older relatives who still tried to earn a living from farming. Everyone felt the tumult of the Great Depression, but families with farms found some measure of self-sufficiency in being able to grow most of their own food and make their own clothes.

Industry wasn't the only change that arrived in the mountains in the 1900s. The mountain communities would continue to be perceived as remote and backwards for decades to come, but more networks of roads were being built, and outside forces continued to influence traditional ways of life. One of the most consequential changes was brought about by the women of the Pi Beta Phi fraternity; with support from the community of Gatlinburg, they established a nondenominational elementary and high school in 1912. Over the years, they expanded their work to agricultural training, renewed interest in traditional arts and crafts, and created a community health center.

Amidst the fits and starts of cultural modernization, the land was changed too. Many of the timbered mountain slopes became unrecognizable from what they'd been a couple of decades earlier. The steep mountainsides were cut bare, leaving loose rock and dirt. This would wash into creeks, rivers, and streams during storms, creating such silt-choked water that nearly all aquatic life was killed. If the mountains got too dry, the opposite problem occurred: a spark or ember from railroad work could cause devastating forest fires. Some people began to worry that a priceless, unique part of the American landscape was being destroyed forever.

Hikers, tourism boosters, automobile enthusiasts, and environmentalists began to pursue the quixotic dream of a national park in the Smokies. They overcame myriad political obstacles, fundraising issues, and lawsuits, ultimately triumphing in the establishment of Great Smoky Mountains National Park in 1934. The national park brought new opportunities and required great sacrifices. Communities within the national park boundary were dismantled, neighbors separated and scattered. Tourism-related work, like running hotels, making candy, crafts making, and offering guide services, began to replace farming and logging as the dominant occupations.

And as the decades passed, the physical scars of logging became less obvious—although perhaps not to those first mountain settlers, if they could see the land today. Hemlock trees once again grew tall and shaded the banks of clear, rocky creeks. Fish began to thrive in the rivers, no longer regularly choked with runoff from denuded slopes. Tuliptrees, maples, and oaks sprouted in pastures that had once produced rows of corn. Black bear, deer, and wild turkey found food and shelter in these second-growth forests.

Today, the National Park Service maintains a network of 800 miles of trail along, around, and between the mountain peaks. People from all over the world visit regularly to marvel at flowers, sunsets, fall colors, and the experience of being in the mountains.

From relying on the mountains for physical survival, to artistic inspiration, to rejuvenation of the soul, the women whose stories appear in this book offer a glimpse into the long and complicated history of this unique place. They are women for whom making a life in the mountains has countless meanings, each as different and varied as the mountains themselves.

Part I: No Place for a Weary Woman

Making a Life in the Smokies

Chapter 1

Lydia Kear Whaley

FROM EARLY DAWN UNTIL DARK SHE TENDED HER CROP, TOOK HER OWN CORN TO MILL, MADE SHOES FOR HER CHILDREN... AND OFTEN FOR THE SUM OF $1.00 EACH, MADE COATS BY HAND IN ORDER TO PAY THE TAXES ON HER LAND.

LYDIA KEAR WHALEY · 1840–1926

—Agnes Wright Spring, "Thirty Years on Little Pigeon," The Arrow of Pi Beta Phi, December 1941

Lydia Kear Whaley

The year 1864 was particularly difficult for people living in the Great Smoky Mountains. Three long years into the Civil War, the men were mostly off fighting, or dead. The women and older family members they left behind had maintained the crops and livestock as well as they could, but food was scarce. What little anyone had left was increasingly vulnerable to raiding parties of lawless vagabonds and desperate soldiers.

Lydia Kear Whaley was twenty-four. As a child she'd been described as "high-spirited" with a penchant for satin and hair bows, but in 1864, she grew up quickly. She was pregnant with her third child when her son Perry, not yet four, died in August. Less than a month later, her husband John, a self-enlisted Private in the Union Army, was dead as well. Lydia was left to raise their one-year-old daughter, Isabelle, and their unborn child.

Much has been written about the strength and self-reliance of mountaineers, but the life Lydia built from loss and hardship as a young mother exemplifies the toughness required to flourish in the Great Smoky Mountains in the mid-1800s. Not only did she take care of her family, she went on to later earn the title of "Aunt Liddy"— "aunt" being a title given only to the most respected, influential women in the mountain communities. Both locals and newcomers to the mountains sought her advice, on everything from birthing babies and curing colds, to increasing mountain children's access to education. Lydia was steeped in the traditional ways of the mountains, but she shrewdly saw the ways to a better future for her community and worked to make them reality.

In 1850, when Lydia was ten, her parents Joel Kear, a first-generation Scottish-American, and Sarah Huff, the daughter of Irish immigrants, moved from flatter Tennessee land to a new farm in the Sugarlands community a few miles outside of present-day Gatlinburg. The first European-American settlers had arrived in the Tennessee mountains fewer than fifty years earlier, and wilderness dwarfed their meager farmsteads. The trees were so large that farmers didn't always bother with cutting them down—instead they hacked a ring of bark away, deep enough to begin to kill the tree, a process known as "girdling," then cut it up when it fell. Gradually, fields took shape from days of hard labor. When the family moved, Lydia was the second oldest of eight children; by 1854, two more brothers had joined the brood, making the total number of Kear children an even ten: five boys and five girls.

Like many people in the mountains, Joel Kear could read the Bible, but didn't have much education beyond that. Unlike many people in the rural community, he valued "book learning" for his children—rare in a time when offspring were mostly seen as free farm labor. Shrewd man that he was, Joel offered to let the county build a new schoolhouse on his land for free. Consequently, his children didn't have to spend as much time walking back and forth to school—and were better able to attend to their farm chores without sacrificing education.

Smart, talented Lydia married bold, outspoken John Brabson Whaley on February 9, 1860, when the country was on the brink of the Civil War. A tough young man two years Lydia's junior, John had a reputation as a rowdy bear hunter, and carried his head turned slightly to the side as the result of a broken neck that had somehow healed without paralysis. He was a blacksmith, and perhaps because his work involved hefting heavy iron and sweating in front of a blazing fire for hours, he was drawn to the hotbed of local politics, which became increasingly keen in the mountains during the war.

Although Tennessee officially joined the Confederacy in 1861, many East Tennesseans maintained their loyalty to the Union, including John Whaley. He enlisted in the Union Army, along with hundreds of other young men from the mountains who risked their lives to travel to Kentucky where they could sign up. In 1862, Confederate Major General Edmund Kirby Smith summed up these East Tennessee pro-union sentiments with, "No one can conceive the actual condition of East Tennessee, disloyal to the core, it is more dangerous and difficult to operate in than the country of the acknowledged enemy...."

For years, John had been an outspoken critic of slavery, and vigorously opposed the "rabble from West Tennessee" trying to take over control in Union-sympathetic Sevierville and Gatlinburg. On

September 5, 1864, he tried to rescue a wounded Union soldier from being taken hostage by Confederates near Fort Harry's Ford, not far from today's Chimney Tops trailhead. He was killed in the confrontation, and his body was later brought down to be buried in the main Gatlinburg cemetery. With no end to the war yet in sight, Lydia found herself on her own to raise baby Isabelle, with another child yet to be born. She became tough, and resourceful.

Later in life, Lydia would tell stories of the hardships of the Civil War to visitors, recounted here by Martha Rawlings in 1956:

"[W]e used to come up to old Aunt Lydia's little old log cabin and sit on the porch. And we'd bring her an apple or bring her some candy or something and we'd sit out on the porch and she'd tell us about her life when the war was going on and how they'd hide their meat in the loft, and she even took up the puncheons in the floor to show us where she hid her potatoes and showed us everything she'd hide and how [the soldiers would] come in and they'd take their horses out of the barn and take em with em...and how [she] took the cow up on this mountain and hid her away so [the soldiers] couldn't find her... what a hard time they had a living...."

After the war, the federal government eventually began sending Lydia a pension of eight dollars a month as compensation for John's death. It took five or six years to get the paperwork for the payments straightened out, but when the money finally came, it alleviated some of the financial worries of raising her daughters Isabelle and Larinda, and keeping her farm. She never remarried.

Her cabin and farm were nestled into the steep slope of Ski Mountain, close to modern day Gatlinburg's Chalet Village. The nearby creek had been known as "Holly Branch" because of the evergreen trees that grew in abundance around it, but Lydia insisted it be called "Holy Branch"—"it seemed more fittin'" she supposedly claimed— and her preference has endured.

In addition to maintaining a vegetable garden, she grew her own corn and cotton, raised sheep, chickens, and cows, and kept a beehive beneath the large apple tree behind her cabin. To protect her face and hands from stings, she devised custom beekeeping gear: the bee bonnet covered her entire head and neck; to cover her face she wove a shield from horsetail hairs which she fastened to a round hoop and sewed onto the front of the bonnet. She also wore specially knotted gloves, thick and tough enough to thwart stings.

A decent shot with a rifle as well, she hunted wild game for her family, an undertaking traditionally seen as men's work. In her later years, her son-in-law John Vesley Huskey carved her a cider trough where she mashed the fruit from her apple tree and fermented it into apple cider vinegar, although the fresh cider was drinkable too. She farmed according to the *Farmer's Almanac*, and believed that certain signs in nature would indicate the coming weather. In particular, she held that the weather from Christmas to New Year's Day would set the pattern for the following year, with each half day representing a month.

Her cabin never had electricity; instead, small brass lamps, each about the size of a teacup, sat on the mantle and burned kerosene. A single stone fireplace served as stove and oven, and heated the entire cabin. To bake, she would use a deep, cast iron Dutch oven strategically set in front of the fire; for frying she would place a skillet over the front coals of the fire. The two store-bought items she purchased regularly were sugar and coffee.

In addition to tending the farm, Lydia ran a side business as a tailor—she made suits by hand. To start, she would shear her own sheep, card the wool and spin it into yarn. She would then weave the cloth and dye it from roots and bark. Her mother had taught her how to identify different kinds of trees and herbs, and which combinations would keep the color from fading. Black walnut bark in particular yielded a rich brown color. She sold these completely handmade suits for a dollar, the equivalent of approximately two hundred dollars in today's economy. She wove linen as well, but instead of dyeing it, she would leave the naturally dark cream-colored cloth out in the sun to bleach to white. And to round out an outfit, particularly for her daughters, she'd hand make leather shoes with a wooden shoe mold and a specially designed cobbler's hammer.

She was also a medicine woman, often known as a "grannywoman" in mountain communities. Legend has it that one morning while collecting eggs from her hen house, Lydia was bitten by a copperhead snake. Copperheads are known to have an extremely painful, sometimes fatal bite—but Lydia treated and cured the wound herself. This in part contributed to her reputation as a healer in the rural community. Trained doctors were scarce in the mountains until the latter part of the 20th century. It was too hard to travel, too difficult to ship in supplies, and not worth the trouble for doctors to keep regular contact with rural patients. It didn't help matters that the mountaineers often distrusted these strangers, preferring instead to seek aid from medicine women within the community. Like Lydia, these women were known for their knowledge of herbs, their steady hands, and nerves of steel. They had to be prepared to rush away from their own work at only a moment's notice—whether to deliver a baby or extract a bullet from a hunting accident. Lydia had an oblong "doctor bag" made of coated fabric to protect it from the elements, with a metal clasp and handle, to easily transport her "doctoring" things.

In the mid 1920s, Smoky Mountain journalist Laura Thornburgh interviewed Lydia several times, and reported this conversation in her book *The Great Smoky Mountains:* Lydia said, "…hit's a fact, thar's a lot of things growin' wild that's good for folks, if they only knowed it. Take pennyrile—that little green weedy thing with teeny weeny leaves that grows in the field—hit makes good tea for colds, an' so does mullein, an' catnip—not all together, but what ye can git handiest." She also showed Laura a bottle of medicine from the doctor and explained, "He charged me twenty-two dollars for it….. But I larn't to make it and I'm goin' to tell pore folks how to git it free."

She brewed common medicines like yellowroot tonic, used to cure mouth sores and stomach ulcers and settle nerves, and boneset tea, for reducing a fever. Many traditional treatments involved swallowing drops of turpentine or kerosene, albeit with a spoonful of sugar. Moonshine was often used as a disinfectant, anesthesia, and ingredient in tonics and teas. Among other things, Lydia kept a flour sack filled with dried rosemary collected "in September, or August, soon's ye see the little blue flowers" and a "piece 'o pine" in the cabin, which was a large piece of green kindling, so she would have easy access to the pine resin for her medicines.

Although Lydia was well versed in the extensive native herbal and medicinal knowledge, she had a "doctor book" too. In the late 1800s, thick compendiums of the latest medical knowledge, with titles like *The Practical Home Physician* and *Encyclopedia of Medicine*, became popular with doctors, and Lydia got her hands on one of them as well. She would consult the book if someone came to see her with an affliction she didn't recognize.

The life, death, and joys found in the mountains also gave Lydia a powerful sense of the presence of the Lord. Church was central to the small communities in the mountains, and faith and prayer were guiding forces in Lydia's life. When her father passed away in 1871, she inherited his Bible, one of the few possessions her father's father had brought to America from Scotland. She could quote countless biblical passages from memory, but also spent time reading the book itself diligently—studying, memorizing, and reflecting on the power of the words. Her conviction in the Lord, and belief in the power of guidance and help from the Divine, gave rise to her reputation as a "preacher woman," in addition to her other talents.

In 1908 Lydia began exchanging letters with women of the Pi Beta Phi fraternity (founded before the use of the word "sorority" became standard) about the possibility of a new elementary school in rural Tennessee. After nearly two years of correspondence with Lydia, in October 1910, Dr. May Lansfield Keller arrived by train via the Smoky Mountain Railroad to see firsthand where they might build a school to provide better access to education for mountain children. Charlie Ogle met Dr. Keller with his buggy in Sevierville and took her via bumpy, winding mountain roads to Lydia's house, where she stayed while assessing whether or not a school might be feasible (and desirable) in Gatlinburg. Dr. Keller, who would go on to become Dean of Westhampton College in Virginia, later praised Lydia as being "one of the most dynamic thinkers I have ever been in contact with."

The Pi Beta Phi Elementary School in Gatlinburg opened its doors in 1912. But that was not the end of Lydia's collaboration with the Pi

Beta Phi women. As the Pi Phi teachers who came to Gatlinburg in those early years became more familiar with the locals, they realized that even as the children were becoming more "book-educated," the area's great traditions of weaving, basketry, and other handmade crafts were being forgotten. With all of the backbreaking, time-consuming work that running a farm and raising a family entailed for mountain women, buying certain necessities in the store instead of making them seemed like a great timesaver to the younger generations.

To prevent this loss of traditional knowledge, the Pi Phis decided to create an economic incentive for making crafts. But someone had to teach. Even though Lydia was in her early seventies, she agreed to become the handicraft school's first basket-weaving instructor. Her father had taught her how to make baskets and she'd become well known for a design that had been in her father's family for three generations. Woven from willow bark that Lydia prepared herself, each basket was an impressive work of art. The distinctive style produced an oval basket with a single handle. It was sometimes referred to as a "melon" basket, because the bottom weaving cinched a little in the middle, making it seem as if the basket had been shaped around two melons placed side by side. Once the basket was finished, she would occasionally add decoration with paint, though most were left plain.

She also taught dozens of women and girls the traditional arts of spinning and weaving, demonstrating how to use a loom, spinning wheel, cards, and a heckle reel. From linen and wool she and her students fashioned towels, scarfs, and bedspreads. The handmade items were bought and promoted by fraternity sisters around the country, thus establishing a "handicrafts industry" which had the added benefit of providing a little income for mountain women, along with the preservation of a unique style of practical arts and crafts.

The mountain handicrafts industry got another boost in the 1920s as tourism began increasing in the Smokies. Visitors to Gatlinburg eagerly paid guides for the opportunity to meet "authentic mountaineers" like Lydia. She received guests to her cabin graciously, for the most part, although it was said that she became a little eccentric in her old age. Agnes Wright Spring, a Pi Beta Phi teacher, reported that "Her first question to all women visitors was: 'Be ye married' If the answer were in the negative, she would say: 'Why ben't ye? Ye be old enough." Sometimes a hiking party would catch her being a little grouchy, perhaps because she received so many visitors, but she was always kind to children. "Divorce, bobbed hair, and knickers are the most outstanding evils of modern society," she told a newspaper reporter, when she was in her late 80s.

With no stores yet established to hawk trinkets or postcards, tourists often asked to buy items in the mountaineers' cabins as souvenirs. This was one of the only ways they could get proper mementos of their hikes into the mountains. While Lydia was willing to sell anything that could be easily replaced, she repeatedly refused to part with her spinning wheel, candle mold, and her brass candlesticks—but she would sell her baskets. In her lifetime, she sold over 5,000 baskets and used the profits to buy a mountain farm for each of her daughters. Clarence Darrow, who defended John T. Scopes in the famous July 1925 Scopes Monkey Trial, is rumored to have bought her entire stock of baskets when he visited her cabin and left orders for others to be sent to his Chicago home. An "Aunt Lydia" basket came up for auction in Knoxville in 2008—it was estimated to sell for between $175 and $225—but the winning bid was $880.

Darrow's visit came about a year before Lydia's health began to decline. She had several bouts of heart-related illness which doctors expected would kill her. She recovered at least once, with the help of one of her homebrewed tonics involving anvil dust, star root, and sourwood leaves boiled together. "They didn't think I'd ever get up out o' bed, but I fooled 'em," she explained to journalist Laura Thornburg. "I cured myself of that thar dropsy with herb medicine." But Laura wrote that Lydia was "frail," still, "with white hair and eyes much younger than her face."

As the dark, cold bleakness of winter settled over the mountains in 1926, Lydia passed away on December 4. Her hands, which had created so much in her lifetime—from baskets to blankets to safely guiding babies into the world—were finally at rest. She was buried next to her husband John in the Gatlinburg cemetery.

From 1931 until 1961, some of Lydia's possessions—her eyeglasses and case, doctor bag, chairs, baskets, metal bucket—were displayed at Mrs. Edna Lynn Simms' Mountaineer Museum in Gatlinburg. Mrs. Simms was a freelance journalist and reporter from Knoxville who had fallen in love with the culture of the mountains. With Mrs. Simms' death in 1961, the museum collection was donated to Berea College in Kentucky and now forms the core of their Appalachian Studies Teaching Collection. It is a long-reaching legacy for a tough, generous mountain woman whose myriad talents and strong sense of independence distinguished her life in the Smokies.

Chapter 2
Mary Elizabeth "Lizzie" Caldwell

LIZZIE CALDWELL · 1855–1937

—*Lizzie Caldwell, to Granddaughter Hattie Caldwell, recounted in* Recollections of Cataloochee Valley and its Vanished People in the Great Smoky Mountains.

Lizzie Caldwell

Snow swirled around the horse-drawn buggy as Methodist preacher T.A. Groce and his seven-year-old son made their way through the mountains, clattering over the winding road, "rocky, rocky, rocky all the way," as he would later remember. It was the first Saturday of November in 1909, and the circuit-riding preacher and boy pulled the buffalo lap robe tight around them as the hours and miles dragged by. The clatter of hooves on rocks echoed harshly in the snowy stillness of the forest as they made their fifteen-mile pilgrimage from Hemphill to the community of Cataloochee, deep in the Great Smoky Mountains. Preacher Groce was newly arrived from South Carolina, traveling for the first time to the handful of rural North Carolina communities where he would give monthly sermons.

Once they reached Cataloochee, they'd been instructed to stay with Hiram Caldwell and his wife, Mary Elizabeth, whom everyone called Lizzie: "if you don't, [Hiram] won't come to church the whole time you are there," their host in Hemphill had warned them. After four hours of riding in the cold, the travelers caught sight of a large white house in the fading light. The barn was nearer to the road and they stopped there first to talk with the tall, mustachioed man who was feeding his animals and settling them in for the night. He turned out to be their host, Hiram Caldwell. He directed them on to the house where Lizzie was waiting to greet them. While she looked stern at first glance, her dark hair pulled back into a tight bun and her dress made from dark cloth with long sleeves and a high collar, her eyes twinkled with delight. She loved to have the preacher stay at her house and welcomed them enthusiastically, ushering son and father into the warmth inside.

Lizzie made sure they were settled comfortably by the fireplace in the living room, then disappeared into the kitchen. The preacher and his son warmed themselves, trying to ignore their rumbling stomachs as delicious smells wafted into the room. Around nine o'clock, the nearly starving guests were invited to eat. "I tell you, Aunt Lizzie had really fixed a fine meal," T.A. would later reminisce. The abundance upon their table was the product of his hosts' constant hard work and devotion to their farm.

A feast worthy of feeding to a preacher included both fried ham and fried chicken, an assortment of vegetables that had been canned as winter provisions, homemade bread with yellow, fresh-churned butter, cornbread, apple stack cake, and smaller tea cakes (particularly favored by all the children of Cataloochee). "Me and Junior ate and ate," T.A. said. "I was so hungry I just kept eating. Finally Uncle Hiram looked over at me and said, 'Preacher you don't need to bother about hurting yourself. We plan to have more food here in the morning.'"

From her festive, dish-laden table to the acres of cropland and livestock that had provided her cooking ingredients, Lizzie's life epitomized what it meant to be a well-to-do mountain woman: a big house, a bountiful farm, and constant hard labor to make a comfortable life. She and her husband Hiram were influential members of the relatively remote Big Cataloochee community, which was home to over 1,200 people in 1910. Lizzie had lived there since 1880, when she arrived as Hiram's young bride from the nearby town of Waynesville. Although she didn't know it at the time, it was the beginning of the community's heyday—decades of fertile farming, improved roads, and larger, more comfortable houses.

Such prosperity would not ensure the survival of the community, however; Lizzie, her children, and grandchildren would together be part of the exodus from Cataloochee—a confused time of grief and sacrifice, as the lands in their beloved valley were acquired by the federal government and protected within the boundaries of the new national park. But on the night when Lizzie and Hiram first entertained Preacher Groce and his son, no one had reason to believe the future would hold such catastrophic changes. Their ability to thrive in the mountains seemed to lie in their hard work and the grace of God.

Once the meal was finished and prayers concluded, Preacher Groce and his son were shown to the upstairs guest rooms, where they slept well on beds and pillows stuffed with goose-down Lizzie herself had plucked, under quilts that she had pieced and sewed. Lizzie and Hiram's house was two stories and had nine rooms, a number most mountain families could only dream of in their one or two-room cabins. A long covered porch wrapped around two sides, and shingled

14

gables gave the house an elegant facade. It was a symbol of modern Cataloochee—completed in 1903, it was constructed with boards made at a sawmill, not the rough-hewn logs of the earlier settlers. The walls were lined with hand-finished tuliptree and white pine; upstairs rooms were multi-purpose and could be adapted into bedrooms or quilting rooms, and included a pantry that could hold over 500 jars of handmade canned food.

This prosperity had been nearly impossible to imagine when Lizzie was a little girl. She'd been born on St. Patrick's Day, March 17, 1855, in Cove Creek, several miles from the entrance to the main Cataloochee valley. Although details of her early life are scarce, it seems that her father was killed on a cattle drive in South Carolina when she was very young. Her mother, unable to raise five children on her own, sent Lizzie to live with two uncles. This was fairly common; aunts and uncles often took in children when one or both parents died—anything to avoid sending them to the orphanage. (As an adult, Lizzie, too, would raise at least one niece in addition to her own children.) Although she and her mother stayed close for the rest of their lives, Lizzie's uncles, Burder and Garland Ferguson, had a profound influence on her.

The Ferguson families were prominent members of the Waynesville community. Lizzie's new home was a stately brick building at the crossroads of two main streets in town, and she was given the same opportunities and encouragements as the Fergusons' own children. She excelled at school and became a model Methodist parishioner, participating in family prayers and Bible readings. But this domestic tranquility was shattered by the Civil War. Lizzie wasn't yet seven when Burder and Garland enlisted in the Confederate Army and left home. Burder fought at Vicksburg and Atlanta, among other campaigns; Garland nearly died from several wounds and from being held as a prisoner of war. But they both came home to Waynesville, grateful to see their families again. Their experiences had deepened their devotion to worship of the Lord, and for the rest of her life, Lizzie would observe the Fergusons' daily routine of praying in the morning and evening, and reading the Bible often. The memory of hardship during the Civil War seemed to stay with Lizzie. Although she was naturally a kind and thoughtful person, she was rarely mirthful, as if the weight of her worries as a young girl never truly left her.

When Hiram met Lizzie in Waynesville in the late 1870s, she was in her twenties and teaching school in the Fergusons' brick house. The handsome, charming mountain man, who could dance with such rhythm and style, swept her off her feet. She agreed to marry him, and move to his family's farm in Big Cataloochee.

When Lizzie arrived in the valley as a newlywed in February 1880, she and Hiram lived in a large log house with his mother, Mary Ann Colwell (whom everyone called Granny Pop), his stepfather Jonathan Woody, and some of Hiram's younger brothers and sisters. Hiram's father Levi had finished building the two-story log house in 1858—the first home in Cataloochee to have a closet!—shortly before the start of the Civil War. But he was fated to never fully enjoy living in it. In 1863, Levi was captured by Union soldiers and marched across Tennessee. He finally escaped and over the next year, made his way home. But he was so weakened by the long journey, he died a month after returning to Cataloochee.

Like the rest of the Caldwell family, newlywed Lizzie woke every morning before the sun broke over the mountaintops. She and Granny Pop would fix a hearty breakfast for the men, who would head out into the fields or mountains to tend crops and livestock. Making any kind of living by farming in the mountains required constant hard work by every member of the family. After the men had left the house, Lizzie and Granny Pop began the many other tasks required of a mountain farm woman: continuing to cook, tending the garden, raising the children, making clothes, washing clothes, cooking lard into soap, canning, and more. If fried chicken was on the menu, she'd kill the chickens. At hog-harvesting time, she'd make a special rub for the hams, collect hickory wood, and tend a smoking fire for several days to cure the hams.

Lizzie did her part to contribute to the functioning of the family farm even though she became pregnant shortly after moving to Cataloochee. She still helped Granny Pop tend the garden through the summer and preserve the fruits and vegetables to eat through the long winter months. She gave birth to her first daughter, Harriet—called "Hattie"—in December 1880, when she was 25. Hiram was often gone for long stretches during the first several years of their marriage. He had been hired as a teamster; paid ten cents a day to drive horses and wagons with goods to Greenville, South Carolina. This income was good enough for him to be able to pay Granny Pop for owner-ship of the log house and purchase more farmland from his siblings, expanding the share of his inheritance from his father to 154 acres.

The land was fertile and flourished under Hiram's attentions. He was particularly skilled with animals and soon was earning good money from sales of his cattle, hogs, and mules. Lizzie cooked and looked after the garden, canned and dried food, sewed clothes, quilted, plucked ducks and chickens to plump up featherbeds, and more. She made lovely homemade dresses that were either black or navy—the only colors she wore—from cloth spun and woven from flax or wool; her main indulgence was using store-bought taffeta for her church clothes. Their family grew steadily as well: their second child, James William, was born in March 1885, followed by Dillard in October 1890.

Each member of the Caldwell family had specific responsibilities, even the children. They would often be found rummaging along the fencerows, a favorite nesting spot for hens, looking for eggs. Or, they'd be given a small jar of turpentine and would prowl through the garden picking bugs off the plants. When they got older, each of Hiram and Lizzie's four surviving children attended school. With Lizzie's back-ground as a teacher, she insisted that education was important and took precedence over farm labor. All of the Caldwells' children fin-ished seventh grade, and at least one attended college.

Life on the Cataloochee farms whirred like a finely made clock, ticking through daily tasks, as well as seasonal ones. Autumn, in par-ticular, was a very busy time in the community, as farmers harvested apples and other crops and brought their livestock down from the mountains—but it was also a very social season. Sometimes there was too much work even for a large extended family to handle efficiently.

When it was time to "put up" beans, a family would host a bean stringing party and invite all the neighbors. The big group would pitch in with needle and thread, stringing the beans along so they could easily hang in the sun to dry. After a long morning of work, the hosts would serve a delicious lunch, usually followed with music, games, and dancing. This and corn-shucking parties were some of the most common ways for young men and women to meet each other.

The autumn of 1896 was a somber one for the Caldwells, however. Hiram and Lizzie's fourth child, a son they named John Connie, died in September, a week before his first birthday. He was their only child who wouldn't live to adulthood. The family grieved as they buried him in the Caldwell Cemetery, with the phrase "Budded on earth to bloom in Heaven" etched onto his gravestone. Lizzie prayed and grieved as she continued to work through the season, for the farm still demanded attention if she was to ensure her family would have enough food to eat during the winter.

The pace of life slowed only slightly during the dark, snowy winter days. Lizzie still spent much of her day cooking and tending the fire. But it was also a time to quilt and knit, weave and sew new clothes. Hiram would take stock of the farm equipment, repairing things that had broken, sharpening tools, or making new leather harnesses and bridles. The entire family often gathered around the fireplace, for warmth and light, making it a natural time for storytelling too—recalling the great hunting expeditions of the past year, friendly gossip about neighbors, or revisiting old family legends.

Lizzie's "change of life" baby was born in 1898. She'd been surprised, at 42, to discover she was pregnant again in the spring of 1897. There was some concern over the fact that the baby would come in January, when it was difficult for a midwife to travel, but on January 8, Reuben Eldridge arrived healthy. The Caldwell children ranged from Hattie, living at home but 18 years old and employed as a schoolteacher, to infant Eldridge. His birth seemed to signal a time of prosperity, building, and growth for the Caldwell family as they contemplated the arrival of a new century.

As the redbuds and dogwoods showered the mountains with color in early spring of 1898, Hiram and Lizzie began making plans to build a new house. It was to be a frame house, the most modern and comfortable they could imagine. Over the next five years, Hiram and other men worked to build the house by hand, taking time off from construction whenever their farms required attention. They set up a water-powered sawmill on the banks of the creek that flowed through Hiram's land, for the specific purpose of making boards for the new house. Bricks for the fireplace, chimney, and kitchen flue were "imported from Waynesville"—meaning a trip of three days for a team of four horses hauling the heavy load over the rutted mountain roads. No one kept track of how many trips were needed to bring all of the materials into the valley. But in 1903, Lizzie, Hiram, their children, and Granny Pop all moved into the splendid new nine-room house.

The second floor, in particular, was designed for Lizzie. She kept her quilting frames suspended from the ceiling in one room; when it was being used as a guest room or bedroom, the quilts would be raised to the ceiling. If the room was unoccupied, the quilt frame could be lowered to lap-height so four women could sit and quilt together. Most of her extra cooking supplies were kept upstairs too, on a wooden rack hung from the ceiling by four strong wires. The rack was loaded with fifty-pound bags of flour, hundred pound bags of sugar and salt, dried beans and coffee, and assorted other foods. Not only did suspending the rack from the ceiling keep it out of the way, but mice had a harder time getting into the supplies. At the far end of the room, a doorway led to a smaller room lined with shelves for canned food. It could hold about 500 jars and was strategically located above the kitchen so the flue ran through the room and kept the temperature above freezing. Additionally, a west-facing window allowed in strong afternoon sun, extra assurance that the jars wouldn't freeze and burst.

Over the next three decades, a revolving crowd of family members, friends, and guests would enjoy the new house. The Caldwells' large, handmade dining table and bench could seat 12-14 people. But this often wasn't enough to accommodate the crowds that Lizzie cooked for, and the table had to be set at least twice: first for the adults, later for the children. The kids would amuse themselves on the porch while the adults ate first, but Lizzie could usually be relied on to slip them some of her tea cakes—homemade cookies sprinkled with granulated sugar—to nibble while they waited. She would also make sure to set aside some fried ham and chicken legs and any other food she knew a particular child really liked.

Although Hiram had bought her a brand new 1904 "Home Comfort Cook stove" to go with their new house, she always preferred to cook over the open fire. The large fireplace accommodated two big pots: one for boiling meat, usually pork, and one for simmering vegetables. The Dutch oven, which she used to cook cornbread, sat in the middle, on the hearth. Lizzie would tuck coals under it, and on the lid. She also baked whole apples and potatoes by nestling them into the hot ash of the fire.

She always made biscuits for breakfast, no matter the day of the week. These could be slathered with yellow homemade butter and assorted jams, jellies, and honey. She baked cornbread for each of the other two meals, dinner (what most people call lunch), and supper. Her granddaughter Hattie remembered the splendor of the meals fondly: "It was not unusual to have a big platter of delicious fried ham, fish, and chicken, along with all kinds of fresh vegetables, and delicious cobblers made of strawberries, apples, blackberries, or huckleberries...."

Although the weekdays were spent keeping the farm running smoothly, for Lizzie and much of the Cataloochee community, weekends revolved around attending church and socializing. Saturdays were mostly spent preparing for Sunday. Lizzie would polish the family's good shoes, then starch and iron clothes for church. If people were coming over for dinner on Sunday—and especially if they were expecting to host the preacher—she would do some extra baking: cake, gingerbread, or cookies. The "frying chickens" were killed and dressed, then kept in cold water in the springhouse—the refrigerator— until it was time to cook them.

On Sundays, people would walk, ride horses, or take their buggies to Palmer Chapel, the small white Methodist church, just down the road from the Caldwell house. Palmer Chapel had been completed around 1900, replacing a much smaller, 40-year-old structure that the congregation had outgrown. The new chapel was lovely in its simplicity: a single room with large windows and simple wooden pews. Lizzie's granddaughter Hattie would later recall, "at one time the walls and ceiling were sky blue. Oil lamps provided light for evening services."

The circuit-riding preacher usually came to Big Cataloochee only on the third Sunday of each month, but Lizzie made sure that Sunday School took place every week. She was the chapel superintendent for twenty-six years, and would often teach the adult and children's Sunday School classes. Lizzie also sang in the choir. "I'll always remember Aunt Lizzie coming to Sunday school with her big black skirt and big black bonnet," Raymond Caldwell recalled. "She'd lead prayer, pray on her knees, with that big skirt all billowed out."

Whether it was Sunday or not, worship of the Lord was central to Lizzie's life. She began each day with prayer before breakfast. Her daughter-in-law remembered, "In the morning when sausage was cooked, coffee made, everything ready but the biscuits, we had prayer, read the Bible, then put the biscuits in the oven. She'd nearly starve me to death." Each day also concluded with Bible readings and long prayers before the children were sent off to bed.

As the years went by, the house began to empty out a bit: the older Caldwell children married and moved to their own homes; Granny Pop passed away in 1917, just shy of her hundredth birthday. Lizzie's youngest boy, Eldridge, was sent away to school. Logging work had begun to replace farm work as a good way for young men to earn money, so when school was out he would work at a nearby logging camp.

But in 1920, when he was 23, he got a message from his parents that they desperately needed his help back at the farm. The Spanish Influenza that had swept the country, killing over half a million people, had finally reached Cataloochee. Eldridge came home to find his parents nearly too weak to stand. Many Cataloochee families had already buried loved ones.

Eldridge managed to nurse Lizzie and Hiram back to health, and handle the farm work as well. But even before the bout of influenza, Hiram had been having heart trouble and was getting too weak to manage the property himself. Lizzie and Hiram made a decision: in return for Eldridge caring for them and the farm, they would give him the home place and 154 acres. They had already given each of their other children land and livestock as wedding presents.

After 1920, Eldridge never went back to school. He assumed most of the responsibility for running the farm. Although it must have pained Lizzie to ask her son to cut short his education, he seemed to feel that things worked out alright in the end: if he hadn't come back to Cataloochee, he never would have met the love of his life.

The same year Eldridge left school, a young woman named Pearl Valentine began working as a substitute mail carrier for her friend in Little Cataloochee, the nearby Baptist community. Given the bad roads, rough mountain terrain, and far-flung rural communities in need of service, mail carriers had to be tough and adventurous. Pearl was originally from the Tennessee side of the mountains, in Caton Grove, but had recently moved in with family in Little Cataloochee. Eldridge heard the gossip about the pretty new mail carrier, and when he finally met her, he was smitten. He would wait for her at the post office, then ride with her part of the way on her route between Big and Little Cataloochee.

For the Caldwell family, love and sorrow intertwined in those early years of the 1920s. Eldridge and Pearl were falling in love. But Hiram, who had suffered heart trouble for a long time, was becoming more ill. He kept up his strong sense of humor, one of the many fond things Pearl would later remember about him. "[Hiram] was a joker, teased a lot. Lizzie liked to argue. Hiram, he would listen a while then finally say, 'Oh, Lizzie, you ought to have been a lawyer.'" A few weeks shy of his seventy-first birthday, Hiram died in nearly the same place he'd been born, and was buried in the family cemetery. Lizzie greatly missed her jovial, good-humored husband. He had been her softer side. But she was far from alone—Eldridge was still living at home, and Pearl visited quite often too.

In the following winter, after two years of courtship, Eldridge gave Pearl a ruby engagement ring. They were married at the courthouse in Newport, Tennessee in February 1923.

Lizzie Caldwell

The newlywed couple lived in the big white house with Lizzie, who found herself taking on Granny Pop's role as matriarch of a younger, budding family. Eldridge and Pearl's first daughter, Nell, was born in 1924. Their second daughter, Hattie, was born in September 1927. One night, when Hattie was only a couple of months old, Eldridge noticed sparks coming from the roof. The roof of handmade shingles, now almost 20 years old, had caught fire. Chaos ensued as Pearl ushered Eldridge, who was on crutches because of a broken foot, out of the house and handed him baby Hattie. Nell and Lizzie got to safety too, as did Pearl's sister Mae and her two children. Fearing that they might lose all of the food they'd put away for the winter, along with the rest of their belongings, they ran to the neighbors for help. Rousted out of bed, men and women quickly formed a bucket brigade from creek to house and poured water over the roof beams to keep the whole house from going up in flames. At last only a burned hole remained; the worst of the damage had been avoided. In the next few weeks, Eldridge would replace the old wood shingles with metal ones.

The Caldwells felt lucky that they hadn't lost their house as winter approached. They settled in for another season of quilting and mending farm tools, telling stories around the fire, and praying. Although they didn't know it at the time, their years in the Cataloochee house were numbered. Congress had authorized the establishment of Great Smoky Mountains National Park in 1926, and the Cataloochee valley lay within the boundary line of the new park.

One Sunday in 1928, Reverend Pat Davis stood behind the pulpit in Palmer Chapel and looked out at the congregation. He had more than the word of God to share with them that day; he deeply regretted being the bearer of the news that residents would have to eventually give up their homes and land to the government. The general reaction to the news was disbelief—tempered only by the acknowledgment that the preacher had said it, and he wasn't given to lying. People's reactions to the news ranged from despair to fury. Lizzie had spent hours praying, singing, and teaching in Palmer Chapel. She had lived in the valley for almost fifty years, and thought back to Granny Pop's stories of taming the land. Being forced by the government to give it up was a bitter and grievous thought. She prayed for strength.

Some Cataloochee men advocated for dynamiting the road, or perhaps murdering government employees. Eldridge and a few calmer friends urged their neighbors to be reasonable. As the details unfolded over the following months, the park commission relaxed the move-out standards, allowing residents to sign lifetime leases for a reduced price on their land. Many families, including the Caldwells, chose to take this option.

Even in the midst of heartache, the community carried on, although the Caldwell family would soon experience another tragedy. As they contemplated losing their house and farm, Lizzie's granddaughter Nell, who was five, became very sick. The doctor diagnosed her with spinal meningitis and said there was nothing he could do to cure her. How Lizzie must have prayed, knowing the pain of burying her own son as a baby. Pearl was seven months pregnant with her third daughter when Nell died, on January 4, 1929. The same phrase was etched into her gravestone as John Connie's, and countless other mountain children: *Budded on earth to bloom in Heaven*, and she was buried in the Caldwell cemetery.

Nine months later The Great Depression sent the country into a tailspin, but the fertile land in Cataloochee insulated the Caldwell family from much of the hunger and joblessness that wracked the rest of America. The farm still yielded corn, beans, tomatoes, and more; the hogs still fattened on acorns; and Eldridge could still hunt wild game. There was no money for paint or making repairs to houses or barns, or to buy fertilizer for soil, but families in Cataloochee remained largely self-sufficient. Despite the sadness and worry about being forced out of the valley, the community tried to ensure the last years were good ones. Lizzie, accompanied by grandchildren, liked to walk over to the old log house Levi had built in 1858 and tell the kids stories about the old days, hoping they wouldn't forget that everything was once made by hand.

In the early 1930s, the Caldwell house was a popular place to be on a Sunday. Eldridge was a good barber, and families would come by for a trim, then stay to enjoy some of Lizzie's cooking. Lizzie was in her

70s but was just as handy at making biscuits and pie as ever. Pearl, and Pearl's sister Mae, were excellent cooks in their own right; together the three of them could make a proper feast. Each good meal was, as always, followed by a Bible reading and prayer, led by Lizzie.

Pearl and Eldridge's youngest child was born in 1931, a boy named Ken. But his memories of life in Cataloochee would only be hazy at best. As the nation's economy began to recover, residents of Cataloochee felt increasing limitations on their traditional lifestyles. Because the park land around them was protected, they couldn't send their livestock into the woods and mountaintops for the summer anymore, nor could they hunt wild game. Even if a bear killed livestock, there was no recourse. The National Park Service also established strict restrictions on fishing and cutting firewood. Eldridge, and many others, felt like they were being strangled by rules, which made it increasingly difficult to feed their families. The Caldwells made the heartbreaking decision to buy land outside of the national park and leave the valley.

In March 1934, Lizzie's grandnephew Kyle Campbell rumbled up to the white house with a large truck. The family packed for the entire afternoon. Men loaded heavy, handmade furniture into the truck, then packed in softer, smaller belongings. Kyle spent the night with the family. At 4 a.m. Lizzie and Pearl cooked the last breakfast they would ever make in Cataloochee. Some of the Caldwells drove out in Eldridge's car; Lizzie, with her granddaughter Hattie on her lap, rode with Kyle. They left the valley before the sun came up, headed to their new house in Maggie Valley, just outside of the park boundary.

Lizzie was 80, weary and saddened to leave the place she'd known and flourished in all her life. She was a lynch pin of the community that had scattered to distant towns, cut loose from her former neighbors who were each attempting to make ends meet on new farms. Now she had her family, her memories, and still, her faith in the Lord. On Pearl and Eldridge's new property, Lizzie found a peaceful place between the house and garden, a shady spot in the forest with the small creek nearby, to kneel on the ground and pray.

The end of life in Cataloochee also made Lizzie think about preparing for her own death. As someone who spent countless hours in prayer, she had some definite ideas about her funeral preparations. She asked a preacher in the nearby town of Dellwood to make a casket for her— she also insisted no undertaker have anything to do with her funeral. The preacher completed the walnut wood casket in 1936, and it was delivered to the Maggie Valley house in a wagon. Lizzie lined the coffin with fancy white cloth, satin or taffeta. She also carefully sewed her own funeral clothes, a white dress, the color of angels' robes.

When she died on August 25, 1937, Preacher T.A. Groce, who had spent so many evenings with Hiram and Lizzie during the heyday of the Cataloochee community, came from Asheville to preach her funeral service. Her coffin was brought back over the rocky road into Cataloochee, where she was buried between Hiram and her infant son, John Connie, at the Caldwell Cemetery. Her friends, former neighbors, and relatives gathered around her, united in Cataloochee once more, to remember her as a generous, intelligent mountain woman who had been such a strong presence in the community.

Lizzie's granddaughter, Hattie, grew up to be Cataloochee's historian. She was determined that the richness of the valley community wouldn't be lost. Hattie started with her own memories, and her mother's, then began to interview other former residents. She quickly became a widely-recognized expert on Cataloochee history, publishing multiple books and guides about the magical place.

The human effort to tame Cataloochee valley has faded in the decades since the last families left. But a few significant buildings remain, including the Caldwell house. It's still white, with blue trim, although the smell of fresh baked biscuits, or cinnamon wafting through the air with fresh apple stack cake has long faded, to be conjured only by imagination.

Lizzie Caldwell

Chapter 3

Dora Cope

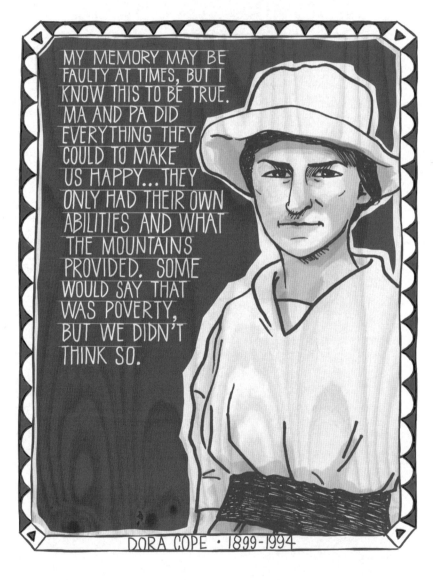

MY MEMORY MAY BE FAULTY AT TIMES, BUT I KNOW THIS TO BE TRUE. MA AND PA DID EVERYTHING THEY COULD TO MAKE US HAPPY... THEY ONLY HAD THEIR OWN ABILITIES AND WHAT THE MOUNTAINS PROVIDED. SOME WOULD SAY THAT WAS POVERTY, BUT WE DIDN'T THINK SO.

DORA COPE · 1899–1994

—Dora Cope, *sharing stories of her life with her daughter, Florence Cope Bush, published in* Dorie: Woman of the Mountains *(University of Tennessee Press)*

On a frosty January day in 1912, twelve-year-old Dora Woodruff, her little brother and sister, and their parents packed their belongings into a couple of wagons and left their family farm in the rolling mountains of Boogertown, Tennessee, a small community in the foothills of the Great Smoky Mountains. Like many other mountain families looking for better economic opportunities, the Woodruffs laboriously navigated the rutted, rocky wagon road that led more than twenty miles higher into the mountains, to the logging camp run by the Little River Lumber Company at Fish Camp Prong.

RV Woodruff, Dora's father, had been working as a supervisor for railroad expansion higher into the mountains, but the entire family's move was spurred by a new opportunity for her mother to earn a decent income as well. Delilah Woodruff, with Dora's help, would run a boarding house for logging men. With the pay from logging and income from boarders, the Woodruffs hoped to earn a reasonable living—able to buy clothes and food, pay for school, and save some money for emergencies. The family had already moved several times in Dora's short life, trying to eke out a living from various farms in the rocky mountain soil. Although the farms produced enough food for their immediate family, there was no guaranteed surplus to sell, resulting in little more than a subsistence living. Working for the logging company was a way to change their lives.

Small logging operations had been established in the Smokies throughout the 1800s, but the difficulty of building railroads and the generally harsh conditions of the region deterred major industrial expansion. As timber resources in the more accessible regions of the northeast U.S. and Mississippi Delta became scarce, larger companies eyed the virgin timber in the Smokies with great interest. Innovations in railroad building and skidder technology around the turn of the century had made it easier to log the rough terrain in the southern Appalachians, and in a few short years, timber companies were the major landholders in the mountains. The Little River Lumber Company, one of the largest of the eighteen companies operating in the Smokies, owned 86,000 acres on the Tennessee side of the mountains. Construction on the Little River Railroad into the mountains began in 1907, with men generally earning fifty cents a day for ten hours of labor. This was a much better income than most families could hope to earn from farming, although the frequent moves took a toll on family life.

To get from the logging camp to his family's cabin, RV Woodruff would generally walk 12-14 miles. More often, he paid for a room at a logging camp and didn't see his wife or kids for long stretches of time. The Woodruff's new opportunity to run a boarding house for loggers would enable the family to be closer together and earn more money while RV continued to work on trestle building, overseeing construction of the railroad bridges which spanned streams and rivers.

Although Dora didn't know it at the time, the railroads her father was helping to build would shape her life, moving her from lumber camp to lumber camp with her husband and children in the decades to come. Many years later, Dora would reminisce about all that she'd experienced with her daughter, Florence Cope Bush, who wrote and published *Dorie: Woman of the Mountains*, an insightful, personal look at the changes in mountain life in the early 1900s. The farm-based self-sufficiency and barter system Dora's parents had known would be replaced by wages paid in cash and company stores; and without a garden to maintain, or room to store hundreds of jars of canned goods for the winter, the responsibilities of mountain women began to shift as well. But these changes were unanticipated and unconsidered as the Woodruff family made their way into the colder, steeper mountains.

Light snowfall and a layer of brittle ice coated the wagon track. The horses began to have difficulty keeping their footing, so the children and Delilah got out of the wagon and walked. Dora later remembered passing by an orchard with "Winter John apples," and the family collected as many as they could to thaw and eat later.

The wagon road led only as far as the logging town called Elkmont; to get the rest of the way to Fish Camp required taking the logging railroad. There was no other way. The Woodruffs spent the night at Elkmont before continuing higher into the mountains. It was still dark when Dora's mother shook her awake. They needed to be on the first train to Fish Camp. The Woordruffs climbed into a chilly boxcar and huddled together to keep warm. After a little while, the train stopped in front of a long bunkhouse. The bunkhouse, where the Woodruffs would live and take care of boarders, was still so newly built the pungent smell of fresh lumber hung heavy in the air. The two ends of the house had rooms with built-in bunks, with boarders in one end and the family in the other. The kitchen and dining areas divided the two wings. The logging work paid well enough that men migrated to the mountains for work, including people from other countries. Two of the Woodruffs' boarders were German, and they heard tell of a camp of Italians in the logging operations out of the Greenbrier area further to the northeast.

The move to Fish Camp marked a significant change for Dora, the oldest of the Woodruffs' three children. Symbolically, her mother had made her leave her only doll with one of her cousins in Boogertown; at the boarding house, she was expected to help her mother run the place—no longer a child who attended school and was mostly concerned with winning spelling competitions. She would clean, do laundry, and help her mother cook for the family and eight boarders, all men. "The days were long and tiring," Dora remembered. "Ma and I got up before the sun to cook breakfast and pack lunches for Pa and the eight men…. My days were spent in the house, cleaning or washing dishes…. I couldn't go to bed at night until every dish was clean and the table set for tomorrow's breakfast. We didn't get a day off because the men worked seven days a week. They cut and hauled timber six days a week and cut wood for the skidder on Sunday. There was no church or school for me to go to anyway…."

But it wasn't all drudgery. The boarding house was well situated near the river, so it was convenient to haul water for washing clothes and dishes, and for bathing. Best of all for Dora's mother, the river was filled with brook trout. She was a talented fisherwoman, and delighted in serving her boarders freshly caught fish.

The lumber camp was growing and developing as a community. As more women and children arrived at Fish Camp, the lumber company executives decided to provide a school and a church for their employees. Although any denomination could schedule meetings at the church, Colonel Townsend, the owner of the railroad, was a Methodist, and encouraged the loggers to attend Methodist services. RV and Delilah had regretted taking their oldest daughter out of school, but when a teacher was hired to educate the lumber camp children, Dora was able to begin her lessons again. The Woodruffs sensed that an education would be important for her future, although she still helped with boarding house chores.

Boarders came and went as they were assigned different jobs. One of the young loggers who eventually came to stay at the Woodruffs' boarding house was Fred Cope. His father had been hired as the Little River Lumber Company bookkeeper in 1912, but didn't like life in the mountains very much and relocated to Knoxville. Fred didn't want to leave the mountains, though, and was worried he would have to work in a cotton mill. So one evening, he put a few clothes in a paper bag, snuck out the window in the back bedroom of the Knoxville house, and headed back to Elkmont, traveling most of the way on foot. Unbeknownst to Dora, she had caught Fred's eye. He moved into her family's boarding house around 1914. Fred began to invite her to go walking with him on Sundays—courting couples often strolled the railroad tracks or wandered along paths through the forest.

He bought a ruby and pearl ring from the jewelry peddler, Red Foot, who came through the camp every few months. During a walk on Dora's sixteenth birthday, he proposed. Delilah, who had married at the much-older-than-average age of twenty-three, strongly disapproved of such an early wedding, but Dora and Fred were determined. Although she didn't fully approve, Delilah sewed Dora a new linen dress—navy blue—with a lace collar, for her wedding.

Fred borrowed a beautiful buggy pulled by two black horses to take Dora to meet the preacher in late May. Their wedding was a secret, or so Dora thought, as they rode toward Gatlinburg. They were surprised to meet the Reverend Ownby on the wagon road—riding his horse over to the Oldhams' Creek Church for a service. He suggested that he could marry them on the spot. Although they had both planned on being in a church or perhaps the Reverend's house for the ceremony, the beauty of the mountains in spring seemed like a perfect setting for their wedding. In keeping with the lack of pomp and circumstance, when Dora and Fred got back to the boarding house she helped her mother with the dirty dishes as usual. But just as they were falling asleep, the door to their bedroom burst open and men snatched Fred out of the room to be carried around the camp with much whooping and hollering, a proper shivaree for the newlyweds. Women helped Delilah set out refreshments—coffee, pies and an apple stack cake—in honor of the newlyweds, and to feed the raucous revelers.

Dora and Fred lived at her parents' boarding house for two weeks, then moved into a nearby cabin at Fish Camp. The cabin came with an extra bunk, which they initially rented out to a logger. But Delilah had never had the time or patience to teach Dora how to cook and she found looking after the man to be extremely stressful. After three weeks, she insisted he leave. "...I didn't want anybody in my house for any amount of money. Most people who grew up in the mountains never thought they had a right to privacy. It was a rare cabin that had two rooms. Everybody lived together in one room, sharing all activities and illnesses."

Dora craved a different life, and saw her opportunity. She later reminisced that after Fred went to work and she had cleaned the cabin, she had no one to look after other than the cat, and herself. "I had nothing to do except indulge myself. I read everything I could get my hands on. The lazy, summer days were blissful... Fred was getting good wages on his job, and we didn't have a place for a garden. All this meant I could be as lazy as I wanted to be without feeling guilty. Things had changed for the mountain women. The lumber companies had brought the outside world to us. The men made the money and the company brought in goods to spend the money on. I would never have to work like Ma did when she was young."

But Dora's free, lazy days were numbered. In August, she found that she was pregnant. Excitedly, she and Fred pored over the Sears and Roebuck catalog, wanting store-bought clothes for their little one—only the best. But store-bought clothes had a drawback—the mail delivery was slow and unreliable, and Dora worried that she'd have the baby before its clothing arrived from Chicago. Two weeks before Dora's seventeenth birthday, on April 27, 1915, she gave birth to healthy Wilma Katherine Cope. And her clothes were waiting for her.

Soon after Wilma's birth, Fred announced they were moving. As a reward for being a dependable worker, the lumber company had given him the opportunity to raise his family in a better house. They left Fish Camp for the Three Forks logging camp, higher in the mountains. Their new house was a "setoff house," the formal name for a railroad car converted into a house. This kind of housing, scattered across the mountainside, was also called boxcars or cracker boxes. Since each setoff house was portable, it couldn't be larger than a railroad flatcar, which was fourteen feet long by eight feet wide. The house was completely covered, inside and out, with rough wood, with tar paper used to insulate between walls and a bit of linoleum on the floor. But it was generally considered an improvement over Fred and Dora's previous cabin. The "house" had four windows, with curtains provided by the company—a treat since most cabins never had curtains "because windows were small and set high in the wall." They also had a coal-burning heater, with coal provided by the lumber company. The heater, Dora would later discover, wasn't quite enough to keep snow from settling inside the house—"The tar paper didn't fit snugly, so there were small cracks which let snow sift into the railroad car during winter storms. When we got up in the morning, the floor and beds would be covered with silky snow," Dora later remembered.

The lumber camps also had staff doctors on hand because of the danger inherent in logging, and the remoteness of the mountain communities. While the doctors should have made life easier, Dora repeatedly found that "modern" medicine was inferior to the home-made remedies her mother taught her. The doctors, in her opinion, placed too much faith in the "curative powers of calomel, castor oil, and iodine." When her daughter Wilma stepped on a yellow jacket nest, the company doctor put baking soda on the welts. The little girl still got a fever and could barely walk, so Dora did what her Ma told her—adding tobacco juice to the soda compress. Wilma was better by morning.

By this point, the sustained fifteen-plus years of logging were beginning to have significant ecological effects on the mountains. Floods were a constant worry, as heavy rains could dislodge huge amounts of denuded mountainside. In dry weather, the opposite was common—a spark thrown off from metal grinding on metal from the railway could ignite a forest. The trains themselves could be deadly; wrecks regularly hurt, maimed, and sometimes killed men.

In April 1916, Dora and Fred's converted boxcar was pulled higher into the mountains, to a camp called Peawood Hollow. Dora remembered, "We were stuck on the side of the mountain like bugs on flypaper. Just behind the house, the earth stopped and plunged into a deep hollow. The sides were straight up and down, seemingly without a bottom." Not long after they had moved to Peawood, a log train fell over as it passed the house. The terrifying incident was over before Dora fully realized what had happened—a metallic squeal from the train, booming logs hitting the ground, and then silence as they rolled over the edge into the deep hollow.

They shared their Peawood Hollow boxcar with four boarders. Cooking and cleaning for the men consumed Dora's days because the small, bubbling spring, from which she hauled all their drinking, bathing, and cooking water, was half a mile walk away. Dora also kept a cow who was free to graze around the mountain, but had a little stall she always returned to for milking. One morning, the cow seemed to have disappeared—until baby Wilma and Dora looked over the side of the ravine. The cow had fallen and broken its neck. Dora remembered her parents' jokes when they were trying to farm in the North Carolina mountains—about how the cows would have shorter legs on one side from standing on the mountain slopes. But one had never fallen to its death. Despite the dangers, Dora loved the beauty of the hollow. She and Wilma would pick wild strawberries and flowers that grew along the railroad tracks. Ramps, a mountain delicacy related to onions, grew abundantly too.

They stayed at Peawood Hollow for "the season"—generally as long as weather permitted logging—then moved back down the mountain to Higdon Camp. Higdon was the center of a large logging operation, and once again Delilah Woodruff was running the boarding house.

She'd used some of her earnings to buy a sewing machine. This partic-ular piece of technology changed her life and the lives of many other women in the mountains. The sewing machine, combined with lum-ber company stores that sold all kinds of cloth—calico, gingham, flan-nel, and more—made spending long days spinning and weaving un-necessary. Delilah and Dora started copying dress styles from the Sears and Ward catalogs, since few mountaineers could afford mail-order clothes. The traditional ways in the mountains were changing—and women's lives were getting less burdensome.

Dora and Fred moved in with Delilah and RV again, so Dora could help take care of the eight boarders. She was pregnant with their sec-ond child, and pulled out the large bibbed aprons to "cover her con-dition and make her presentable."

In 1917, a terrible forest fire burned into Higdon Camp. Fires were always a concern, particularly because friction between trains and tracks created sparks that could easily set a blaze on a dry moun-tainside. Sometimes they burned out quickly, and sometimes they wreaked havoc. The loggers, including Fred, had to dash through the burning woods, fearing that the camp was already ablaze, their loved ones possibly dead. Thankfully, the fire was moving more slowly, and a train was provided to ferry people further down the mountain and out of harm's way. RV and Delilah decided to stay and try to protect the house and their belongings. "For the first time, they had things worth saving and couldn't bear to leave them behind." Fred and Dora stayed to help, and so did all the boarders—adrenaline from the sounds of the roaring fire fueling their efforts as a bucket brigade. They were saved by a shift in the wind that came shortly before dawn. Their house was only one of three houses that survived the fire. About a half mile up the river, their neighbor Harrison Watson had moved all of his belongings onto stones in the river, to spare them if his house caught fire. When all was calm again, though, his house stood un-touched, while flying debris had burned all of his possessions.

Other families returned and searched the burned houses for any-thing to save, but the setoff houses, all tar paper and thin, dry wood, were highly flammable. After the fire, "Everywhere we looked was desolate. I'd never seen such ugliness… Dirt and debris washed down the slopes into the river, turning it into a muddy, sluggish stream. Rainbow and speckled trout washed up on the banks, smothered by ashes and mud. Nature would reclaim the mountains, but not for a long time."

The lumber company took charge of relocating the families from Higdon Camp, which was too destroyed to remain functional. But the experience had been too close a call for Dora's parents. RV got word that a farm on Upper Middle Creek was for sale for eight hundred dollars. He bought it, spending his seven hundred dollars in savings, with the promise to pay back the additional hundred over the next year. Dora and Fred decided it was time to try something different as well. They waited to move from Higdon Camp until their son Paul was born, and then joined Dora's parents on their seventy acre farm, in September 1917.

And so Dora brought her new baby and two-year-old Wilma back to the way of life she'd grown up with, born on an isolated farm in North Carolina. One of little Wilma's first memories was hog-killing time on the farm. She "crawled under a bed in the back room" in horror but was later happy to eat the meat provided by the sacrifice. Sometimes Delilah would pickle the pig's feet—Wilma's favorite. Delilah regularly prepared every other part of the pig, from ribs and tenderloin to "souse meat" made from cooking the head, feet, ears, tongue and liver. She also grew her own cotton to weave the fabric for quilts, often asking little Wilma to help pick seeds out of the soft white balls of cotton.

In *Dorie: Woman of the Mountains*, Dora reflects that it was a hard, Spartan life by most standards, but when it was the only thing a child knew—particularly with the mountains as an endless playground—it was easy to be happy. Still, making anything more than a meager subsistence living from farming had been difficult. Earlier, her father had taken a job in a cotton mill, but the work didn't suit him at all—the system of overseer/management and ordinary mill worker resulted in social dynamics that weren't to the liking of a mountaineer used to working for himself and not being judged for his poverty. They were welcomed back to the Tennessee mountains to stay in a cabin on family property in Boogertown and help run the farm, until logging income had lured them away in 1912.

After five years on the Middle Creek farm, they were still barely making ends meet, even though the entire family worked together to plant the corn and tend the garden. Dora recalled, "The farm had poor soil, used up generations ago and never replenished. It was doubtful we would grow enough for our own use, certainly none to sell. The tobacco crop would probably bring in the only cash we could make from the farm." Fred partnered with RV to rent a gristmill too, charging a fee to grind other families' corn into meal. But they still couldn't make enough money for two families to live on. The work was hard, just as hard as logging, and the income was miniscule. After Dora's third child, Mary Edith, was born on the Middle Creek farm in January 1920, Fred began to look for other options to support his growing family.

In search of opportunity, Dora, Fred, and their three children moved to Gaston County, North Carolina to work in the newly established Cramerton Mills in June 1922. Although Fred had dreaded the prospect of working in the mills as a young man, it was harder to resist the income they promised now that he had a growing family. Fred was hired as a supervisor at Cramerton. The company housing provided luxuries like indoor plumbing, two big bedrooms, hot and cold running water, and a stove that you could cook at while standing, instead of crouching over a low fireplace. A butcher brought fresh beef once a week—a treat for mountain folk for whom it was generally too profitable to sell a calf than to be tempted to eat it.

Shortly after they had settled in at Cramerton, they got news that Dora's sister Lola was sick and they hurried back to Middle Creek for a visit. Lola recovered, and after hearing Dora and Fred's talks of "Cramerton as a wonderland," Delilah and RV decided to join them. But there was inequality and oppression in the cotton mills, and politics as well. Union labor and workers' rights disputes were simmering. Communist activists Fred Beal and George Pershing were agitating for strikes. To avoid confrontation, the Cramerton Mills were closed.

Disappointed to have lost the economic opportunity of the mills,

RV and Delilah, along with Dora, Fred, and the children, all returned to the upper reaches of the Smokies, back to the farm. But they had savings from the mill work—enough that Delilah paid to have a telephone installed in their house. Dora's brother, Luther, had stayed in the mountains as a logger and had earned enough money to buy a Chevrolet Touring Car. These luxuries were still rare in the mountains, and unheard of from Dora's childhood. Luther became the family chauffeur, happy to give slow, bumpy rides over bad mountain roads. Everyone except for RV would take him up on the offer, but Dora's father preferred to walk or take the wagon. RV got his old job back with the Little River Lumber Company, supervising trestle building and furthering the expansion of the railroad into the mountains. Fred and Dora stayed on at the farm. For the present time, Fred oversaw the crops and also cut and sold acid wood and tanbark, which were used to turn animal hides into leather. It wasn't a good living, but they eked out a year of it, before deciding to return to the life of a logging family.

Fred's new position at Little River Lumber Company meant they would live in a railroad car house on Jakes Creek, a section of the mountains being logged for the second time. Dora's two oldest children, Wilma and Paul, walked to the one room schoolhouse. Fred got promoted to being a supervisor on the skidder, the heavy machinery used to move felled trees out of the forest and onto railroad cars, after the Jakes Creek job was finished. Their house was hoisted onto a flat railroad car and they were all moved to Wildcat Flats, just below the bustling logging town of Tremont. Dora later remembered that the Tremont community had a building that looked like a church—complete with small steeple—but was really an "all purpose building." It was a church, school, movie theater, and on Saturday nights, a wrestling arena. Women were welcome to attend the wrestling matches, but only the boldest dared go. The joke was you could find education, salvation, and damnation all in the same place. And every December, Mrs. Townsend, the wife of the railroad company owner, would have a Christmas tree put up and send beautifully wrapped gifts for all of the employees' children.

Despite the holiday cheer, December 1926 was a frightening one for the Copes. Fred caught typhoid fever and nearly died. Dora nursed him back to health, but he missed two months of work—which meant they had no income. As well as a logging job paid, it didn't come with any sick days at all. The Copes relied on their precious few canned fruits and vegetables, and meager savings, to get them through his illness. When Fred had recovered and resumed work, they moved again, to the upper end of Lynn Camp called Stringtown. "We had to move so much we didn't mind it anymore."

But with fires and floods getting even worse, there were murmurings of saving what was left of the mountains and turning it into a national park. The mountains had been well pillaged, and the stock of valuable trees was dwindling. Dora recalled, "We loved the mountains and wanted them to remain beautiful, but the timber was our bread and butter." Fred, looking to develop other skills, began taking courses to understand electricity installation. He ordered pamphlets from the Cones Electric School of Chicago and taught himself, studying at night after putting in a long day of work for the logging company. Fred only had a ninth grade education, so he'd ask the lumber company bookkeeper to help with some of the math problems. For one of his assignments, he built a working electricity generator—the assignment came with two light bulbs included. "Suddenly the whole room was filled with a clear steady light many times brighter than the kerosene lamp. It was a miracle…" Neighbors came to marvel at the light, wondering how a few wires and a tiny machine could be so bright.

But as long as he could, Fred kept logging—and they stayed in Stringtown for five years, the longest they'd been in one place since they were married nearly fifteen years earlier. Dora had another baby, William Wayne. The logging town was a vibrant community, with a good school and plenty of opportunity for neighborly visiting and fun. But Fred's last real logging job meant the family had to move again, to Marks Cove, just below Clingmans Dome, the highest point in the Smoky Mountains. It was an isolated, harsh environment filled with spruce and fir trees evocative of Canadian forests; the Copes occupied "the last [house] at the end of the line." The logging company added an extra room onto their house so they could have four boarders. Dora only cooked for them—they took care of their own laundry. The temperature reached twenty-eight below a few times—a brutal temperature in a little wood and tar paper portable house. But they made the best of the harsh winter, in ways like eating snow cream—fresh white snow mixed with sugar, vanilla and milk.

The lumber company was being more selective about which trees could be cut—they had to meet certain size standards, so "only the biggest and best trees" still standing were logged. This meant Fred's jobs became shorter because there were fewer trees to cut. In 1929, they moved again, back down the mountain slopes to Sams Creek, about a mile above the large logging town of Tremont. The schoolteacher on Sams Creek, Eulah Fox Broome, had started a small library. Dora had been collecting books, mail-ordered along with other things from Sears & Roebuck, which she shared with other camp women and older children. Their collection included an impressive number of Zane Grey novels and Tarzan books. Grace Livingston Hill, a romance writer, was popular among women in the camps, and her books were often traded around.

During their stint at Sams Creek, Fred suffered his worst logging injury, nearly losing his legs when he fell into the log pile and was pinned. Miraculously, his legs weren't broken, but the family once again had to live on their small savings while he recovered. Since he couldn't be a part of any logging operation, he studied electricity. Lumber work was being phased out as the national park took shape, and many men were already leaving, looking for new ways to earn a living.

With the onset of the Depression, Dora and Fred, along with her parents, lost nearly everything. "They never had anything to do with banks anymore," Wilma, Dora's daughter, remembered about her grandparents. "I've seen them stuff their money in a quart jar... And [they would] stuff it in under the straw ticks [a home-made mattress], between the straw tick and the springs. And when Granny died, she had eleven hundred dollars pinned to her gown."

But Fred's foresight in learning about electricity helped ease some of the strain. He was able to work occasional jobs across East Tennessee building power lines, often away from the family. He briefly returned to logging—one of a handful of men hired during the Depression, as the family scraped by. Dora had more children: Dwight Arnold in 1930, and Vida Florence in 1933, and Don LeVerne in 1935. In March 1937, the Copes finally left Tremont and joined Dora's parents once again at the farm on Middle Creek. After enjoying life in a small community in Tremont and the other logging towns, Dora found that the isolation of her parents' farm bothered her. She longed for someone to talk to besides her own family and a few traveling salesmen or the mailman.

Fred was often gone too. He kept working on installing power lines, but would be laid off when a job was finished, left to wait to be called for the next one. In spring of 1938, the last tree was cut by Little River Lumber Company, hauled out of Spruce Flats Branch. An era that transformed the local economy, boosted standards of living, and created widespread ecological havoc had ended.

By the late 1930s, Fred had been hired as a full-time, long term employee by the power company. He was working in Knoxville and wanted the family to join him. In 1943, they moved to Knoxville with their six children still young enough to live at home, to a house so newly built wood shavings still littered the floor. Slowly, they began to settle into a new rhythm of life, with the mountains only a distant blue outline on the horizon. They brought their cow with them to the city—they'd made arrangements to pasture her nearby, but kept her in the yard for a little while as they unpacked and settled into the house. They were sensitive to being seen as uncultured backwoods folk, particularly with the cow around, but as the months passed, they began to settle into the city suburbs.

Yet, as Dora shared her story with her daughter Florence, told in *Dorie: Woman of the Mountains*, she came to realize she was part of the last generation to make a full life in the high altitudes of the Great Smoky Mountains. She treasured those memories, later recalling of her childhood, "When the leaves on the hillside began showing their full blaze of color, we knew the cold, crisp air would come down from the north and remind us to get ready for winter. And, oh, the harvest moon—at night it looked like a big ball of white ice floating in a sea of purple velvet. It shone so brightly that only a few stars were visible in its glow. From where our house sat between the mountain ranges, it looked twice the size of the moon that I see since I became older."

Chapter 4

Ella Costner

OH! THAT YOU OF
THE CITIES AND
HOSPITALS · COULD
WALK THE WOOD-
LAND, THERE
BE MADE
WHOLE ·

LISTEN TO
THE SONG
OF THE BIRD
AND INSECT · AND
THERE TO LET
SOLITUDE FLOOD
YOUR SOUL ·

ELLA COSTNER · 1894–1982

—Excerpt from Seasonal Splendor (In The Smokies), *Ella Costner*

Caught up in her storytelling, Ella Costner leans forward in her metal chair, not noticing the light breeze that tugs a few strands of her snowy white hair loose from the bun piled high on top of her head. Her sense of humor and clear voice, with a soft Southern twang, draw an audience to her like bees to a flower. Perhaps her listeners at the Folklife Festival in Cosby, Tennessee have heard that Ella is the "Poet Laureate of the Smokies," a title bestowed by the Tennessee House of Representatives in 1971 after publication of her book *Lamp in the Cabin*. Or perhaps, in the way she speaks and the magnetism of her presence, they can sense that this woman has lived an unusual and adventurous life.

There is something regal about the way she confidently commands attention that belies her childhood of poverty in the mountains. Ella embodies some of the stereotypes of Appalachian living—from growing up in a tiny log cabin to earning a living from moonshining—but as an Army nurse she led as far-flung a life as anyone of her generation might have dared dream. She traveled extensively, worked in places from Hawaii to New York City, but no matter how far she roamed, she always returned home to the mountains.

Her eyes twinkle as she tells stories of lost treasure buried by early loggers in the Smokies who were paid in gold; her grandfather's hunting excursions with President James K. Polk; and tales of ghosts and unsettled spirits haunting travelers on lonely stretches of mountain roads. Listeners familiar with the history of Cosby, Tennessee might have recognized her as the sister of notorious moonshine distributor Ike Costner, who served time in Alcatraz. Ella herself successfully operated a moonshine business in Cosby in the 1930s, and had her own risky encounters with The Law.

She shared some of her moonshine exploits in *Song of Life in the Smokies*; her part memoir, part story collection. Only a few men made whiskey in Cosby until the double-hit of Prohibition and the Great Depression, when everything changed: "At that time a lot of people were out of a job, and moonshine whiskey was selling for twenty dollars a gallon. So you see the inevitable happened and a few million people became INVOLVED," she later wrote.

Ella didn't initially plan to become one of the few female moonshiners in Cosby, but she was shrewd and recognized the opportunity
when her other undertakings failed. The Appalachians were infamous
as an economically depressed area, and jobs were as scarce (or scarc-
er) than anywhere else in the country. Money from moonshining fed
families, paid for warm winter clothes, school fees, and doctor's visits.
With such large rewards and few other options, moonshiners were
willing to undertake the sensational risks that made them folk he-
roes. Many of the early white settlers in the southern Appalachians
were Scots-Irish, and through the proud traditions of their ancestors,
distilling and brewing were an integral part of life, an inalienable
right. The rocky soil wasn't much good for bountiful produce and the
bad-to-nonexistent roads meant it was difficult to get crops to market
in a timely fashion anyway, so turning corn into a non-perishable,
more easily transportable, and more profitable liquid was a reasonably
practical undertaking. From the Depression until the mid-1970s, Cosby became the epicenter of moonshining in the Smokies. The saying
was the "sugar comes in dry and goes out shakin'."

In 1933, Ella rented a six-room house and five acres in Cosby, posted a "For Tourists" sign and announced the opening of The White
Rock Inn. She was forty years old and had worked in hospitals from
New York to Panama, but returned to her family in the mountains
during the Depression. Although Great Smoky Mountains National
Park was yet to be officially dedicated, the scenic, remote area was
already a draw for city folk looking for clear air and adventure in
the mountains. Along with the Inn, she ran a little store and filling
station nearby. She hadn't planned to become a moonshiner, but as
she recounts in *Song of Life in the Smokies*, with the heroine "Katie"
a pseudonym for herself, it seemed that she was being set up for it
whether she wanted to break the law or not. At a certain point, so
much of Cosby's population was making moonshine, the mentality
became "if you're not with us, you're against us."

Ella had planned to provide a bed and breakfast solely for tourists,
but quickly reconsidered. Her next venture began innocently enough,
with the suggestion of a grand opening party. "Two men came from

the little town to see [Katie], and asked if they could bring some musicians some evening.... Katie agreed they could do that, not discerning their intentions.... So a few nights later there came to the Katie Hart Inn a crowd of people which took Katie by surprise so much that she was almost speechless." While some of the partygoers were interested in meeting her and seeing her inn, quite a few others had come for the promise of "Ole White Mule." The night ended with a half dozen of her "guests" in jail, and a haze of ill-repute hanging over Ella and the White Rock Inn.

A few weeks later, she realized that the "young men who lived on farms in the backwoods" who hung around her store being friendly and telling stories, occasionally buying pork and beans or some Vienna sausage, were actually peddling jars of whiskey to cars that drove past. Still attempting to salvage her reputation, she banished them. But she also began to wonder if she might have a very successful enterprise on her hands.

Her first undertaking at moonshining, with the help of her cook, was a valuable learning experience. The cook turned out to be a plant from the Alcohol Tax men, who raided the property and destroyed her equipment before the whiskey mash got beyond fermentation. It was Memorial Day, Ella remembered clearly—she was wearing "a poppy red dress, with white lace cuffs and collar; he was wearing a poppy in his coat lapel."

The raid didn't frighten her; on the contrary, she became more desperate that she wouldn't be able to care for her aging parents if she didn't manage to start a whiskey business. So she "got in her car, went to Cosby, loaded two cases of whiskey, returned to her place and soon when the cars came by the store there was a new boy there to go around the corner and make the delivery. They made a new batch of Home Brew, and soon it was whispered that she had the best Home Brew in the whole county."

And so it began. Ella's reasons for becoming a moonshiner may have been a common motivation—to earn enough income to support herself and her family—but prior to the 1930s, Ella's life had been anything but usual for a mountain woman. Unlike many "blockaders," she already had a breadth of experiences far beyond the horizon of the Smokies, and had come home to take care of her ailing parents during the difficult post-Depression years.

Her ambition to see the world had led her far from the Great Smoky Mountains as a young woman, but she always considered the mountains home—they pulled her back to Tennessee even when she didn't want to return, and welcomed her when she settled down at last, to write her memoirs and books of poetry.

Aspects of her childhood were not so unusual for a girl in the mountains at the turn of the 20th century, although Ella herself was very different from her peers. She was born on February 20th, 1893, in a two-room log cabin near Cripple Creek, deep in the remote valleys of the Great Smoky Mountains. The tiny community was known as Mountain Rest. Ella and her siblings helped tend the family farm, but also ventured into the mountains, reveling in the woods as their playground. She found playing in the wild beauty of the mountains to be an outlet for her "primal urge to creativeness," as she would later describe it.

She was a talented student, able to recite hundreds of lines of poetry, and when she'd memorized all the books she had access to at school, turned to the spelling book and memorized it. She drew great inspiration from Rosa Bonhuer, a realist artist, and the writer George Eliot. James Russell Lowell's poem "Aladdin" moved her deeply: "*When I was a beggarly boy/And lived in a cellar damp/I had not a friend nor a toy/ but I had Aladdin's lamp/ When I could not sleep for the cold/I had fire enough in my brain/ And builded with roofs of gold/ My beautiful castles in Spain*" The words resonated with Ella in her mountain cabin, with snow blowing in through the cracks and settling on top of the home-stitched blankets on her bed. "I too, had fire in my brain, I too dreamed of castles in some far of place. But the thing that I longed most in all the world to do was to build a poem like this, that would make some little girl happy as I had been made happy by this one. To do that was the supreme thing, to write something so poignantly beautiful as that to so stir the soul of another as it had stirred me, would be all that one needed to live for and when that was accomplished one could die peacefully. And so all the days and all the years were colored with aspirations such as this."

She later wrote of her adolescent view of the world beyond Mountain Rest: "Someday she would go out there into that world. She knew for certain she would; just how, she did not know. It was far, very far from the end of the road in the Smoky Mountains. Sometimes the men went out there and came back telling fabulous stories of wonders they had seen... But none of the women ever went. None of them. [She] was a little sorry she was a woman; but just the same, *she* would go!" This eagerness to see the world may have been spurred by two things: her voracious reading, and by the love of her life, Robert "Mac" McMahan who joined the Army and reported for duty in far away places. Mac was also a good deal older than she was; when he left for the Philippines, Ella was still in grade school.

Her ambitions notwithstanding, her father felt that education was not relevant to her preparations to be a mountain man's future wife, and tried to remove her from school (thus saving money) when she was ten. Her mother sensed this would be a great disservice to her daughter and insisted Ella be allowed to continue her studies. But Ella noticed the difference in how she and her brothers were treated. "With my brothers it was different, they could do their homework while I washed the dishes, they could sleep while I helped with the breakfast, each had his special duties to perform, but I still think the women had by far the most work to do. The men and boys were the ones who could sit before the fire and dream, pile on another stick and go on dreaming."

When she was fifteen, in 1908, she fled Mountain Rest to escape vicious rumors that one of her married teachers had had an affair with her. In her telling of the events in her 1971 book *Song of Life in the Smokies*, she maintains that she was the innocent victim of persons eager to spread malicious gossip. Her neighbor, Lewis Williamson, agreed to give her a ride out of the highest hills into the lower-lying town of Newport in his apple wagon. The larger town was twenty-five miles away, a distance that took them an entire day and night to travel, and Ella spent most of it walking beside the wagon to keep warm in the chill November air. Her step-grandmother lived in Newport and took her in for the night, but the following morning, Ella was on her own. Her saving grace came in the form of employment as live-in help with the local druggist's family, assisting his wife, Cora Massey Mims. With a place to live, Ella was able to continue her education.

She attended Newport High School, then studied teacher education at the State Normal School in Johnson City about sixty miles to the northeast, which had opened in 1911 (and later became East Tennessee State University). Although she could have taught at Mountain Rest, she was wary of returning to the insular mountain community. Instead, she applied for a job at the Singer Sewing Machine Company. She became a demonstrator and bookkeeper, which enabled her to support herself while staying in Newport.

In her memoirs, she recalls reading an article in the November 1911 issue of *Woman's World Magazine* which inspired her to become a nurse. She found the opportunity in San Antonio, Texas where one of her aunts lived. With her aunt's recommendation, a "kind old German and his wife" agreed to hire Ella as live-in help and a caretaker, and paid her railroad fare from Tennessee to Texas sometime around 1915 or 1916.

By 1917, Ella had enrolled in nurse's training at the John Sealy Hospital School of Nursing in Galveston, Texas. She excelled at the work, attaining a position of supervisor before she graduated. Once she had her nursing degree, she was offered a full position at the hospital. She recalled, "...I worked my way through high school and one year of college. Then I decided the odds were against me and gave it up for a nurses' training school, and after a thousand years, which, as time is counted were only three, I graduated." She soon left John Sealy for employment at a hospital in Knoxville, but wasn't happy there either. While she'd been in Texas, her childhood love Mac McMahan had gotten married, despite his affectionate letters to her. It was the first in a long series of heartbreaks—she may have wondered at times if her romantic life had been put under some kind of curse.

Ella began to feel restless in Tennessee and looked for other employment opportunities. Bellevue Hospital in New York City accepted her as a nurse almost immediately upon receiving her application and so she headed north, timing her travel so that she could attend the Presidential Inauguration of Warren G. Harding in Washington, DC. Her position as a night nurse at Bellevue—a schedule which she selected purposefully—gave her freedom to explore the opportunities for fun and learning offered by the immense metropolis. She was methodical, and held herself to a schedule: three visits to museums, art galleries, and other cultural institutions each week. She took advantage of opportunities to go to lectures at Columbia University, and befriended the woman in charge of social outings for the nurses, which guaranteed her the best opera tickets available.

After about a year in the city, a nurse friend of Ella's mentioned that she had turned down a civil service nursing position in the Canal Zone in Panama. Ella pounced on the opportunity and was accepted. She arrived at the Colón Hospital in the summer of 1922, to a land of palm trees and lush tropical elegance. She thrived in the social scene of the Canal—people found her witty, and she could make up a toast for any occasion, reveling in being the life of the party. One of her patients, an entertainer who had adopted the pseudonym Marion Richmond, took a fancy to her pleasant nurse Ella, nicknaming her "Happy." When she recovered, Marion promised, she would "do something nice" for Ella in return. Shortly thereafter, Marion invited Ella to a party and informed her that a gentleman friend would be her escort. The man, Juan (Ella called him John) Arosemena, "enthralled" her, and he clearly fancied her in return as they cast glances each other's way throughout the evening. Ella found out during a few toasts at a second party that he was the Governor of Colón, a province of Panama.

For the second time in her life, she'd managed to begin building an affectionate relationship with a man married to someone else. She maintains in her memoirs that she was respectful of Arosemena's family, and their close friendship never became more than a platonic, cerebral affair. She accompanied him on a tour of Panama which inspired quite a few of her poems, later published in *Barefoot in the Smokies*. Although Arosemena invited her to be his secretary for his diplomatic appointment to France, she felt her presence would be harmful to his family, and perhaps recognized that she would also be at the mercy of his good will. She declined, but they wrote letters to each other for years. He later became President of Panama, from 1936 to 1939, his leadership characterized by major initiatives in health and education—perhaps because of Ella's influence.

While she was in Panama, Mac McMahon tracked her down and visited her. His first wife had died, and he proposed to Ella before he returned to his posting in Venezuela. She was overjoyed, but then "his letters ceased without any explanation—NOTHING!—as if he had suddenly passed out of being." She later found out he had gotten a Chilean woman pregnant, and abiding by the woman's Roman Catholic faith and his responsibility to the child, he agreed to marry her.

Only one man ever made her forget her disappointments with Mac. Every so often the nurses in Panama would return to the United States on leave. Ella had been working in Panama for three and a half years when, during one of these leave visits to New York City, she met the charming Al Whitfield (sometimes spelled Winfield) from Chattanooga in a chance encounter. She was looking to meet a friend at a theater, and asked him for directions. Throughout the play, she scribbled silly poetry to Al on her program, and mailed it to him the next day. They quickly fell in love. He proposed, she accepted. The one small catch was that she had to return to Panama, resign and collect her things, then return to New York to marry him. But when she returned, having left her job and friends, Al didn't meet her at the dock as she disembarked from the ship. After a few frantic days of trying to find him, she discovered that he had died of pneumonia three days before her ship arrived. Stunned and heartbroken that a man she could be happy with, who had wanted her to be his wife, had died so suddenly, Ella retreated to the mountains in 1927. She was overcome with grief, later writing, "I did not eat or leave my room for three days. I felt it was the end of the world for me…. Then I came home to drabness and mostly poverty [in Tennessee]."

Back home she worked as a private nurse for a little over a year. She later recalled one of her nursing adventures during this time:

"On a winter day a doctor sent me out to Upper Cosby in the Smoky Mountains, to nurse a man with a bullet hole through his lung. It was snowing and the snow was getting deeper by the minute. Someone said they hoped it would get knee deep to Elmer Jones, the tallest man in town. And it did, almost. My job, as an RN, was to prevent, if possible, the wounded man from getting pneumonia in the good lung. And for the record, I succeeded."

But she found little joy in her life in the mountains and worried that she had given up too early on her childhood dream of seeing the world. She decided to return to the place where the world had opened for her before: San Antonio. This time, however, she befriended a homeopathic doctor and friends of his who were devotees of the Theosophical Society and its theories on reincarnation and karma. Ella was enthralled by the intellect of the people she met at the Society's study sessions. They were a social, well-mannered group, if a bit odd. One of the gentlemen in the group, Dr. Hoygard (first name unknown), a Norwegian chiropractor with piercing eyes, began to fancy vivacious Ella. She later admitted that although they were opposites in nearly every way—she, outgoing and friendly; he, brooding and quiet— she still agreed to marry him.

The wedding was held in Tennessee, although Ella recounts in her memoirs that she had misgivings and tried to run away. Perhaps her friends and family were just delighted to get the thirty-six year old Ella to the altar—she found no help in eluding her bridegroom. Her wariness about Dr. Hoygard foreshadowed the misery she would feel as his wife. He was controlling—tight with his own money, possessive of hers—insisted on driving their car even though he couldn't drive, and, her worst fear, he was a charlatan. Shortly after their marriage, he joined a scheme to sell people "healing magnetic blankets" that Ella, as a nurse, knew wouldn't help address any kind of affliction. She left him on their "honeymoon" in Chicago and went back to Tennessee. After three weeks, he arrived to reconcile with her, and they returned to San Antonio, perhaps trying to find again the happier days of their courtship.

More disaster ensued. Dr. Hoygard was rumored to be a hypnotist, and Ella felt he was repeatedly trying to put a spell on her. The stock market crash of 1929 left the country in shambles just as they arrived back in San Antonio and they could barely find any work. Finally Dr. Hoygard was hired at a health resort in Kenedy, Texas, and they both regained steady employment. Ella was a hostess, nurse, and dietician; the doctor oversaw therapy treatments. But their better economic footing didn't help their marriage. The doctor was descending into a habit of physical abuse with Ella, and after he nearly broke her neck, she fled.

Safely back in Tennessee, she filed for divorce. Dr. Hoygard had disappeared with all of her belongings that she'd left at the health resort in Texas, and had controlled her finances for the past year. She had very little money left. Mac McMahon reappeared in her life, and explained his sudden disappearance after proposing to her in Panama. She was shocked and stunned to learn he was remarried and had a son. Once again she found herself heartbroken and nearly penniless. And so began her enterprise with the White Rock Inn and moonshining.

Her story of moonshining continues with her "pitting of wits" against the revenuers. She remembered, "It was a beautiful Day in August. Katie [Ella's alter ego] had her place shining, and real early in the morning she had bottled what kegged whiskey she had and refilled a two gallon keg. She put the keg in the oven of her coal and wood stove with a slow fire. She took the bottles out and hid them under the back steps. She had two gallon jugs in a tow sack out by the back fence in a clump of rose bushes." A little while later she had just pulled the keg out of the oven when "two deputies rushed in at her back door, served a search warrant on her, and started going through her most private possessions. One went in her bedroom and one went upstairs." They didn't realize that she was standing in a daze between them and the keg sitting right there beside the stove.

As they searched upstairs, she recovered her wits and hastily put the keg back in the oven, then built a big fire up to make it seem like she was getting ready to cook something. She hurried out the back steps, retrieved the bottles of moonshine and tossed them into a saw-brier patch on the other side of her property line. She looked up and her heart stopped as she realized a Cosby deputy, whom she knew, was standing in the doorway of her store. He was "laughing fit to bust" as he watched her. "Why don't you come on down and take me in?" she asked. He said, "It ain't my raid" and kept laughing.

Relieved that her friend seemed to be getting a kick out of her out-smarting the two deputies in the house, Ella quickly put the two gallon jugs in the sawbrier bush, then went back in the house and began frying ham while the deputies searched her basement. They finally "came back in the kitchen, stood in front of the stove and told her she had a clean house. Then they left." She retrieved the keg from its second heating in the stove, but found it charred. Luckily the bottles she'd thrown in the sawbrier patch hadn't broken and were ready to be sold that day. She "was a great admirer of Kipling; she now brought to mind his lines: I pitted my wits against the wits of men, Sometimes they won, and sometimes I won."

Although that was a satisfying, if stressful, encounter with the law-men, Ella wasn't interested in making a long career of moonshining. As winter approached, she and her brothers packed up and closed the doors to the house, store, and gas station. Ella left, leaving the title of best Home Distiller in the area to be claimed by someone else with a higher tolerance for law-breaking.

But her exploits with the law weren't over, although the fault lies mainly with her brother Ike Costner. Ike's success as a moonshine distributor was partly attributable to the fact that he was a member of a gang with ties to Al Capone, among other unsavory characters in Chicago. The gang robbed a U.S. Mail truck in Charlotte, North Carolina on November 15, 1933 and made off with $105,000. Some of the money was buried in jars along the Pigeon River in the Smokies. During a flood several years later, the jars broke, spilling money into nearby fields. Locals went into a treasure-hunting frenzy. Ella's elderly father was arrested, and in her attempt to keep him from the harsh conditions of a jail cell, she told the officers where to look for the money. When they couldn't find it, she told them, "Well, I guess I can find it. I didn't put it there but I'll see if I can find it." When she successfully uncovered the money, they immediately arrested her.

The jail was not to her liking: "There wasn't but one cot, and it didn't have a mattress.... Somebody had cut the mattress all to pieces and crammed it down the toilet, stopped up the toilet and the whole place was flooded." After a sleepless night perched on the cot frame, Ella was cross with the deputies who asked if she could make her bond. "I said, 'Make my bond? If I can make my bond this morning, I could have made it last night,' I said... 'I may never see the inside of a jail again and I'm a staying awhile.'" But she did eventually post the $2,500 bond and came home. Her brother Ike was sent to Alcatraz for thirty years, and her brother Rufus was sent to the federal penitentiary in Atlanta.

Despite her family's brushes with infamy, Ella was still able to find work as a private nurse when the economy began to recover in the 1940s. Mountain Rest had been absorbed into the boundaries of Great Smoky Mountains National Park, and her parents had moved out of their remote cabin. In Newport, Ella became head nurse at a clinic run by Dr. Mims, the pharmacist whose wife had taken her in as a fifteen-year-old runaway. But the specter of another war was looming over the United States, and she felt her nursing skills could be useful to the war effort. She enlisted in the Army by lying about her age on the application form—at almost fifty years old, she was technically too old for service, so she claimed to be thirty. Apparently no one noticed (or cared) and she was sent to Camp Forrest for training.

Camp Forrest, in central Tennessee, was one of the largest Army bases of World War II, and despite the threats abroad, the nurses and reserve soldiers spent the months relatively pleasantly, "with time for picnics, swimming, a trip home, a walking horse show at Shelbyville, and the Cotton Ball at Chattanooga." But the attack on Pearl Harbor changed everything. After December 1941, a request would come regularly for a certain number of nurses to volunteer for overseas duty. One of these was particularly urgent—the volunteers would be on the train to the West Coast the next morning. Ella was one of the fifteen who departed in a whirlwind, without time for ceremony or long goodbyes. None of them knew where they would be sent "overseas" or when exactly they would leave the country. She spent several chilly months in San Francisco taking classes "on everything from the detection of gasses to the many tropical diseases. We learned how to put on and take off a gas mask, and got used to wearing steel helmets." Even when she boarded the ship to head to her post in March 1942, she was only told the destination was "somewhere in the Pacific." But on the eighth day, someone recognized Hawaii on the horizon and "we rounded Diamond Head and sailed into Pearl Harbor. There was the ARIZONA just as she had capsized, holding tragedy within her embrace."

Ella took the chaos that still gripped Hawaii in stride. She had always been an exceptional nurse, and she was extremely popular with her patients. Not only was she adept at giving them medicine and taking temperatures, fluffing pillows and bringing water, she also talked to them about their families, their homes, their loves. She even read to them, sometimes poems or stories she'd written, sometimes popular novels. The same skills that made her the life of a party, made her a beloved and effective nurse.

In Hawaii, the literary ambitions she had harbored all her life were given substance. She was photographed for a piece in the *Honolulu Star-Bulletin* on "Pictures of Women in Uniform" and used this as an entrée to ask the newspaper's editor Riley Allen whether she might contribute some poetry or other writing to the paper. In December 1944, she was transferred to Guam to treat injuries from Iwo Jima, and she continued to send short pieces to the editor in Honolulu. Fan letters made their way from Hawaii to her tent in Guam, and she delighted in responding.

She wrote to her editor toward the end of her post, "When I pick up newspapers all over the country there are letters from service men and women in them…. I believe there is more morale building in a human interest story about the boys who are doing the fighting than there is in a thousand moving pictures, or in many of the USO or Special Service Shows. Now that Ernie Pyle is dead, who will replace him? The boys write from their foxholes and tell about having read my stories. I answer every letter."

After a jeep accident in May 1945, she was sent back to the mainland to recover for three months. She was then summoned to Seattle to await another deployment. She remembered, "While waiting there the bomb fell on Japan, and all of we older nurses were ordered to stations where we would be let out of the Army and sent to our homes. While on the way back on the train, the ceasing of hostilities was declared. I had a heart attack and could drink nothing but water to celebrate."

As life began to return to normal with the end of the war, she retired as a second lieutenant and went home again to the Smokies. By this time her parents were quite elderly and their health was fragile— her father was nearly blind; her mother a semi-invalid—and Ella felt it was her responsibility to focus her care on them.

Throughout her life she read voraciously and sought out a self-directed education from museums, public lectures, and well-informed friends. But as she approached her 60th birthday, she decided it was time to go back to school. Perhaps the encouragement, or discouragement, of Riley Allen at the *Honolulu Star-Bulletin*, had something to do with it—he wrote, "If you seriously contemplate taking up journalism—and that is at best a hazardous step for you—your best experience will be gained in some good mainland school." She enrolled in Carson-Newman College in Jefferson City, Tennessee in 1951. Four years later, she graduated with a BA degree in English.

Her niece Jean, one of Ike's daughters, suggested that Ella consider publishing some of her poems. Ella quickly warmed to the project, publishing her first book, a collection of poems about the Smokies called *Lamp in the Cabin*, in 1967. Her second book, *Poems of Paradise* (about Hawaii) was published the next year by Carleton Press in New York. Her writing was described as "far from ordinary, diverse, and constantly pleasing and surprising literary skills," and *Poems of Paradise* was touted as "memories illuminated by the pageantry, beauty, and grace of a changing Hawaii…. She was stationed in this epicenter of contrast between jasmine-scented nights and the carnage of the times…. Word-painting of high order of sensitivity is framed in these pages."

Neither her childhood in the Smokies, nor her subsequent returns to the mountains, were ever the happiest circumstances for her, but she seems to have made peace with her homeland as she grew older. Her third book of poetry, *Barefoot in the Smokies*, published in 1969, included many poems inspired by the beauty of the mountains. She dedicated it to "all poets who ever tried to sell a book of their verse." On December 31st of that same year, she was awarded a Certificate of Merit for "Distinguished Contributions to Poetry" by the Board of Editors of the International Who's Who in Poetry.

In 1971, she published *Song of Life in the Smokies*, part memoir, part collection of stories, and part genealogical record of Cosby. She was also recognized as the Poet Laureate of the Smokies by the Tennessee state legislature with Joint Resolution #108. Her niece Jean Schilling and Jean's husband Lee had started the Folk Festival of the Smokies, which Ella was more than happy to participate in as a storyteller, continuing to captivate listeners with skills she'd perfected at glamorous parties and in the stark white hospital wards filled with patients eager to escape into whatever literary world she created for them.

As an unusually intelligent young woman, she seems to have sensed that the life she hungered after wouldn't be found in the tiny community of Mountain Rest. And yet, with all of the enjoyment she found in her life abroad and her travels, she only ever called the Smokies home. Later, she acknowledged their lingering influence on her, writing, "The things that have lived longest in my memory, the things that have been most vivid, what you would call first things... the things that drew me back when I have been on the verge of destruction are the things I remember from my childhood... memory would beckon and I would follow, to some far pine scented hollow and I would run and run in the wind, and at evening I would come home to the little cabin and smell the coffee a roasting, and taste Mother's sweet corn pone; and a million like memoires have sustained me through the years of adulthood, of disappointments unnamable, and heartaches untold."

When she passed away on July 9, 1982, her family buried her in a small, shaded cemetery in Great Smoky Mountains National Park—a privilege accorded to very few people once the government assumed ownership of the land. Surrounded by tall rhododendrons, her grave-stone lies very near the old log cabin home site where she was born—brought back to her humble beginnings after a life of adventure so grand it staggers the imagination of even modern mountain residents, preserved in her memoirs and books of poetry.

Ella Costner

Chapter 5

Phyllis Higginbotham

IN THE MANY MONTHS WITHOUT A DOCTOR IN THE AREA, WE WERE DEPENDANT ON OUR OWN RESOURCES. WE IMPROVISED SPLINTS, APPLIED PRESSURE BANDAGES, USED SUCTION FOR SNAKE BITES AND TOOK CARE OF AXE CUTS, GUNSHOT WOUNDS, CONVULSIONS, AND BEAR SCRATCHES.

PHYLLIS HIGGINBOTHAM · 1890-1978

—*Phyllis Higginbotham, nurse 1920-1926, in "The Arrow of Pi Beta Phi" newsletter.*

Marjorie Chalmers

Pi Beta Phi
Health
Center

IT WAS A NEW WORLD TO ME, FRESH FROM A
CITY HOSPITAL... THE WORK WAS NEW AND
INTERESTING, BUT I TRUST NO ONE KNEW, IN THOSE
FIRST MONTHS, OF THE UTTER PANIC I FELT AT THE
HEAVY RESPONSIBILITY AND MY IGNORANCE OF
HOW TO SHOULDER IT.

MARJORIE CHALMERS · 1893-1986

—Marjorie Chalmers, nurse 1933-1965. Introduction of her memoir, Better I Stay.

On a late spring evening in 1923, Phyllis Higginbotham made her way up the path towards the twinkling lights of the medium-sized bungalow she shared with the other teachers at the rural school in Gatlinburg, Tennessee. As the first "community health nurse" at the elementary school established in Gatlinburg by the Pi Beta Phi Women's Fraternity, Phyllis's job was to educate mountain schoolchildren and their families about sanitation, nutrition, and disease prevention. But because no doctors were able to travel to the community quickly, and none had established a nearby practice, she was asked to do much more.

She had spent this particular day as she had many times before: riding her horse along steep, narrow paths as she made house calls to families living on isolated farms. Looking forward to relaxing with some of the teachers, she entered the house and found a note addressed to her: a baby was sick with symptoms of diphtheria, a virus that killed many children before immunization became common. "It was about the farthest place in another community," she later wrote. But she knew that if she didn't hurry, the child was likely to die. "Taking all the emergency antitoxin I had, one of the teachers drove me as far as possible in a Ford, then we walked through the woods to the house and gave the antitoxin by the help of a smoky lamp and a flashlight.... The child couldn't have lived till morning so there was no waiting to get a doctor—the nearest one couldn't have been gotten under six or eight hours provided he was home when called."

As the only medical professional available to the hundreds of families living in one of the most remote parts of the Smoky Mountains, Phyllis must have often felt the weight of life and death on her shoulders. Although a car could sometimes get her to her destination, she more frequently rode a horse because the roads were rocky and rutted (or there was no road at all).

Of course, a car would generally have the advantage of staying parked where she left it; one night she emerged from a cabin around 3 a.m. and discovered her new horse, Prince, was nowhere to be seen. "We scoured the fields in the moonlight," she remembered, "then one of the men discovered fresh prints on the road leading to the

Burg, and half a mile down the road we caught up to him, cropping the early spring plants as he walked homeward." Although she tried to be prepared for anything—her saddlebags always packed with a set of medical instruments and first aid kit, and she kept a flashlight handy—many things about her work were impossible to anticipate. There was nothing routine about nursing in the mountains.

Over four and a half decades, Phyllis Higginbotham's, and her successor Marjorie Chalmers's, efforts created a fundamental change in the way mountain people understood, reacted to, and treated health and sickness—from tooth brushing to pregnancy, to bee stings and broken bones, to treatments for diphtheria and smallpox. The nurses found that people in the Smokies were completely unaware of pre- and postnatal care and that babies never received standard immunizations. Treatable conditions like poor eyesight and clubfeet were taken as "God's will." No one had regular doctor's checkups, malnutrition was common, as were advanced-stage hookworm infections that brought on anemia. No doctors visited the area with any regularity, and many afflictions went untreated, or were remedied with traditional medicines. Burns, snakebites, colds, and other illnesses were treated with folk medicine—turpentine, sugar, mud and tobacco juice, or corn whiskey…with varying degrees of success.

The Pi Beta Phi Settlement School nurses immunized schoolchildren, provided educational programs about prenatal and "well-baby" care, and taught better home sanitation, although that was difficult to achieve given the fundamentals of mountain life. Large families crowded into one or two-room mountain cabins. Children usually shared a bed with multiple siblings—making it nearly impossible to prevent the spread of illness to other family members. Additionally, schoolchildren regularly drank water from the same ladle and bucket, easily spreading disease among families. Because of poor soil in the mountains, family gardens and farms rarely yielded enough food for the family to eat over the course of an entire winter, and their diets were limited, starch-based (corn, potatoes, beans) and lacking in nutrient-rich vegetables (carrots, spinach, broccoli, etc.…). Older children drank coffee instead of milk, because the cows rarely produced enough for an entire family (which Phyllis attributed to lack of good feed for the cows themselves).

The nurses' work in the midst of such deep-rooted public health problems and enduring faith in folk medicine was endless and difficult. It was also, above all, transformative for generations of families living in the remoteness of the mountains. But that positive outcome was by no means certain when Phyllis arrived in Gatlinburg.

The Pi Beta Phi fraternity had successfully opened an elementary school for mountain children, known as a "settlement school," in 1912 as a national service project to celebrate their 50th anniversary as an organization. Classes were initially held in an abandoned building that had previously doubled as a church and schoolhouse. By 1914, the Pi Phis had acquired property, completed a six-room new schoolhouse, and enrolled 75 students. But it was clear to the teachers and staff in those early years of the Pi Beta Phi Elementary School that achieving their education goals depended on a more holistic approach than schooling alone. In particular, the Pi Phi women noticed the general poor health of the overall population, the absence of modern approaches to nutrition and disease treatment, and lack of access to doctors.

The women knew they needed to hire a nurse, and perhaps build her a clinic to work in, but World War I slowed their fundraising campaign. Over the first four years of the settlement school's existence, the teachers did what they could for their students and families. They improvised during the war years and the long winter of 1918 when the Spanish Flu pandemic ravaged the mountains, as it did much of the rest of the country, killing more Americans than died during battle in World War I. The teachers at the settlement school began asking for a community health nurse with renewed vigor just as the post-war economy was boosting incomes. In 1919, the Pi Beta Phis had secured enough funds to hire twenty-nine-year-old Helen Phyllis Higginbotham, a woman with exemplary nursing credentials, to join the settlement school staff in Gatlinburg.

Between the time she was officially hired and her arrival at the Pi Beta Phi Settlement School, Phyllis spent time at the Henry Street

Settlement House in New York where she learned how being a settlement school nurse differed from regular nursing duties, namely that she would be working on her own instead of with a network of supportive, well-trained professionals. She then traveled to the Hindman Settlement School in Kentucky where she "gained valuable insight into the cultural standards of mountain families," she later wrote. In the fall of 1920, she arrived in Gatlinburg. It was difficult being the first nurse because the community didn't know what to expect from her, nor she from them. But Phyllis bravely blazed a trail for the Pi Phi nurses who would follow, performing her work so admirably that she was asked to become the first state supervisor for public health nurses in Tennessee in 1926.

A succession of nurses staffed the Pi Phi Clinic for the next ten years until Marjorie Chalmers, a widow from Illinois, took the position in 1936. Like Phyllis, she loved the mountain people and the wild beauty of the mountains themselves. She stayed and worked until the clinic closed in 1965. Its closing was a sign of shifting health care resources—the government had begun taking on more of the public health burden. But it also signaled a great success for the Pi Phi nurses themselves, for they had fundamentally changed the community's understanding of health and preventative care through their clinic.

The fraternity's newsletter *The Arrow* reported that when Phyllis began work in October 1920, "there was nothing for her to work with: no office, no supplies—nothing but a great need." She accepted the position knowing she was making a personal sacrifice—letters from the fundraising committee openly acknowledged that her salary of $75 per year was a pittance compared to ordinary nursing compensation. And the workload was staggering, with long and unpredictable hours.

Phyllis later wrote about her initial work, "The people had as vague an idea of a nurse as I had of what comprised nursing in the mountains. Their experience was limited to a few private nurses, so a nurse to them meant someone who would make an indefinite stay and relieve the family of all responsibility...consequently as a Public Health nurse I was neither fish, flesh, fowl, nor good red herring; being variously called the doctor, the nurse, the cook or the waiter—and since I wouldn't diagnose and prescribe, or go and spend weeks with a typhoid case, the people were much puzzled to know of what use I could really be."

Myriad concerns vied for her attention, from health education, to access to doctors, to malnutrition. A lesser woman might have been paralyzed by the scope of the problem, but Phyllis was brilliant, organized, friendly, and comfortable on a horse—attributes necessary for anyone hoping to improve the current health practices of the population.

Phyllis was born in the rural western ranching country of Lethbridge, Ontario Canada in 1890. Although her father was the town pharmacist and postmaster, she grew up riding horses and loved the ranching culture. Perhaps the people in the Smokies reminded her of the stoic, hardworking people she grew up with, and her familiarity and fond memories of folk who earned their living from working the land helped her relate to and bond with the Southern highlanders.

Phyllis studied modern languages at the University of Toronto, then nursing at Johns Hopkins. After graduating in 1918, she joined the American Army and served in France for a year. She then received a Red Cross scholarship to continue her studies at Columbia University and earned her master's degree.

Her dedicated professionalism was balanced by a sense of humor, and a willingness to laugh at her own initial reactions to some oddities of mountain culture. She explained in *The Arrow* that, "I am not as sensitive as I once was about always being asked, for months afterwards, if I was with 'so and so who died.' I used to resent the implication that I had hastened their departure."

She admired many of the traditions of the mountain people, and even though her goal was to modernize their approach to healthcare, she appreciated and enjoyed many aspects of Smoky Mountain culture. Not long after she arrived at the Settlement School, she suggested that the Pi Phis organize an annual "Old Timer's Day" to celebrate traditional Appalachian customs. The Settlement School director, Evelyn Bishop, liked the idea, and the first one was held in 1921. It quickly became one of the community's most anticipated events of the year.

The atmosphere of the heritage festival was reminiscent of the "frontier round-ups" Phyllis had grown up attending, with competitions ranging from sharpshooting, quilt making, and vegetable canning to a corn husking contest (to see who could husk ears of corn the fastest) and hog-calling (the art of summoning hogs). Competitions were taken seriously, but music and laughter pervaded the day. In addition to the pride and glory that came with victory, the mountain people relished the opportunity to gather together on the Pi Beta Phi school grounds, a break from their relatively isolated farms.

Perhaps because her own work was so taxing, her burden of care so great, Phyllis understood what it meant to the hardworking families to come together and have fun. In her first two years, working without a clinic, Phyllis made over 2,000 house calls. She generally limited her visits to five miles or less in any direction from the Settlement School, or roughly 200 families. Going farther into the mountains often required an entire day for a single visit and wasn't efficient—especially because there were no accurate maps of the area, so it was easy to get lost.

For two years, Phyllis tried to attend to the community's health needs basically out of her saddlebags, storing bandages and supplies in a corner of the school headmistress's office. But the spring of 1922 was a watershed season for Phyllis, Gatlinburg, and the Pi Phi fraternity. The remodel of a four-room farmhouse was completed, providing Phyllis with a brand new clinic on the Pi Beta Phi property. The Jennie Nichol Memorial Health Center, named for a Pi Phi founder who died shortly after obtaining her medical degree, opened on May 8, 1922. Phyllis delightedly reported on the arrangement of furniture and supplies, all donated by various alumni clubs, in the bathroom, waiting room, office, and workroom. The latter room, with its porcelain sink, slop sink, work table, and three-burner stove also doubled as a laboratory one day a week for the five high school students taking science classes.

Phyllis was able to persuade four doctors in Sevierville and Knoxville (14 and 40 miles away, respectively) to each keep monthly office hours in Gatlinburg. Between all of them, she could guarantee a doctor at the clinic each Wednesday afternoon. One of her "nose and throat" clinics resulted in thirty examinations and a few "light operations." This was one of the ways Phyllis made inroads on treatable health conditions that had gone unaddressed by traditional mountain medicine. Although the Pi Phis did their best to compensate doctors for their time, many of these clinics were run at financial loss for the doctors, because the patients were unable to pay. But the doctors did it, persuaded by Phyllis who said they "have been most helpful and loyal, and have often made trips at great personal inconvenience, and more cost than reward."

The clinic's first year was "an especially hard one" as the October 1923 Pi Phi newsletter reported "an unusual amount of sickness both in the community and among the teachers." Phyllis made 1,171 house calls, and traveled over 2,000 miles within the mountains. These were still early years for community health work, and most of her focus had to be on curative care, addressing sickness as it arose instead of focusing on longer term understanding of immunizations, nutrition, pre- and postnatal care, among other issues. Hookworm, an intestinal parasite, was an epidemic throughout the South, and the mountains were no exception. A majority of the schoolchildren were infected, some so badly that they suffered from anemia.

Some funding for medicines was provided through state health programs, but Pi Phi members and alumni clubs gave most of the money, supplies, and furniture for the clinic. In the newsletters, Phyllis repeatedly thanked them for their generosity, but wasn't shy about asking for more. Midwives in the mountain communities had traditionally collected unneeded clothes or blankets from more well-to-do families and distributed them to the poor—their presence in cabins and awareness of general family health gave them a good idea of need and poverty. Phyllis continued this service from the health clinic, asking the Pi Phi women to send unneeded items like outgrown children's clothing or old bathrobes for distribution at the clinic. In particular, baby clothes were in high demand.

Phyllis was also determined to do something about the lack of nutrition in the typical mountaineer diet, which consisted largely of soda biscuits, corn, sorghum, eggs, and edibles foraged from the forest. Even the fruits and vegetables that women canned after the harvest rarely lasted very long. (Except, Phyllis recalled, in the ironic case of one childless household that had "three hundred cans of fruit and vegetables to be moved out of the room we decided to use as an operating room....")

Apple season, which she noted didn't happen every year, often resulted in the kids' consumption of too much of the acidic fruit, causing intestinal problems and "accentuating sores." Some fresh fruit was good, of course, but Phyllis hoped to introduce a wider variety of nutritious foods. In an inspired moment, she wrote to a Tennessee Congressmen for the district and asked for a variety of vegetable seeds to feed the fifty or so schoolchildren who attended Pi Beta Phi elementary. Then, to her "utter horror and amazement," she reported, she returned from several days away from Gatlinburg to find two mail sacks full of seeds, dumped out in the back of the store where the Pi Phi's postal deliveries were sent. Seeds were collected in everything ranging from dish pans to wash tubs and wastepaper baskets, "and [the Pi Phis] gave out seeds to everyone we could, for several years." Unfortunately, this was one of her least successful initiatives and resulted in little improvement in the community's enthusiasm for new vegetables. She wrote that she would patiently hope for "the domestic science department to cultivate the taste for vegetables new and untried."

Assisting with childbirth was another significant part of Phyllis's work. As a community health nurse, her official responsibilities stopped short of delivering babies, but she never refused a request, as long as she had confirmation that a doctor had been sent for and couldn't make it. The communities also had a long tradition of midwifery—although skill level varied widely among the women—and Phyllis often worked with these "grannywomen," welcoming any capable assistance during a birth. Ever looking to improve understanding of modern practices among the community, she organized training classes so established midwives could learn more up-to-date sanitation practices and handling of newborns. She also learned, as did her successor Marjorie Chalmers more than a decade later, that when men showed up at the clinic and "didn't know what was wrong" with a woman, it was most likely childbirth-related. One of the oddities of mountain culture Phyllis had to get used to was that women explained very little about what was wrong, leaving husbands to awkwardly relay problems secondhand. "I have had to get used to getting more of a woman's symptoms from her husband," she reported. This, combined with the fact that pregnancy was viewed as an embarrassing female condition, to be hidden under generously sized aprons, made directly addressing issues of women's health very difficult.

In spite of Phyllis's capability, progress on health education and preventative care was slow. Even after a year of operating out of the clinic, Phyllis reported, "Later on it may be possible to emphasize more of the preventative and instructive work, but at present my work is largely care of the sick, and the people are usually sick, too. Infectious diseases are apt to be severer than one finds in the cities." But she loved the work. "Nursing in the mountains may sound like nothing but problems and difficulties, but the compensation more than makes up for them… nowhere does one find such people and such scenery as in the mountains, and the longer one stays the more fascinating the work becomes," she wrote to her fraternity sisters in the June 1923 newsletter.

Despite the hectic schedule of administering first aid, making emergency house calls, and organizing doctor visits, Phyllis kept meticulous records. She set up a filing system with a card for every patient, often listing an individual's medications so she could easily fill prescriptions without consulting a doctor. She also kept detailed records of her work: "field visits," office visits, vaccinations, inoculations, family conferences, health talks, and more. Nurse Marjorie Chalmers would later explain the challenge of maintaining the record keeping: "The index file is vastly interesting, for nearly everyone in the community has been in at one time or another. Filing must be done with care for there are so many of the same name…. There are index cards for six hundred and ninety-three Ogles from Aileen to Zula. There are nine Charles Ogles, five Stella Ogles, six Tom and eight Don Ogles…. It is hard enough to keep records straight, but when two or three of the same name have fathers of the same name, things can get complicated...." And yet, Phyllis's attention to detail helped the center function smoothly in the midst of what often seemed like chaos.

In 1925, a doctor from the State Medical University in Memphis visited the Health Center and observed Phyllis's work and record keeping firsthand. He wrote an extensive report and recommended that the clinic be used as a model for rural health centers throughout the state. The next year Phyllis was offered the newly created position of state supervisor of public health nurses, which required leaving Gatlinburg. The community, which hadn't quite known what to make of her when she arrived only six years earlier, felt her departure keenly. And if the Pi Phis who hired her feared she was irreplaceable, they were almost correct.

For the next ten years, a handful of nurses arrived and left the Settlement School. The work was hard, the pay was low, and the area was very remote, although that was slowly changing. Roads were improving, the logging boom brought job-seeking men, sometimes with families, to the mountains; and in response to the logging, a movement to preserve the natural beauty of the land as a national park began to take shape. The tourism industry had been steadily growing since the mid-1910s and was developing into a mainstay of the local economy.

In the midst of this time of upheaval, Marjorie Chalmers, a middle-aged widow from Galesburg, Illinois, was hired as the Settlement School public health nurse in 1935. As she wrote in the beginning of her book, *Better I Stay*, about her experiences nursing in the Smokies: "I still don't know how it all happened. Why this blind leap into a job of which I knew nothing? 'School and Community Nurse' was an imposing title, but it could cover a lot of things. The whole thing was very indefinite.... I couldn't even find Gatlinburg on my map of Tennessee.... Even as I drove southward, I wondered at me. Far from being an adventurous soul, I prefer my life uncluttered by change. This, then, was most upsetting."

Marjorie had wanted to be a nurse since she was a young girl in Illinois. Her father, however, had refused to pay for her education because he didn't like the nursing school, so she studied to be a teacher instead. After a few unsatisfying years as a first grade teacher, she convinced her father to let her go to Minneapolis, where some of her cousins lived, and study nursing at the posh Eitel Hospital which served the city's wealthiest citizens. (It featured sun porches with Navajo rugs and private rooms with brass beds and mahogany furniture.) She and her cousins didn't tell her father that Marjorie wasn't actually living with them—she was staying across town to be closer to the hospital since she worked twelve hour days, with only half a day off each week.

At the start of World War I, she tried to join the Red Cross but hadn't yet completed three years of nursing nor passed the state board exams. When she could meet the qualifications, she volunteered for the Army and began treating wounded service men at a hospital in southern Indiana in October 1918, a month before armistice was declared. She spent the majority of her career working in larger hospitals, but after her husband died in 1933, she found herself looking for something new and challenging to take her mind off his absence. She couldn't have guessed how completely the new job in Gatlinburg would take over her life, but as she would later write, the days at the Health Center were "far from monotonous."

Marjorie's predecessor stayed a week to instruct her in the clinic routines, show her around the town, and make a few introductions. Then she was on her own. She maintained the previous nurse's office hours—opening the clinic at 8 a.m., but felt it was inadequate. Mountain children and sometimes adults, would already be waiting patiently for her on the front porch. These were usually folks needing simple first aid, and Marjorie used those skills to make friends—which she knew would go a long way towards helping her gain the community's trust.

Building friendship and trust with people who still had their own traditions and medical lore was key to Marjorie's success. Like Phyllis, she quickly realized that the work would be what she made of it. There would always be more to do than she had time for, so it was up to her to address as much as she could take on at a time. "It was a new world to me, fresh from a city hospital. The little village, the narrow valley beside the river, the heavily wooded hills and the steep, winding trails were sheer beauty. The work was new and interesting, but I trust no one knew, in those first months, of the utter panic I felt at the heavy responsibility and my ignorance of how to shoulder it," she remembered. "It took more courage than I would have thought possible to make those first calls. Had I met with antagonism I might not have continued. But mountain folk are kind."

Her first winter in the mountains was bitterly cold, and one of the first real tests of her mettle came on a morning when it was seven degrees below zero, with a dusting of snow. She was eating breakfast with the other resident school staff when word arrived that a woman called Aunt Crettie had died and the family wanted Marjorie to prepare her for burial. The two school cooks generously agreed to accompany her on the trail—it was too dangerous to travel alone. Marjorie had packed the supplies in a knapsack, "so our hands would be free for climbing." She anticipated well, for the trail was steep and slick with ice. "…when we couldn't stand up we sat down and inched ourselves backward, or crawled, clinging to the bushes."

When the nearly frozen trio finally reached the cabin, Marjorie found Aunt Crettie's body laid out in the one-room home on a bed at the opposite end from the fireplace. It was so cold at that end of the room that some spilled water had frozen on the floor. Thirteen people huddled close to the fire, "but the room was so still I could hear the movements of the hound dogs tied under the house. I felt on trial, for I was the new Yankee nurse, and I knew almost nothing that was expected of me in such a situation." After a few moments, however, one of the family members stepped forward and quietly offered to help, dispelling her fears. Together, they prepared Aunt Crettie for burial.

The journey back to the Settlement School was equally cold and treacherous, and Marjorie found she had no appetite for dinner. When the school caretaker brought hot water bottles, Marjorie, not normally prone to crying, dissolved into tears of exhaustion and appreciation at the thoughtful gesture. Gradually she adjusted to the pressure and constant surprises of healthcare in the mountains, learning to trust that she, too, would receive help when she most needed it.

There were two major changes between Phyllis's tenure at the health center and Marjorie's. First, when Marjorie arrived, there was a doctor in town. He was Gatlinburg's first local doctor who had established his practice in 1935. They helped each other out with difficult cases, surgeries, and emergencies. Eventually, though he moved away and Marjorie assumed the heavy responsibility of being the only accessible health professional for miles until 1950, when a new doctor opened a permanent practice in town.

The second significant difference was that the road conditions had improved so much that Marjorie found a car more useful than a horse. Not only did she not quite feel as at ease on horseback as Phyllis had, but she found she could generally drive most of the way to a patient's house before continuing on foot along trails that led further into the woods. The car enabled her to make house calls that were twice as far from the clinic as Phyllis had traveled. It also increased her scope of regular nursing duties. In addition to being responsible for community health in Gatlinburg, Marjorie was the nurse for children at the Settlement School, high school, and the six rural one-or-two room schoolhouses in several nearby communities.

That's not to say that travel was easy. The farthest flung community of Big Ridge was so remote that she could only get there when it hadn't rained recently: the road, which ran part of the way through a creek bed, was regularly impassable. Most of the roads were steep, narrow and winding, and nearly impossible to travel when it was raining. Marjorie didn't care to count the close calls—the time she almost backed over a ledge; the time the rotted bridge almost sent her plunging into the raging river; the time she almost turned over in a gully as she swerved to miss a black bear crossing the road. Night driving, or "night riding" as she called it, was an all too frequent part of her work, and her fearlessness made her effective at reaching her patients in the nick of time. She drove about a thousand miles each month, and traded her cars in every two years because the mountain roads were so bad. "The boys at the garage watched over those cars with a very personal interest," she said, "for no one knew when they might carry them or one of their folk on a fast emergency trip."

And Marjorie learned to answer a call as quickly as the bad roads would allow, for as she soon discovered, folk remedies often made it more difficult for her to address an injury. Many of the older mountaineers still practiced folk medicine, putting mixtures of soda and molasses on burns, or cobwebs in a cut to lessen the bleeding. These, in particular, Marjorie found only increased the chance of infection, although she was careful to treat mountain traditions with respect even when she disapproved of their application. In fact, she found greater reception for new techniques by encouraging people to tell her about the old ways and looking for similarities between her approach and theirs. An article Marjorie found about researchers "trying to find out why the onion's volitil oil was efficient in the treatment of respiratory diseases," which hearkened to the old-timey use of "onion-poultice" for pneumony-fever, was particularly well received.

As Marjorie acknowledged, "Some folk were born, lived a full life and died without ever going to a doctor. A woman, and a man as well, in the old days had to have a practical knowledge of treating many sorts of accidents and illnesses...." But she also wanted to understand what kinds of treatments she might have to work around, and what long held misconceptions of healing she would need to dispel in the children. To get a better sense of the treatments the children might receive from home care, she asked them to talk to their parents and write things down for her. In her book, she listed some of the more common responses, such as "Red-root medicine is good for toothake. Wilted cabbage leaves is good for colds. The bark of a sassafras tree is used to inrich the blood...." To treat hookworm, it was common to boil the seeds of Jerusalem oak and mix it into molasses which, when cooled, was cut into "candies," a treatment which was sometimes remarkably effective.

Like Phyllis, Marjorie realized that getting adults to shift from "curative care"—treating health issues as they arose—to preventative measures like inoculations, regular ear/eye exams, and good hygiene was difficult and slow. While she was always happy to do what she could for adults, she focused her teaching on the younger generation. The health habits of children improved by leaps and bounds with the introduction of the Blue Ribbon Day, a personal health and hygiene program instituted in Sevier County in 1933. Under Marjorie's leadership, the program flourished from the late 1930s through the 1950s. The genius of the program was that it made a competition out of healthy habits, much in the same way that the modern day President's Fitness Challenge encourages a basic understanding of exercise and good nutrition.

The Blue Ribbon Day reward was a shiny pin, worn as a badge of honor and pride on a dress or overall strap, and a trip to Sevierville for a ceremony and parade. To earn the pin, the child had to meet several requirements over the previous year: proper hygiene, which included brushing teeth, dental visits and eye exams, taking vitamins and drinking milk, and being up to date on inoculations. Some mountain parents remained suspicious of modern medicine's enthusiasm for shots, but withholding permission meant a child knew he would be automatically disqualified from getting a Blue Ribbon. And suffice to say, children found ways to be persuasive that the nurses could not. Thus Blue Ribbon Day became a major factor in achieving the Pi Phi's goal of establishing new norms in the community's approach to preventative care, nutrition, and hygiene.

Attending to first aid needs and emergencies continued to be a significant part of Marjorie's work. She treated the Settlement School kids at recess, administering daily first aid for about twenty students. Burns were common from open fireplaces in many cabins, as were cuts from handling axes and knives, scalding from getting too close to boiling water, and sprains, bruises, and boils. On Friday afternoons she held "open house" hours for community members to come by and ask questions about health problems, or just to visit. Marjorie gave booster shots and inoculations, weighed babies, and administered first aid as needed. She continued to encourage the clothing exchange Phyllis started—mountain people brought in outgrown clothes and acquired new, better fitting ones, and the Pi Phis donated useful, used items for the clinic patients from their own homes.

When Marjorie occasionally had free time in the afternoons, particularly when she was new to Gatlinburg, she would drive down roads and stop at houses, introduce herself, and learn about the families that lived in the most remote parts of the mountains. Even on sick calls, she found, there were moments to get to know people. There was often time to visit while a kettle of water boiled, or waiting to make sure medication would take effect. Marjorie would sit with the mountain families, often by a fire, and rock a baby in her arms, and ask questions about life in the Smoky Mountains. These were often unguarded moments, when people were at their most relaxed and friendly.

Like Phyllis, Marjorie was enchanted by the uniqueness of mountain traditions. Music captivated her most of all. She tried to learn the music and lyrics to old ballads from nearly everyone she met. "I learned them as I could—while sitting in a home, while watching a weaver at her work at her loom or winding a warp, or [as I was] carrying folk about the country in the car." To her delight, the young schoolchildren at some of the more rural schools would occasionally perform a "program of old songs" for her as she made her rounds. She loved the songs without accompaniment, appreciating their "unusual harmonies and haunting minors." But often the singer would be accompanied by someone on banjo, fiddle, guitar, or Marjorie's favorite, the dulcimer. She tried to find one for sale for many years, and finally stumbled upon her prize in North Carolina. It was old and in need of repair—but she found its original maker and had it fixed. It became one of her most treasured possessions.

After several years in Gatlinburg, Marjorie herself had a significant health scare in the early 1940s. Her hand became severely infected, contaminated from a patient with a virulent abscess that she had been taking care of. It became so serious she required treatment at the hospital in Knoxville. Osteomyelitis and gangrene developed and three quarters of her left thumb had to be amputated. She very nearly lost her entire left hand, and it took weeks before she was back to full duty. "Lord Ha' mercy, Miss Marjorie," a woman told her, "I thought you had died out." Always delighted by mountain phrases, Marjorie was amused by the thought of "dying out" and wondered lightly how it might be different from just dying.

Unable to go on house calls and attend to first aid as she usually did,

Marjorie began to focus more on teaching. She offered a simplified first aid course, attended by about one hundred high school students. Next, she offered courses in home nursing to both high schoolers and adults. The classes were rewarding, but she found herself still marking time until she could get back to her regular routine. The Massachusetts club of Pi Phis had sent a new black leather doctor's bag at about the time Marjorie contracted the infection, and after many months of recovery, she relished being able to resume house calls and get some good use out of the beautiful new bag.

By this time, the health center had been around for over twenty years and had established a good reputation in the community. More people sought out Marjorie's advice, or came to the regular doctor's clinics and educational classes she offered. The construction of the main road through Gatlinburg, simply by making travel easier, also contributed to an increasing number of patient visits. But the constant use of the clinic, combined with harsh weather and termites, was beginning to take its toll on the building. Reflecting back, Marjorie wrote, "Sometimes it seemed as if the old white building gathered within its slightly warped walls all the problems of living for half the community. That was inevitable, for birth and death, health and sickness; the stark, unadorned struggle for existence, and the love and the beauty of living—these were the things that passed through the cottage day after day."

Agnes Wright Spring, one of the settlement schoolteachers, reported in the March 1944 newsletter that "large rocks... are used to prop the warped doors shut or open as desired... The basement is moldy and the foundations are wobbly from the constant attack of termites." Marjorie too struggled in the dilapidated building: "Equipment, instruments and books, shoes and clothing must be carefully watched for rust and mold. It is discouraging, trying to keep things clean and efficient." The Pi Phis recognized the need to renovate and update the clinic, but World War II strained their existing resources and hampered fundraising. Finally in 1947 plans for a new health center were approved, and the building opened in the summer of 1948.

The new building had a classroom, first-aid room, and clinic, as well as an office. Its roof was gray slate, and the façade was made from hand-hewn white pine shingles. It faced the main highway through Gatlinburg, very conveniently located for town residents, as well as those who traveled in from farther afield by horse or car.

The health center's role expanded briefly during the Cold War years—it was appointed the "rallying point for civilians, soldiers, and government employees in the event of a Soviet nuclear attack." This, thankfully, was one crisis situation it did not need to meet.

After operating for forty years, the clinic was becoming more popular than ever, a sign of its firmly established reputation as the main health resource in the community. The 1960 *Arrow* newsletter included a brief listing of Marjorie's work for the previous year, which included over 500 field visits and over 3,700 office calls. She distributed small pox vaccinations, typhoid inoculations, booster shots, tetanus shots, made over 250 "family conferences" and gave over 200 "health talks." And as Marjorie later discussed in her book, she was finally beginning to see the results of her work. Children who had never used a toothbrush before the advent of the clinic had grown up and started their own families, passing on their improved healthy habits to their kids. People had begun to move into town as the tourist economy, stoked by visitation to the national park, began to become more robust—managing hotels and shops were now occupational alternatives to farming. With the increase in population, a doctor or two had found it feasible to establish permanent practices, relieving Marjorie of being the only locally-based health professional.

Additionally, responsibility for community health education was beginning to shift from public service organizations to the city and county governments. In 1965, the Sevier County government took over public health programs and outreach, and began to hold classes at the newly opened Gatlinburg Health Center, effectively replacing the services of the Pi Phi clinic. With this shift of responsibilities, the Jennie M. Nichol Memorial Health Center quietly closed on August 31, 1965, marking the end of a remarkable half-century transformation of community health. While there would always be health issues to address, the Pi Beta Phi nurses had largely achieved their initial goals of advancing modern knowledge and community well-being. Marjorie retired at the closing—she was seventy-two—but stayed active in civic projects and served on the board of the County Welfare Department.

She wrote a book about her experiences, *Better I Stay*, published in 1975, in which she reflected on the achievements of the Pi Phi community health program and what life in the mountains came to mean to her. "[And] with the hill folk I have found a wealth of good things—faith and courage, wit and wisdom, and a kindliness that shares even 'the widow's mite.'"

While neither Marjorie nor Phyllis was born in the Smoky Mountains, each became an integral part of mountain life. They had to understand and work within the peculiarities of a culture long accustomed to self-sufficiency and folkways. They brought a humility to their work that made them successful as they attended to urgent matters of cuts, broken bones, burns, measles, pneumonia, birthing babies and other serious matters, while at the same time striving to transform the entire community's approach to health. And, as they would be the first to acknowledge, with much help and goodwill from others, they succeeded.

Phyllis Higginbotham, far left, with Dr. Christenberry, two nurses, and Dr. John Massey at the Pi Beta Phi Settlement School, circa 1920.

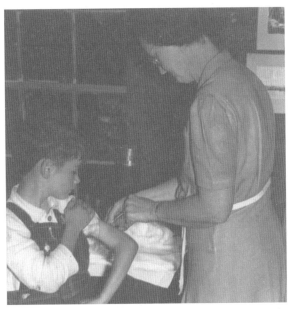

Marjorie Chalmers administers a vaccine to a Smoky Mountains patient in 1941.

Chapter 6

Hattie Ogle McGiffin

MOST WOMEN LIKED TO BUY PRETTY CLOTHES. I WAS ALWAYS INTERESTED IN BUYING PROPERTY.

HATTIE OGLE McGIFFIN • 1898-2002

—Hattie Mae Ogle McGiffin, interview by Lois Reagan Thomas, "A heritage of hard work, property purchase," Knoxville News-Sentinel, April 29, 2001.

The hunters arrived at Isaac Maples's general store on horseback or on foot, with bearskins, mink, and other furs bundled up to trade for store goods or money. One by one, they'd present the hides to Hattie Mae, the storeowner's vivacious fifteen-year-old daughter. She'd look at the size of the pelt, the quality of the fur—and make them an offer. She knew she needed to be shrewd but fair, or the men would trade their skins elsewhere—and she'd gotten so good at this part of the business that her father had put her entirely in charge of it. Often the men would buy a little sugar and coffee for their families while they were at the store, before making the winding journey back to their farmsteads farther up in the mountains. When she'd bought enough pelts to fill a wagon, Hattie and her father would hitch up their mule team and make the fifty-mile, two-day trek to Knoxville from Gatlinburg to resell the skins. Over the next ninety years of Hattie's life, she would be an active presence in the town's business community—and even when tourists replaced hunters as the folks she most often worked with, Hattie never forgot how she got her start with bearskins.

When Hattie Mae Maples was born on chilly February 24 in 1898, Gatlinburg was a sleepy mountain hamlet, home to only a handful of families. She was the first child of Jimima Whaley and "Squire" Isaac Levator Maples, who owned 300 acres and a large white house that sat close to the banks of the West Prong of the Little Pigeon River. Hattie loved growing up near the water, listening to the river splashing over rocks as she played along its banks. But the closeness to the water was a practical choice: Jimima used the river water to wash their clothes, retrieved bucketsful to heat and use for bathing, and to keep milk and butter cold. Gatlinburg, unlike most of the cities and towns in America which had installed public utilities by the mid-1800s, still had no municipal-run gas, electricity, telephone, telegraphs, sewers, or running water. A letter from a person in Gatlinburg to a friend in a neighboring community was delivered by a mail carrier on horseback, and post offices were run out of homes or general stores. Nor was there much organized town leadership—Isaac Maples, Hattie's father, was the citizen closest to being a mayor, mostly because he had served on the local county court. This was how he acquired the nickname "Squire."

Squire Maples, who had attended Maryville and Carson-Newman Colleges was one of the few mountain folk who had much more than an elementary-level education. He operated one of the general stores in town and built a small dam to manufacture electricity around the turn of the 20th century. He charged neighbors 50 cents a month for access to electricity. In addition to his business savvy, he had a penchant for three piece suits and always looked dapper. His oldest daughter inherited his shrewdness, but not his enthusiasm for snazzy dressing. She preferred to buy property.

With Squire Maples' mix of resourcefulness and ingenuity, Hattie's family was one of the most successful and educated in the mountains. But even such relative prosperity didn't spare them from the harshness of rural life. Hattie was four when Jimima lost an infant son; when Hattie was nine, another infant brother died shortly after birth. Four other siblings survived—two brothers and two sisters. Hattie's family was wealthy enough to call for the doctor in emergencies—she would listen for the sound of his galloping horse and look for his familiar black leather satchel. She once watched the doctor remove one of her grandfather's eyes, without using anesthesia. Grandfather (David Crockett Maples, Sr.) was a tough old mountain man, though—he'd once gotten caught in a blizzard and his feet and legs had frozen so badly they had to be amputated at mid-calf. Undeterred, he'd made himself some artificial legs and was able to get around on his own.

But doctor's visits were rare, reserved for major health problems; for routine dental work or eyeglasses, Squire Maples would load his kids up in the family wagon for the two-day trek to Knoxville.

When Hattie was 14, in 1912, she started working in her father's general store, surrounded by shelves lined with candies, flour, sugar, coffee, bolts of cloth and clothes, shoes, toys, farm tools, and more. While she could run the register as well as anyone, dealing with the hunters became her specialty. But she was still just a kid—and occasionally impulsive. On one of the more memorable trips to resell furs in Knoxville, Hattie spent the first part of the trip sitting on a chicken coop in the back of the wagon, snacking on a piece of cheese. She realized later that she had made a big mistake. As they made camp for the night and Squire unpacked their dinner, he discovered that they had nothing to pair with their bread. So they both went a little hungry that evening.

Squire had benefitted from more schooling than most mountain children, and he wanted his own children to be educated as well. The Pi Beta Phi fraternity had opened their Gatlinburg school in 1912, and Hattie attended for several years. The Pi Phi curriculum was more comprehensive than other mountain schools, and featured a variety of after school clubs and social gatherings. Hattie's entrepreneurial spirit thrived with her membership in the Tomato Club, which grew, canned, and then sold tomatoes. Like many other mountain children, she also looked forward to spelling bees, which doubled as social events for the community. The Pi Phis also encouraged greater investment in the town infrastructure beginning in 1913, with the construction of a pedestrian boardwalk along the main street and a few side roads so that people didn't slog through mud every time it rained. They also augmented Squire Maples' electric dam with a generator, which powered the school and a few local homes. And their work to bolster the local handicrafts industries—particularly weaving—made a big impression on young Hattie.

She was still just a teenager when she fell in love with one of the local boys, Charles Austin Ogle. He happened to be the son of the man who owned the other general store in town. "He and I were competitors," she said. "I'd try to take all his customers and he'd try to take all mine." The family later joked that Hattie decided the best way to get rid of her competition was to marry him. The ceremony took place on November 2, 1917, a few days after Charles's twenty-fourth birthday. Hattie was nineteen. With their marriage, she closed her father's store, which she'd been running, and began to manage her husband's. The next year, she gave birth to their first son, Charles Earl. A daughter, Elizabeth Anne, followed in 1920; her second daughter Antoinette (Annette) was born in 1923, and her fourth and final child, Thomas Austin, was born in 1929 just as the Great Depression sent the country into economic chaos.

In addition to the broader economic upheaval of the Depression, many of the mountain communities around Gatlinburg were in crisis because of the establishment of the national park. Squire Maples was a staunch park supporter, perhaps because he could envision the growth potential for Gatlinburg if it became a tourist destination. The park boundary lines, which displaced many mountain families, stopped short of the majority of the Maples family's landholdings, providing Squire with a robust business opportunity. Hattie shared her father's vision of Gatlinburg as a resort destination for wealthy vacationers, and she saw her business efforts as a way of bringing growth and prestige to the town.

In 1932, when her youngest son was four and her oldest was fourteen, she opened the Bearskin Craft Shop, the first craft shop in Gatlinburg that wasn't affiliated with the Pi Beta Phi fraternity. She'd asked her husband for a $100 loan to get started, but she soon paid it back. The store was crowded with baskets, linens, quilts and much more, made by mountain women. Pottery lined the floor-to-ceiling shelves. Furniture and iron work were also displayed in the cozy shop. About twenty-five women relied on the income they made from supplying Hattie's shop. "They'd bring their materials in and I'd buy them, and they'd go over to my husband's store and spend the money," she remembered, smiling. Hattie also made buying trips over to North Carolina for Blenko glass products, made in the Appalachians in West Virginia, and to the Cherokee Indian Reservation for baskets—in fact, she became known as "the basketwoman" to many Indians. When President Franklin D. Roosevelt and First Lady Eleanor Roosevelt stayed in Gatlinburg for the national park's dedication in 1940, she gave the First Lady a hand-woven tie for her husband. Hattie also wasn't above making sure that her artisans were keeping up with the latest fashions—when nylon placemats became trendy, she bought nylon yarn and gave it to her weavers.

The Bearskin Craft Shop also served as a gathering point for the community—a small red cross painted on the door signified that it was where people should come for safety in case of fires, floods, war, or other disasters. Just like Hattie, Annette, her daughter, would work in the craft shop after school. Later on, grandchildren worked at her other properties—she didn't have a lot of employees and she expected a lot from them, even if they were family.

Hattie straddled the line between modernism and her past in some interesting ways. Running her businesses was her first priority—she paid others to take care of the rest of things, which ranged from having a housekeeper who looked after the children most of the time, to women who harvested and canned her vegetables for her. Any good mountain woman knew the produce needed to "be put up" for the winter—Hattie didn't do away with this tradition, she just hired help. Her secretary and right-hand-woman Irene Mize worked for Hattie for 45 years. Although Irene was over 20 years Hattie's junior—nearly the same age as Hattie's children—the two women respected each other greatly. Hattie later said, "I credit my long time secretary, Irene M. Mize, as having most influenced my life."

As Gatlinburg began to develop a reputation as a quaint resort town, Hattie saw a need for more tourist lodgings. Andy Huff, a prominent landowner, had built the first hotel in 1916. Over the years he'd expanded the Mountain View Hotel to three stories and three hundred rooms. In the early 1940s, Hattie built a few little cottages on land that had been one of her family's cow pastures and called them the Bearskin Tourist Home, a tribute to her earliest business enterprises. The property consisted of a house and seven cottages made from local stone, with interior woodwork of rare and valuable wormy chestnut, with cozy fireplaces. "The people loved them," she later remembered. As the Bearskin Tourist Home gained a reputation, Hattie tore down the original house and built a 15-room motel. She was devoted to making sure her guests enjoyed themselves, not only because she wanted them to return and stay with her again, but because she'd inherited her father's sense of civic duty: she saw her successes as part of making Gatlinburg a more robust, economically prosperous town. Her daughter Annette remembered that her mother's philosophy was "you did it first-class all the way, even if you had to go back to the bank." Hattie made sure the cottages and motel always felt fresh and new, replacing linens, carpets, and anything else that was getting a little worn on. Later on, a pool was added, custom-made in the shape of—what else? A bearskin.

Hattie kept farmer's hours her entire life: she'd wake up between three and four in the morning and get to work. Instead of milking cows or harvesting eggs, though, she grabbed a broom and started sweeping. "I'd sweep out the yard where the men would sit at night and smoke cigarettes and throw them on the yard," she explained. "I'd be so mad at them, but I'd go out and sweep [up the cigarettes anyway]." Sometimes she'd sweep the sidewalks all the way along Gatlinburg's main street.

First-class accommodations also meant providing liquor to her guests, despite the fact that Gatlinburg was dry for all intents and purposes. She and an employee or family member would make regular trips to Knoxville for booze, because "she knew guests from the North expected it." Her grandchildren also learned that when guests asked for drinks, it meant larger tips than usual. Hattie's reputation for hospitality extended far and wide, even up to large cities like Chicago, where mobsters heard about the little towns in Tennessee where their illegal liquor came from, but which were also sleepy and off the beaten track. When things got "too hot" for certain members of the mob, they'd book an escape down to the Bearskin Motel.

Hattie would do anything for her guests—"room service" in fact meant that Hattie would put something on a tray for you and bring it to your room herself. Once, she was delivering a breakfast tray to some guests on the second floor of the motel when two girls who were leaving their room asked if she served coffee in bed. "I said, 'Yes'," Hattie recalled with a laugh, "and these two girls got back in bed and called for me to bring them two coffees." She liked the idea of the continental breakfast and was the first hotelier to serve it in Gatlinburg. She'd originally planned to keep things simple with coffee and donuts, but when one guest asked for juice, she incorporated it into the menu, along with milk for kids.

On December 10, 1945, Hattie's husband, Charles, died of a heart attack. She worked through her grief by completely immersing herself in running her businesses. She cared very little about how she dressed, rarely buying herself expensive clothes. In fact, she generally gave the impression of being a pauper because of her unfashionable dresses. She also had a life-long love of simple foods, like the cornbread and beans she'd grown up eating. But she cared very much about how her home looked, and her businesses; those needed to be modern, comfortable—"the best." She lived in a small apartment at the Bearskin Motel through the 1940s, '50s, and '60s. She paid to have a professional decorator from Knoxville 'do it up nice' with fancy furniture and antiques bought from shops in New York City. But for $35 a night she'd rent it out to tourists and sleep down on a cot in the laundry room. She slept down there for an entire summer once, when some merchants from New York wanted to rent a shop from her but didn't have anywhere to live.

She made sure that her cluster of shops on the main Parkway through Gatlinburg was modern and sparkling clean—with big glass-front windows like you'd see across any town in America, in contrast to most of the rest of Gatlinburg, which still had a log-cabin rustic appearance. She also opened a second craft shop in Gatlinburg, Ogles' Crafts of the Smokies, as well as craft shops in the neighboring town of Pigeon Forge. She added a second motel, Roaring Fork Motel, and the Dudley Creek RV Park. "I'd buy anything I could get my hands on," she said. "I'd borrow money, but I paid it all back. If you do anything, you've got to borrow money."

Several years after her husband died, she met Ira Alfred McGiffin, a "Northerner" who'd vacationed in Gatlinburg and decided to return after his wife died. He was a musician, a talented accordion player, who charmed Hattie. "He was the one who taught her life didn't need to be all business," her granddaughter Sandy remembered. After they were married, Hattie installed an organ in the lobby of the Bearskin Motel and Ira would play for guests. Hattie also kept a tiny office in the motel, with a small safe hidden behind a portrait of her father. This was the primary storage spot for Hattie's social security checks, which she treated as if they were more precious than gold. Her granddaughter, who worked at the motel remembered, "And when the mail came, if there was a social security check, you had to immediately give it to Hattie."

As she became wealthier, she began to give back to the community in ways that were clearly influenced by her rural upbringing. Religion was a pillar of mountain life, and she'd been a member of Gatlinburg's First Baptist Church since she was born. She donated money to help modernize the church's building and facilities. She also supported the Mountain Hope Good Shepherd Clinics which provide medical services to local families who generally can't afford healthcare. This is particularly important work in the mountains, since the seasonal, tourist industry jobs rarely provide health insurance. With a handful of other community leaders, Hattie helped establish the Robert F. Thomas Foundation, which provides financial assistance to local healthcare facilities as well as health education and outreach.

As she got older, she began leasing her businesses to tenants and instructing family members in how to manage the properties. Although she was quite shrewd, she occasionally made questionable decisions: she insisted the Bearskin Motel be torn down in the 1970s and turned into a parking lot after the valuable wormy chestnut disappeared while the hotel was under a tenant's "management."

Retirement, for Hattie, meant spending time with her roses and peacocks at a sprawling house overlooking the quiet waters of Douglas Lake with views of the Great Smoky Mountains. Although the lake was quieter than the sound of the rushing waters of the Little Pigeon she'd grown up listening to, she loved to live near water. She'd tend her African violets and always had a "helpful project" for family members who stopped by to visit. Over the years, her children and grandchildren had taken over parts of her business empire, but she still liked to get in the car with her caretaker, JoAnne, and tour the Gatlinburg properties almost daily, "making sure everything was in its proper place."

It seemed that her enthusiasm for real estate, and the pride she had in seeing Gatlinburg grow as a tourist destination, kept her young. She outlived two of her children, Charles Earl and Elizabeth Anne, who died in 1998, the year Hattie turned 100. She passed away at home, of pneumonia, a few months after her 104th birthday on June 21, 2002. Her funeral service was held at the First Baptist Church in

Gatlinburg, which she'd belonged to her entire life. She left her family with a very specific request for her funeral arrangements. When she was growing up, there was no florist, no commercial purchase of flowers for burial ceremonies. Instead, little girls carried baskets of flowers picked from home gardens and wild meadows. Hattie wanted those flower girls, that old tradition, at her own funeral. And so, in they processed, with baskets of flowers as if at a wedding, beneath electric lights, with air conditioning humming softly through the building's vents—for a few brief moments, they were a bridge, like Hattie had been, between the world of the 1800s and the future.

Chapter 7

Ila Hatter

I'VE ALWAYS WANTED TO KNOW WHAT WAS AROUND ME... AND IF YOU'RE INTO PLANTS, YOU REALLY CAN'T DO BETTER THAN LIVING UP HERE.

ILA HATTER • 1942-PRESENT

—*Ila Hatter, interview in North Carolina's Our State Magazine, October 2011*

On a sunny June morning in the Cosby area of Great Smoky Mountains National Park, a dozen people gather near the beginning of a nature trail and adjust backpacks, sip from water bottles, and lean on walking sticks. Ila Hatter, an interpretive naturalist and expert on traditional edible and medicinal plants, leads the way into the woods. Although the path is shaded and winds along a small creek, the day becomes brutally hot. Still, Ila doesn't rush—occasionally sweat glistens on her forehead, but she's too absorbed in her search for interesting plants to care much about the weather.

She pauses next to the silvery trunk of a sweet birch tree. "Sweet birch contains methyl salicylate, which is similar to aspirin," she says. "So if you're hiking and feel a headache coming on, you can chew on a small birch twig," although she warns that picking plants is illegal in the national park. Long before the area became protected land, settlers brewed "birch beer" from birch tree sap, and added wintergreen tea from twigs (for its painkilling properties) to herbal combinations.

The group continues along the trail, pausing to learn about another edible or medicinal plant as Ila finds it: ginger, black cohosh, chanterelle mushrooms. The mitten-shaped leaves of sassafras wave in the slight breeze as Ila explains how the Native Americans brewed the roots into a tea for a "blood-builder" tonic, curing the early European settlers of scurvy. The tree is now known to contain not only iron and vitamins, but also a blood-thinning compound, which would explain its effectiveness as an old-time remedy for lowering blood pressure. The Cherokee also steeped sourwood leaves and twigs in boiling water to make teas for urinary trouble or bad cases of diarrhea. Sourwood, Ila explains, contains a compound called arbutin which can help prevent urinary infections. "Dr. James A. Duke of the USDA told me about twenty-five percent of the medicines that are produced today in the U.S. are still derived from plants," she says.

Many of her students have never seen the Smokies this way—as pharmacy, grocery store, and livelihood all wrapped up together in rocky slopes of rhododendron and bubbling creeks. As Ila tells them, making a living in remote valleys was dangerous work. Farming and hunting accidents were common—the slip of an axe, malfunction of a gun, rattlesnake in the henhouse—the people of the mountains had to be ready for anything. Children often got burned as they played near open cooking hearths in small cabins. Diseases like pneumonia and measles spread rapidly among family members since children often shared beds. And of course, there were many, many babies to deliver. But the communities were too small and too remote to support a doctor's practice. Instead, midwives and "grannywomen" in the communities understood how to deliver babies, treat injuries, and cure disease with native herbs, plants, and other ingredients.

For centuries before the land became a national park, people's lives depended on figuring out the nutritional and healing properties of the plants growing in the forests around them. Much of the traditional plant knowledge was nearly lost with the rise of modern medicine, but Ila has devoted her life to rediscovering and teaching what the early people of the mountains believed and understood about plants, both as food and medicine. This information isn't found in libraries, or university curriculum—uncovering the old ways, both superstitions and real medicine—requires being the sort of person who can win over a recalcitrant Cherokee grandmother, or spend hours hiking along roadsides looking for plants like toothwort and yellowroot.

Over the past fifty years, Ila has attained a breadth of knowledge about edible and medicinal plants in the Smokies that makes her the go-to expert for anyone from producers of TV shows and movies to authors of books on Appalachian cooking. She takes her teaching very seriously, and has been an instructor with the University of Tennessee's Smoky Mountain Field School for over twenty-five years—often finding that her students share tidbits from their grandmothers and great-grandmothers. She also lives what she teaches: she has yellowroot tonic in a Mason jar at home, makes elderberry syrup, and brews tea from staghorn sumac berries. She'll also add lambs-quarters to her quiches and salads, and toothwort to her roast beef sandwiches for a horseradish-like kick.

But her career didn't always involve walks in the woods—far from it. She spent her twenties and most of her thirties immersed in the high-pressure world of advertising, merchandising, and corporate graphic design. After a year-long stint as a stewardess for Pan American World Airlines, she met her husband Oswaldo. One fateful day in Gainesville, Florida, where they were living while Oswaldo was back in college finishing his degree in urban planning, Ila discovered Eliot Wigginton's book *I Wish I Could Give My Son a Wild Raccoon*, a book about passing on woods lore to a child. "I literally cried over it," she remembers. "I'd lived in cities since I was grown and married but that kind of mountain living is what I wanted." Wigginton's book led her to seek out the Foxfire Series, an extensive compendium of folk knowledge that covers traditional ways of life from making horseshoes to moonshining to hog-dressing and more.

Memories of her childhood came rushing back, and she was overwhelmed with the need to find a way to reconnect to the earth. Seeking sustenance and healing from the land was one of the most significant lessons Ila's parents taught her when she was growing up in Austin, Texas. Her father was forty-seven and her mother was thirty-eight when Ila was born on June 6, 1942. Two World Wars and the Depression had given her parents a profound sense of the need to instill self-reliance and "woods lore" in their daughter so that she could look after herself if she ever needed to—particularly if anything were to happen to one or both of them. So Ila learned to fish with her father and to hunt—her mother was quite skilled at shooting jackrabbits and squirrels, as well as deer. She also learned what plants were edible and, equally important, which ones to avoid.

The family would spend weekends at their lakefront property about an hour's drive from Austin, on the edge of Lake Travis where the Colorado River was controlled by Mansfield Dam. Although her father built houses along the lake for clients, and always planned to build something for his wife and only child, somehow they could never quite get rid of their cozy green canvas tent. It was giant, a Texas-sized Army surplus contraption. Her father built wooden bedframes so they could sleep in comfort and, out of necessity, made wooden cabinets that locked to keep the food safe from raccoons. It was primitive in many ways, but it was also perfect.

Both of Ila's parents worked in real estate; her mother focused on downtown properties and her father specialized in ranches and woodland property. Sometimes the three of them would drive out together to a ranch her father was selling, and Ila and her mother would explore while her father chatted with potential buyers. Once they stumbled upon an expansive field of horsemint, the clean, pungent scent of its beautiful purple flowers filling the air. Ila would always remember her mother explaining how her own mother had harvested horsemint and scattered it around the henhouse to keep the chickens free of lice.

On another family drive into the country when Ila was a little girl, her mother discovered a grove of mustang grapes, a native, wild Texas grape. It was early summer and the grapes hung heavy, purple-black orbs with thick skins. Mother and daughter stood on the hood of the car in the heat and picked buckets full of fruit. Later, back at their house in Austin, Ila's mother let her wear her apron as Ila stood on a chair to watch the dark mustang grape jelly boil. This is the moment, Ila recalls, when she first realized that the woods could provide bountiful food.

Back in Gainesville with Oswaldo and her young daughter Susanna, a few years after Ila first discovered the Foxfire series of books, her in-laws suggested they take a family vacation to the Blue Ridge Mountains in North Georgia. To Ila's surprise, she saw that Clayton, Georgia's heritage center, the Hambidge Center, was hosting a talk by Marie Mellinger, the longtime editor of and writer for the Foxfire Series. "I wanted to go so badly," Ila remembered. But her in-laws were insulted that she'd even consider attending an event by herself—so she stayed with the family schedule. It wasn't until Ila and her husband were separated a couple of years later, that Ila, then in her late thirties, gave herself permission to go back to Clayton to finally meet Marie.

Marie Mellinger was brilliant, but she was also a curmudgeon. She would pursue a plant so single-mindedly that she'd leave her students struggling up steep mountain slopes and through tree branches, desperate to keep Marie in sight. But she was one of the foremost experts on edible plants in the Southern United States, and people loved her in spite of her prickliness. "I'm a Purist," she was fond of saying. Meeting her was transformative for Ila. The morning after her first day learning from Marie, she remembers, "I woke up and went outside and said a prayer—I want to be like Marie." And in that moment, she became dedicated to absorbing Marie's deep knowledge of southern Appalachian plants, their uses as food and medicine—and to seeking out knowledge from others. Ila's warmth and friendliness won over Marie as well, and Ila became her de facto disciple—the person she most relied on to preserve and share her knowledge.

Ila was a member of Marie's "Incredible Edibles" Club for many years. She and the other club members spent countless weekends foraging in the woods, identifying and collecting plants—often harvesting them for dinner—learning from Marie, exchanging knowledge amongst themselves. They left the rest of their lives behind at these meetings—they didn't talk of family or day jobs. Members of the Incredible Edibles Club came for the complete immersion in learning herbal lore, and the only thing that mattered was plant knowledge.

Most of Marie's work and study was centered in North Georgia, but in 1985, Ila moved north to Gatlinburg, Tennessee and settled down just outside the boundaries of Great Smoky Mountains National Park. She immediately felt at ease—the lush plant life in the mountains was a botanist's paradise. "Even though I loved the Texas bluebonnets, and running around on deer trails through the cedar breaks," she remembers, "I longed for a forest—one with a fern-covered floor; now that's a forest!" Her affinity for the mountain trees was so strong she took a job for a while as the camp host at Joyce Kilmer Memorial Forest, one of the most impressive old-growth forests in the country. "I enjoyed saying, 'don't you love my office?'" she remembers.

In addition to immersing herself in the plants of the Smokies, Ila befriended locals who still remembered the rich cultural traditions of European-American herb women and the Cherokee Indians. She and Oswaldo decided to divorce, leaving Ila free to live the life she hungered for. She was forty-three and decided that the Smokies felt more like home than any other place on earth.

Marie Mellinger encouraged her to stay in the Smokies as well—with the national park so close, and so many tourists, she thought it would be an ideal place to both study and teach about native plants.

"People will come to you," Marie told Ila. But it wasn't easy getting established. Ila worked several jobs with flexible hours to support her native plant work. Her first teaching job was with a local tour bus company as a "step-on guide"—she'd hop on a bus headed for open, grassy Cades Cove or across the mountains to Cherokee, North Carolina, and would entertain the passengers with local history and anecdotes. Every so often, the bus would stop and she'd lead the group on a short walkabout, pointing out flowers and trees. She seemed to have a knack for it, so she decided to see if she could find any clients as a private guide. "Well a woman finally called me and was interested," Ila remembered, "but she wanted to know why they needed a guide. And I explained that I knew about plants and would teach them things as we walked, and also I knew what to do in case a bear showed up. She did NOT like the idea of encountering a bear, and I lost that first potential customer." Not yet discouraged, Ila also worked with several campgrounds to promote her lectures and educational walks. She charged five dollars a person to attend her short workshops on native plants and their uses—but it soon became clear she would never earn a living from these intermittent talks.

Teaching at the national park's annual Wildflower Pilgrimage, a weeklong celebration of plant life in the mountains, indirectly provided Ila's big break. Through the Pilgrimage, she got to know botanist and University of Tennessee professor Edward Clebsch. He was impressed by both the depth of her knowledge, and her talent for teaching. So in 1987, when he decided to take a sabbatical, he suggested that Ila replace him as the instructor for his very popular "Field School" class on edible and medicinal plants. Her lack of a botany degree gave the administrators some pause, but Clebsch was firm in his endorsement of Ila's qualifications. His support of her knowledge and teaching skills was a turning point in her work as a naturalist. Ultimately, since the classes weren't for credit and were held in the evening, the university approved her to be the instructor for "Traditional Uses of Native Herbs." Classes were held at the university agricultural campus in Knoxville, so Ila would hop in her Jeep and drive a little over an hour from Gatlinburg to Knoxville to teach.

"The classes ended kind of late in the evening," she remembered, "so some of those drives back home got a little chilly." Her first class was a memorable one: worried that the students might not stick with it to the end, she made "aphrodisiacs" the final topic. "That got people's attention," she remembered. She also had some fun with a segment on "magic potions," which of course had to take place during the right moon phase.

In addition, Ila started the field school tradition of wild food dinners. "I knew that the way for people to realize they could incorporate the "food underfoot" into their meals was to actually taste it and see how good it is." Most classes took place in Knoxville, but Ila made sure that at least one took place closer to the wild abundance of the mountains. "Since I lived in a log cabin near enough to the national park, we could finish the walk at my house and then prepare a meal with what we legally had gathered [outside the national park boundary]," she remembers. Through her work, Ila has earned various nicknames, from the Lady of the Forest to The Mad Hatter, in reference to some "wild edible tea parties" she's hosted.

In 2001, Marie Mellinger gave Ila the publishing rights to her cookbook on wild edibles, Roadside Rambles. Ila edited it and added more recipes and illustrations before publishing the revised edition. Students loved the book, but wanted something more visual—and so Ila and her husband Jerry released three half-hour videos, filmed so that viewers could go on a "wildcrafting walk with Ila" from the comfort of their living rooms. "Wild Edibles and Medicinals of Appalachia" was picked up as part of the programming for RFDTV, and led to other video collaborations and consulting work. When the TV Series "Christy," about a young woman moving to a mountain community to teach, began filming in the Smokies in the early 1990s, Ila was hired as a consultant. She advised the show about which herbal remedies the rural doctor would have used, and she physically prepared the mountain plant remedies that served as props in the show.

Ila is also one of the few people raised outside of the Cherokee tribe who has gained insights into their approach to traditional medicine, through years of patience and friendships. Cherokee medicine is very difficult to generalize, she explains, because it is so individual. Each community might look at plants differently and use them for different purposes. Even medicine men and women had their own incantations and herbal remedies that were rarely shared or taught to others. And so Ila has learned that when someone is willing to speak to her about old ways of healing, she should listen carefully.

She values traditional techniques as a record of mountain culture, regardless of how modern medicine rates their efficacy. Homemade medicines vary in concentration of helpful compounds and dosage amount, and include a lot of superstition that was well-regarded in earlier cultures and traditions. Early settlers believed that reciting particular verses from the Bible could heal, like using Ezekiel 16:6 to stop bleeding: "And when I passed by thee, and saw thee polluted in thine own blood, I said unto thee when thou wast in thy blood, Live, yea. I said unto thee when thou wast in thy blood, Live." Other mountain remedies include boiled skunk fat, turpentine, kerosene, anvil dust, and cooked onion poultice for bronchitis. Moonshine—corn liquor—was a common ingredient in mountain medicines and was also used as a disinfectant.

Although she sometimes wishes she'd had the time and money to devote to a formal degree in botany, the fact that she's learned in a practical way, from many others who were self-taught, makes her easy to approach and less intimidating to students. During a workshop at Tremont in 2003, Ila met an elderly student named Eileen Wilson who'd taken field classes with Dr. Jack Sharp, an internationally renowned professor of botany at the University of Tennessee. Since Eileen was interested in Native American studies and botany, Dr. Sharp had let her copy one of his student's thesis manuscripts to use as a "textbook." It was a study of the medicinal plants of the Southeast Cherokee Indians, written in 1952 by a graduate student, William Banks. Eileen had kept the copy through the years, and wondered if Ila might be able to finally find a publisher for the work. Ila was astounded. She'd heard of the manuscript Eileen was talking about: over a decade earlier, the same Dr. Jack Sharp had told Ila about it. The university library's copy had disappeared and the only other copy he knew of was in his house, in a safe. Although he invited Ila to have a look at it, he and his wife both passed away before she had the opportunity. Ila was overwhelmed at the serendipity of getting a second chance with Banks's rare research—possibly the first study of Cherokee plants conducted since the early 1900s.

Eileen Wilson wanted the manuscript to be shared with the Cherokee tribe. It seemed to be knowledge that had been rarely shared with outsiders and largely forgotten. Ila had the connections to become a champion for the publication of the long-lost work. Ila's second husband, Jerry Coleman, was half-Cherokee. He and Ila had met in the early 1990s, during a prayer circle that took place at the site that celebrated the return of the tribe's Sacred Fire to the mountains from Oklahoma. After they were married, Jerry introduced Ila to Amanda Swimmer, the Cherokee elder who had befriended him and shared cultural traditions. "We started chatting about herbal remedies," Ila remembers, "talking one mother to another. Jerry was amazed because Amanda had never talked to anyone about medicine before—but no one else knew the questions to ask." Ila had learned a lot about Cherokee medicine from other friends and acquaintances through the years, but she and Amanda got to know each other so well they were practically family.

Ila knew that Amanda, who could speak, read, and write in her native language, would be a valuable ally in preparing what William Banks had written about Cherokee plants for publication. She and Amanda spent hours reviewing the manuscript notations, making sure what Banks had recorded was correct— since it wasn't unusual for Cherokee to make jokes at the white man's expense. One of the most exciting elements was Banks's handwritten Cherokee syllabary and phenome set, which gave Cherokee names—in their language— for the plants. This bi-cultural approach was rarely attempted by researchers. Banks had also taken the time to reference all the plants in his book at the university's herbarium to make sure they were correctly identified. These two aspects, in particular, made the book an exceptional resource.

Ila and Jerry also tracked down William Banks himself, to ask his permission to print the manuscript. He agreed, but said that he'd promised his informants that he wouldn't benefit personally from the sharing of the information, and that if he could, he would use the information to better the lives of future Cherokees. They managed to meet that requirement by working with Great Smoky Mountains Association, a nonprofit dedicated to providing information and support for the national park, as the publisher. *Plants of the Cherokee* was published in 2004.

As Marie predicted, Great Smoky Mountains National Park has become an incomparable resource for Ila; it's her most frequent classroom (although she always makes sure her students know that picking plants within national park boundaries is illegal). Ila, with Jerry frequently at her side, has walked countless miles through the national park, pointing out medicinal and edible plants to students. As she tells her classes, the southern Appalachians are now known to harbor some of the most diverse plant species in North America—which gave the early Cherokee Indians and mountain settlers an incredible resource from which to cultivate food and medicine. Even mountain women who weren't known as healers generally raised a few medicinal plants in their gardens: catnip, which was good for colicky babies, and bee balm for colds and flu. But they also knew where patches of wild herbs grew, and would make their rounds to harvest them when necessary.

Going on a hike with Ila and Jerry evokes another, earlier culture— one that survived without grocery stores or pharmacies, pills and vitamins. Instead, the woods offered the only available food and medicine: a slender sweet birch twig for a natural pain reliever, yellowroot for an antibiotic, spicebush for a favorite Cherokee tea (now known to be anti-inflammatory). Ila also looks for ginger, its heart-shaped leaves growing close to the ground, which was brewed into teas for nausea. Each excursion brings delightful surprises: a rare orchid, a prized mushroom, a bear sighting. No day, no walk, is ever the same.

And at the end of her hikes, when students are thirsty, sweaty, and tired, Ila and Jerry will unload some coolers and Tupperware from their dark green van, revealing a deliciously prepared native foods feast. Everyone sits down together to enjoy a spread that usually contains wild greens salads, quiches with lambs-quarters instead of spinach, tea brewed from sumac berries or sassafras. Ila's work, ultimately, is guided by both Psalm 104:14 "He causeth grass to grow for the cattle, and herbs for the service of man, that he might grow food from the earth" and Henry David Thoreau's observation that "The woods and fields are a table always spread." She knows that showing people easy ways to incorporate traditional knowledge into their lives—their meals, in particular—is the best way to ensure that the traditions of the Smokies grannywomen continue.

Some of Ila's favorite recipes:

Sumac-ade

Sumac-ade was traditionally used hot for a sore throat gargle.

Remove sections of berries to make one cup from a "head" of red Sumac (*Rhus typhina* or *glabra*).

Pour 4 cups of boiling water over berries.

Steep at least one hour or until water turns a deep pink.

Strain. Add honey or other sweetener to taste and serve over ice.

Persimmon Passion

I also keep some Persimmon (Diospyros virginiana) pulp in the freezer in case someone calls to ask for it to use for "Thrush"(a yeast infection). Sometimes called "Thrash" here in the mountains. Mixed with water for drinking or plain as a swab in the mouth.

1 box of peach gelatin dissolved in 1 cup hot water.

Add 1 1/2 cups ripe persimmon pulp, 1/4 cup sugar, and 1 cup cold water.

Mix well and pour into a mold.

Chill 3-4 hrs until firm. Unmold and serve with whipped cream.

Spicewood Tea

According to the Cherokee, if you drink spicewood tea all your life "your hair won't turn gray, and you won't have arthritis." At least the second part may have some validity as Lindera benzoin is an anti-inflammatory.

Boil small twigs of spicewood plant, strain.

Part II: Mountains As Muse

Craftswomen, Artists, and Writers

Chapter 8

Mayna Treanor Avent

AS A WOMAN WORKING IN THE SOUTH AS A PROFESSIONAL ARTIST, SHE WAS A PATHFINDER FOR FUTURE GENERATIONS OF WOMEN... SHE WAS ONE OF THE FIRST PROFESSIONALLY TRAINED WOMAN ARTISTS IN THIS REGION, AND HER INFLUENCE EXTENDED WELL INTO THIS CENTURY.

MAYNA TREANOR AVENT · 1869-1959

—James Hoobler, *Curator of Art & Architecture, The Tennessee State Museum* (1993).

Sunlight dappled the mountainside near Elkmont, a small summer community in the Great Smoky Mountains, as Mayna Treanor Avent walked along a winding trail. She carried her smaller, lightweight easel for painting *en plein aire* as she looked for inspiration. The mountains had endless possibilities for paintings: delicate pink rhododendron blossoms, far-off peaks shrouded by clouds, or a portrait of a neighbor.

Her surroundings may have been rustic, but Mayna's artistic training was world-class. One of the first professionally trained female artists in the South, her work opened doors for later generations of Southern women to be taken seriously as artists, considered for commissions, and included in museum shows and traveling exhibitions. She lived in Nashville where she taught art for most of the year, but in summer she was drawn to the mist-filled mountains in the easternmost part of Tennessee.

Almost impossible to imagine in the national park's quiet Jakes Creek valley today, Mayna's summer studio was once in the center of Elkmont, a bustling rural community. The trees that now shade the slopes of the creek are much younger than the cabin they tower over—and when Mayna visited each summer in the early 1900s, she was surrounded by the neighbors' apple orchards, cornfields, and cow pastures. There was a village, church, and store instead of the current Elkmont Campground, all centered around the timber industry and a few very small farms. The main access trail to the cabin today, the Jakes Creek hiking trail, was initially a railroad spur for the Little River Lumber Company.

Neighbors never knew when they'd be invited to sit for a portrait, or would come upon Mayna in the woods, sketching or painting scenes that captured the vibrancy of her summer home. The diversity of her subject matter was complemented by the range of her talent with many types of media: she painted mostly in oils, but was also adept at pen and ink sketching, water-soluble gouache, charcoal, watercolors, woodcut, and graphite pencil. James Kelly, Assistant Director for Museum Programs at the Virginia Historical Society, would later write, "although [she was] versatile in many media, and an accomplished portraitist, outdoor scenes were her specialty and greatest legacy."

Mayna was born on September 18, 1868 and grew up at Tulip Grove, an antebellum mansion adjacent to Andrew Jackson's property The Hermitage, outside of Nashville. She was the third of four daughters of Thomas O. and Mary Treanor. Mayna's family was part of the wealthiest strata of Nashville society, which gave her many special opportunities to pursue her artistic studies. Her parents recognized her talent and encouraged her passion for art when she was very young, fully supporting her pursuit of formal training. She first studied art in Nashville and Cincinnati before leaving for school in Europe in 1888, when she was twenty. Mayna spent the summer in Ireland, traveling, sketching, and visiting family. Then she and a strict chaperone—something every well-to-do young woman abroad was required to have—settled down for two years of art school in Paris.

Mayna enrolled at the prestigious Academie Julian, a private art school that provided the same opportunities and training to all of its students regardless of gender. The turn of the twentieth century was a difficult time to be a female artist, particularly for those who wanted to paint in the classical tradition. Opportunities for women to study under teachers of the same caliber as men were very limited. In most schools, women were banned from learning to draw the human figure from nude models—but the Academie Julian had no such rules. In later years, Mayna delighted in telling how one of her female classmates had, however, fainted when their first model disrobed. The Academie Julian's progressive policies enabled it to attract alumni like Henri Matisse, Diego Rivera and Man Ray—as well as path-setting female artists like Anne Dunn and Sophie Pemberton from Canada, and Jenny Nystrom from Sweden.

Mayna would remember her adventures in Europe, exciting and terrifying, for the rest of her life. On a visit to Rome, she was blessed by Pope Leo XIII—on a procession through the streets, his carriage happened to pause close to where she was standing and the Pope looked out, made eye contact with her, and gestured in the sign of the cross. Although she wasn't Catholic, the experience was deeply meaningful to her. She remembered her time in London less fondly, since she was there during Jack the Ripper's killing spree. Her unsympathetic chaperone made her sleep in a room rented from a medical student, complete with a skeleton stashed under the bed.

Back at the Academie Julian in Paris, Mayna unintentionally caught the eye of a French Count who tried to woo her. He wrote letters pleading for her hand in marriage, and despite her disinterest, followed her back to the United States. Many young ladies might have found the Count's combination of persistence and noble title difficult to resist, but Mayna's mind was made up—she was in love with Frank Avent, a young attorney from Murfreesboro, Tennessee. And so the Count returned to France alone.

Mayna and Frank were married in Nashville in 1891. Their wedding announcement in the *Nashville American* described Mayna as "one of Nashville's loveliest and most accomplished blossoms, having gained a high standing as a pupil of the Nashville School of Fine Arts" and the groom as "a lawyer by profession...but a farmer by predilection." The happy couple moved to his farm, Aventhurst, two miles south of Murfreesboro. Their first child, Mary, was born in the summer of 1892, followed by their son James in 1895. By 1910, the Avent family had moved back to Nashville, into a quaint house on Belmont Boulevard, where they transformed the attic into a studio for Mayna. She lived in the house until she was in her 80s.

Mayna was an active member of the Nashville art scene, but every summer, she packed up her art supplies, and prepared for the long drive to the Smokies with her children. Frank, as the Railroad Commissioner for the state of Tennessee, often had to stay in Nashville for much of the summer, so a handyman would usually drive Mayna and the kids on the long trip to the mountains.

While they missed Frank, they weren't lonely in Elkmont. The little community had started as a getaway for Knoxville's wealthy sportsmen (generally members of the Elks Club), but had quickly expanded into a quaint summer destination for the entire family. The Avent's cabin was close to the town's social hub, the Appalachian Clubhouse. During the height of the season, the clubhouse featured performances from three piece bands from Knoxville, hosted costume parties, and square dances. Other social events included "taffy pulling" competitions and sing-alongs. A half-mile "boardwalk" was constructed from the clubhouse up Jakes Creek so members could stroll home from lunch, dinner, or other festivities without getting muddy. Ice was brought in by train from nearby Maryville; fresh vegetables arrived via ox-and-buggy from Gatlinburg. The gentlemen of Elkmont rounded out the meals with wild game and fish.

Mayna painted regularly, energized by the beauty around her. She approached her work with the indomitable practicality of a devoted artist: when the muse came to her, nothing could stop her from painting—not even the lack of a canvas. One of her paintings, "Indian Pinks in the Mountains" was painted on a large rectangle of tin—presumably because a canvas wasn't available when the artistic spirit moved her. Another time, after having picked a bouquet of magnolias at her home in Nashville, she was overcome by their beauty and inspired to paint them. Discovering she had no canvases prepped, she promptly began painting on a wooden door panel— still attached to the door. When later asked about her haste to begin painting, so the story goes, she exclaimed, "Magnolias just won't wait!" The magnolia-painted panel was later removed from the door and "Magnolias Just Won't Wait" was exhibited at several shows.

Mayna's skill in portraiture came to the attention of officials at the Smithsonian, leading to a commission by the National Portrait Gallery to paint reproductions of a couple of damaged portraits, one of President James K. Polk's wife, Sarah, and the other of Emily Donelson, Andrew Jackson's niece and hostess at the White House. The Vanderbilt University School of Medicine also commissioned a portrait of one of its esteemed chairmen, Dr. W.E. Garrey. The Tennessee State Museum acquired several of her oil paintings, as did the Cheekwood Museum in Nashville, and the Morris Museum in Augusta, Georgia. Mayna's approach to portraiture was informed by her egalitarian sensibility. She cared about a person's character more than ethnicity or economic status, which elevated much of her art. Museum curators and art critics praise her portraits, with subjects ranging from mountain folk to university deans to African-Americans (rare choices for a well-to-do, white Southern woman) which reveal a deep understanding and compassion for her subjects.

When she wasn't painting, she was writing poetry. She enjoyed writing poems all of her life, but only shared her musings with her family and friends, never seeking to publish them. In June 1916, she used some Appalachian Club stationary to write a playful poem titled "Sugarland" about hiking with her daughter Mary: *Below we leave the world we know/ and into fairyland we go/ And if a shower- the balsams shelter/ and if the sun too hot should grow/ the shaded laurel thickens pelter/ blossoms pink and white as snow/ Pelter, shelter us together/ Never mind about the weather/ On we go to fairyland/ O'er the trail called Sugarland.* Mayna turned to poetry as well during the worried years of World War I, when Jimmy was in France. The short verses were a way to channel her emotion and meditate on the tragedy of war: *Wait, wait, waiting on/ Never any news I see/ Since our Jim has gone/ Our sonny Jim of Tennessee.// Tramping through the mud and snow/ Whistling softly "it must be"/ While they stand to face the foe/ With our Jim Of Tennessee...* To Mayna's great relief, Jimmy did return, unharmed.

In 1918, Frank and Mayna bought another log cabin—originally built in the 1850s—on the outskirts of Elkmont. It was closer to their daughter's cabin than their first Elkmont home, and had 18.5 acres surrounding it. It quickly became the primary Avent summer residence. Mayna made the cabin a tribute to the artistic heritage of the Smokies, decorating it with local arts and crafts—hand-woven baskets, paintings, quilts and weavings, books and objects collected from the woods. A spinning wheel sat in a corner of the main room, along with several brightly painted chairs and a small easel, with a place to hang her wooden paint pallet on the wall when it wasn't in use. Brilliant orange curtains framed the main window, and the mantel was painted bright red.

Although comfortable, it was by no means a cushy country house: there was no electricity, water for the sink flowed through a long pipe from a mountain spring, and the outhouse "throne" was a fifty meter walk into the woods, and was popular with spiders. (Bears also frequently stole the toilet paper, festooning the woods with white strips.) Frank and Mayna took advantage of a second icy cold spring, conveniently located between their cabin and Mary's, to build a tiny wooden springhouse. Thus was born a shared "refrigerator" with a submerged wire cage stocked with butter and milk.

Given their mutual interests in hunting, fishing, hiking, and the mountains, the Avent family quickly became good friends with their new summer neighbors in the Smokies, who included local mountain hiking guides and personalities Sam Cook, Steve Ownby, and Lem Ownby who often cared for the cabin in the fall and winter months. (Entrepreneurial Lem was particularly well known around Elkmont—each year he managed to trap about thirty black bears. The fur hides commanded $7 each; he sold the bear meat to the hotel kitchen.)

The following year, 1919, was a big one for Mayna and Frank: their daughter Mary got married and soon after, they began to anticipate the arrival of their first grandchild early in 1920. Their son James (Jimmy) took a job with the Standard Oil Company and moved to China. He would go on to have a long career in China—Mayna visited him there and delighted in using his children's Chinese dolls as subjects of several paintings.

Back in their beloved mountain retreat, Mayna and Frank were noticing changes in the land around them from one summer to another. Industrial-scale logging had increasingly marred the slopes around Elkmont, and Mayna and Frank were supportive of the national park movement. In 1926, a spark from a railroad track had ignited the forest around Elkmont. The Avents worried that their cabin would be lost, but the fire stopped short of damaging the building. The ridge-line across the creek, however, burned so badly that signs of the fire are apparent even today. It was one of myriad signs that logging was impacting the beauty and environmental health of the mountains. The timing for the park movement was right in an economic sense, since most of the profitable virgin timber had already been removed and it was getting harder for loggers to find and cut down large trees.

As the ownership and future prospects of the land around them changed, the Avents undertook some significant construction work on their cabin. Jimmy Avent helped since he was on leave from his work in China and wanted to spend time in the Smokies. He and Frank made several major changes—replacing floorboards, and constructing a loft, chimney, and separate kitchen shed, and installing the eight foot, distinctive window in the southeast wall to let in more sunlight. The large window made the cabin better suited for use as Mayna's summer art studio. That was also the year Jimmy planted a balsam fir tree which came to be known as "the bear tree" because its trunk showed repeated scarring from bear claws.

With her children grown and leading their own lives, Mayna stayed busy by teaching and painting. In the mid-1920s, she and her best friend, Ella Sophonisba Hergesheimer, traveled north to Provincetown, Massachusetts to learn techniques in woodblock printing. Artists in Provincetown had recently invented a new printing technique called white-line woodblock, which used a single block to make a print. Mayna learned the white-line technique, as well as an ancient Japanese approach that used several blocks to create a design.

In July 1934, in anticipation of the official establishment of the national park, she created a vibrantly colored woodblock print of their cabin and wrote "The Log, Smoky Mountains National Park" across the bottom. The official establishment of the national park was a joyful achievement, with a tinge of sadness as well for Mayna and Frank, and the many others who had to give up their homes and land within its boundaries.

Two years later, the Avents put the first visitor log book on the desk by the cabin's large window and began to record their experiences and memories, knowing the years they would be able to stay there were numbered. Extended family, friends, and other visitors left their thoughts as well. The log is now over 300 pages long and is filled with interesting entries from honeymooners, foreign visitors, lost hikers, and others. Acclaimed Southern poet Paul Ramsey wrote a poem in the log, called "Drifted Morning": *Fog on the ridge becomes mist/ In the near trees decades arrange/ Silverberry, hemlock, and oak/ Sleep as an entry foregained.*

Another unusual entry is written in Japanese and then translated into English: "It is raining as if to wash away all the dirt of the world...

[but] how luxurious it is to dine with the light of lanterns." Other visitors from Holland wrote of their delightful visit at "a refuge for all those who seek some peace and rest for the body and the mind, a happiness which we wish many may enjoy in the future as we have enjoyed it now." A couple of Appalachian Trail hikers, desperately seeking shelter from a terrible storm one New Year's Eve, stumbled upon the cabin on their way down from Miry Ridge—they left a note of thanks, along with three dollars as payment for cutting the screen to get inside.

Although Mayna and Frank happily shared the cabin with expected and unexpected guests, there were increasingly lengthy stretches of time when they were unable to visit the Smokies themselves. Both were elderly and found it difficult to travel to the mountains without other family or friends. In October 1941, Frank, ten years older than Mayna, passed away in Nashville at the age of eighty-three. Mayna continued living at their house on Belmont Boulevard and returned to the Smokies when she could, but for the next few years, especially with rationing during World War II, it was difficult for her to visit her beloved mountains.

She also began to have trouble painting with her previous detail and skill as she reached her early 80s. Ever creative and resourceful, she began constructing intricate scrapbooks that wove letters and sketches with the stories of her life. The books were beautiful compendiums of articles and photographs clipped from magazines, along with comments on paintings that impressed and inspired her, written in a delicate cursive hand. This was in part her way of staying connected to innovation and style changes in art around the world. Her clippings reveal much about her artistic tastes and influences; she admired Francisco de Goya and Diego Velasquez in particular, but her marginalia reveals nothing but disdain for Pablo Picasso.

In the early 1950s she moved from Nashville to live with her son Jimmy and his family in Sewanee, Tennessee where, after thirty years in China with the Standard Oil Company, he had retired to take a position with the University of the South. They lived in a large stone house on the outskirts of town, originally built by a cotton king from

New Orleans, and a previous site of séances. The view from the edge of the property was a fond reminder of the scenery the family enjoyed in the Smokies, although the mountains in middle Tennessee are flatter. One of the last paintings Mayna Avent completed is a watercolor of the trees and rolling hills on the property. Aside from the smoothness of the distant blue mountains, it could be a painting of a high mountain bald in the Smokies.

Mayna passed away at the house in Sewanee on January 2, 1959 at ninety-one years old. Her memorial from the *Nashville Banner* said, "The South lost one of its most beloved and dedicated artists in the death of Mrs. Frank Avent... she represented the best in the Southern tradition. Her love for her native land was left of record in a rich heritage of paintings that will keep the name of Mayna Treanor Avent an honored memory for generations yet to come." James Hoobler, Curator of Art and Architecture of the Tennessee State Museum, wrote that Mayna "was one of the first professionally trained women artists in this region, and her influence extended well into this century. For this reason she is worthy of recognition."

In addition to her portraits and landscapes that grace Southern art museums, her name lives on in her cabin in the Smokies. The Avent cabin was listed on the National Register of Historic Places in 1994, after over a year of dedicated work from granddaughter and namesake Mayna Avent Nance to prepare the application, attend hearings, and await the official decision. There were stumbling blocks along the way, including significant discussion of the alterations the Avents had made to the cabin. Eventually the Tennessee Historical Commission concluded that it is common for log cabins to be modified by their owners, and considering this one had been built in the mid-1800s, its alterations were relatively sympathetic to the original use and nature of the cabin as a "single family dwelling." The Commission also agreed that although Great Smoky Mountains National Park is dotted with historic home sites and cabins, no others were associated with an artist of Mayna's stature and regional importance.

Mayna had hoped that her house in Nashville would eventually become a gallery and museum to showcase the works of local artists, but instead it is the cabin in the Smokies, her summer studio, that has been preserved. The cabin's log book now contains hundreds of happy memories and thanks from visitors, including many artists, who make annual pilgrimages to Mayna's uniquely-situated studio. Whether they are from Las Vegas, Nevada or Yekaterinburg, Russia, couples celebrating anniversaries or a University of Illinois ecology class, the visitors find a perfect place to sit and reflect—as Mayna did with her art— on the beauty of the mountains and people who called them home.

Frank and Mayna Treanor Avent, 1938.

Self-portrait, oil on wood panel.

Mayna Treanor Avent, circa 1920s.

Chapter 9

Olive Tilford Dargan

THE MOUNTAINS ROSE
IN EVERY FORM,
CURVED, SWAYING,
ROUNDED, A SPEAR,
SHADOWED AND
UNSHADOWED, THEIR
SPLOTCHES OF GREEN,
GOLD, AND HEMLOCK-BLACK
FLOWING INTO BLUE,
WHERE DISTANCE BALKED
THE EYES AND
IMAGINATION STEPPED
THE CRESTS ALONE. IT
SEEMED EASIER TO FOLLOW
THAN TO STAY BEHIND WITH
FEET CLINGING TO EARTH.
AFFINITY LAY WITH THE SKY.

OLIVE TILFORD DARGAN · 1869-1968

—Olive Tilford Dargan, "Serena and Strawberries," in Highland Annals, New York: C. Scribner, 1925.

Olive Tilford Dargan

Olive Tilford was seventeen when she first saw the southern Appalachians, and she never forgot them. Over the next twenty years, she would romanticize that trip, planning to return someday and make a life in the mountains that had captured her heart. Her unusual path back to the Smokies began with earning a teaching degree from Peabody College in Nashville, then further study at Radcliffe College in Massachusetts. A few years after graduation, she began making a name for herself as a poet and playwright in the cacophony of turn-of-the-century New York City. But the memories of misty mornings and rocky streams still beckoned to her, and as soon as she had the money and opportunity to buy a farm in the North Carolina section of the Great Smoky Mountains, she took it.

The people of the mountains didn't know what to make of her—in addition to being highly educated, she had strong ties to Communist and Socialist politics. She also made her living as a writer—something vastly puzzling to the mountaineers who spent each day producing what they needed to survive. That a typewriter could be used to earn a living was a completely foreign concept. While Olive's life in the Smokies was often more challenging than she could ever have imagined, it sent her writing in a new, enriching direction: she became a chronicler of mountain life to a national readership, a keen social observer of the disruption caused by the formation of the national park and the rise of cotton mills in the South. Amidst literary disappointments and family heartbreak, she sought solace in the hard work that day to day life in the mountains required.

In 1932, *The New York Times* review of her first novel, *Call Home the Heart*, described her uncanny ability to put her conflicted feelings about the mountains into her writing:

> "*There is beauty of an inevitable kind in* Call Home the Heart—
> *the beauty of the mountains themselves, of wooded valleys at sunset,*
> *of a forest fire sweeping up over Dark Moon Ridge, or the morning*
> *mists lingering about the slopes of Cloudy Knob. This natural love-*
> *liness is set in almost painful contrast against the harsh actualities of*
> *mountain life, against the struggle, now bitter and now discouraged*

and half-hearted, with poverty and hunger, against the inescapable human facts of misery and dirt and disease and death."

Call Home the Heart was a surprise sensation, published at exactly the right moment to be well received by readers. It was inspired by Olive's observations of mountain life, the lure of prosperity promised by difficult, dangerous cotton mill jobs, and the real-life events of the Loray mill strikes that took place in Gastonia, North Carolina in 1929. In all, six novels were inspired by the Gastonia strike, but Olive's writing was distinguished by her talent for developing characters, and that she never let her political passions trump telling a good story. *Call Home the Heart* went into its fourth printing only a few weeks after its initial release, and was rumored to be a contender for the Pulitzer Prize. Edward Mills, the president of the Longmans publishing house, said it was the finest novel they had published in his time at the press.

Olive had been a well-established writer in New York City before she moved to the Smokies in 1906. But less than ten years after she graduated from Radcliffe, sister college to all-male Harvard, her writing career took off. Her earlier plays and poetry were influenced primarily by classical mythology, history, and literary figures. Her editor, William Crary Brownell, also worked with literary lights like Edith Wharton, and her publisher, Charles Scribner's Sons, represented F. Scott Fitzgerald and Ernest Hemingway.

During these early years in Manhattan, Olive's communist sympathies began to take shape, particularly through friendships with Rose Pastor and Graham Stokes, leaders of the socialist movement. Although Olive could never give up her writing to dedicate herself to social change the way she sometimes wished she could, Rose was her best friend throughout her life. They wrote to each other regularly until Rose's death from cancer in 1933, often discussing political and philosophical affairs, as well as personal aspirations and daily life.

Despite her successes, Olive wasn't happy in New York. The city was dense with crowded slums—1,000 people per acre in some areas—and she believed that the pastoral beauty of the mountains would benefit her writing, and her health.

The money for the down payment on the North Carolina farm came from the sale of the stage rights to *The Shepherd*, from her second published volume of plays. Olive had finally gotten the opportunity to fulfill her vow made on that first camping trip before starting school at Peabody College in Nashville: if she ever owned her own home, it would be in those beautiful mountains. And so in 1906, she and her husband, Pegram Dargan, a Harvard-educated poet, moved south to a farm near Almond, in Swain County, North Carolina.

From the beginning, life at Horizon Farm was challenging. In a letter to one of her good friends, Olive explained she and her husband were "half camping in a tiny room by the riverside, on our own bit of land." The winter of 1906 was harsh, and Pegram found himself working part-time in a blacksmith shop. Olive confided to a friend that despite working twelve-hour shifts, Pegram still was barely paid enough to cover their expenses. That the situation, wrote Olive, "discourages him greatly at times, but the *work* is the main thing now—the other will come."

Olive had grown up in small, remote towns and was no stranger to hardship. Her parents, Rebecca Day and Elisha Francis Tilford, were teachers who moved frequently, seeking a climate that wouldn't aggravate Rebecca's fragile health. Olive was born on January 11, 1869 near Leitchfield, in western Kentucky. The family soon moved further west to Doniphan, Missouri, hoping that drier air would improve Rebecca's health. It didn't, and so they moved on to Warm Springs, Arkansas, an almost-abandoned resort town in the north of the state. Following in her parents' footsteps, Olive herself took charge of a school when she was fourteen, teaching all subjects to a full class of students ranging in age from six to twenty.

When Olive was seventeen, she heard about a scholarship for teachers to study at Peabody College, in Nashville. To be considered for the scholarship, she had to take an academic exam offered nowhere near her home. With her family's support, she rode twelve miles on horseback to the county seat, where a hired wagon ferried her the remaining twelve miles to the railway station. Having missed the train, she waited alone in town until four a.m. for the next one.

She was a most unusual sight: a young woman traveling unescorted. Her tenacity paid off though—she was awarded the scholarship to Peabody, graduated in two years, and spent time teaching in Missouri and Texas before attending Radcliffe College in 1893.

And so, despite her elite education, Olive had a deep familiarity with rural hardship, although perhaps she had imagined her life on Horizon Farm would unfold differently. Their first two years in the mountains were a time of great change for the Dargans. Pegram was considering leaving the farm and relocating to the West Coast—Oregon seems to have resonated with him the way the Smokies drew Olive southward. But Olive had discovered she was pregnant at thirty-eight, and was reluctant to accompany him into the wilderness. Instead she traveled north to stay with her wealthy friends, the Stokes, at their mansion on Caritas Island, Connecticut.

Some of her letters indicate she had decided early in life not to have children, but she had begun to look forward to motherhood. Devastatingly, her baby, Rosemary, survived only two hours. Olive wrote to her friend Alice Blackwell, "I had persuaded myself that the babe was coming for some great and true purpose beyond my desire to see. I *had* to be fearless for the child's sake. I had to believe it was right and best. Then when I had succeeded, and even permitted myself to indulge in the most joyous hopes, everything was changed again and so quickly that I was almost stunned by it... I don't know yet what the experience means, but I shall find out sometime and put it in my philosophy, for it surely has a place there, which I am too driven and blind to understand."

From late 1907 until early 1911, Olive struggled through her grief, seeking a balance between farming and writing in the mountains and traveling back to the East Coast. Pegram was injured in a riding accident in winter of 1908, leaving Olive the only one doing chores on the farm in the brutal weather. She did "the nursing, and all of the work indoors and out, taking care of the pigs, chickens, cows, and a crippled horse." She spent time with her tenants, and gradually became accepted into the community as a friend, not a foreigner. Perhaps she became a little too well-liked, as she wrote to her editor in January 1909, "I might get along very well if my cooking were not so popular. In later years some record hunter may come this way with the query, "What about Mrs. Dargan, of Round Top?" and I predict the answer: "By gum, she was the best cook in Swain County!" When literature seems to be on the other side of the world, as it always does now, I am at least permitted to feel that I'm good for *something* on this side."

In 1911, Olive and Pegram left the farm under their tenants' care and traveled separately. He pursued business interests while she sailed to England, sponsored by her dear friend, the accomplished and independently wealthy sculptor Anne Whitney. In London, she met many radical thinkers and writers, particularly members of the Fabian Society, a socialist organization, and the developing Labor Party: George Bernard Shaw, George Lansbury, Ramsey McDonald, Harold Laski, and Walter Lippmann.

Olive had been interested in workers' rights and women's rights for many years, and was already quite sympathetic to the aims of socialism and communism. Her longtime friend Sylvia Latshaw once told an interviewer that Olive "would have invented [communism] if nobody had done it first." Olive's experiences in England greatly influenced her feelings about the role women could play in revolutionary activities and were a powerful force in her later novels. She wrote frequently to Alice Blackwell, who was working as the editor of *Woman's Journal*, about riots, bombings, and abuses of suffragists.

When she returned to the United States in 1914 as the shadow of World War I began looming over Europe, Scribner's published a book of her poetry, *Path Flower and Other Verses*, and she seemed to be finding her writing rhythm again. But the following year was very difficult for her—her friend Anne Whitney died in early January, and later in the year, Olive received news that Pegram, who had sailed to Cuba, had drowned in an accident at sea on the return trip. In an interview many years later, Olive's friend Sylvia Latshaw confided that Pegram's death might have actually been part of a suicide pact made with his brother after their joint business venture failed and some of their friends lost their investments.

No Place for the Weary Kind

Olive poured her sorrows into a new book of poetry, *The Cycle's Rim*. Published in 1916, it was her tribute to Pegram, a sequence of Shakespearean sonnets dedicated to his memory. It won several awards—the Patterson Memorial Cup, an award for North Carolina writers; and a $500 prize and "best book of the year" designation by the Southern Society of New York.

The effort to put her feelings for Pegram into words seems to have drained her of creative energy for a while, and she turned to the North Carolina farm. The hard physical labor its upkeep required was the perfect antidote for too much thinking, and for loneliness. Olive wrote to Alice Blackwell in April 1916 that she was busy, "mending fences, digging ditches, carrying rock, cutting poles and other incredible things." One of her more "incredible things" was orchestrating the construction of a road, with help from her tenant farmers, so the fallen timber could be transported out and sold—to provide funds for much-needed upkeep on her farm. She wrote, "For forty years people have said, "What a pity a road can't be built to Round Top!" …But I believed that a good wagon road was possible, and set about it. We now have it two thirds done, far enough along to see that it is a success, and people who discouraged us are now coming up the mountain to admire the road and congratulate us."

Successes like the road were diminished by other challenges, particularly as the deadly Spanish flu swept through the mountains in 1918. Olive did what she could to help take care of her neighbors, running errands, looking after children, preparing food, and more. She wrote on December 19th to her editor, Brownell, "I've no fear of contagion. You would know that I am immune could you see me in some of the places I visit. Only once have I thought I was taking it. I was re-setting asparagus roots, which means a *lot* of digging. When the unpleasant feelings began I said, "This is the flu, and I shall die. Shall I go in and write a last poem, or stay by the job? I will stay by the job. Gras [asparagus] will last longer on the planet than literature anyway." So I dug on, and got well! But I didn't fool myself. I knew that I was afraid I couldn't write the poem."

The farm, and her neighbors, were increasingly filling a void that literature wasn't. In July Olive wrote to her editor William Brownell that she cared, "more and more for poetic living and less and less for writing about it." Perhaps as she helped build a pig-proof fence "down a perpendicular hillside" and prepared pea seeds for planting, she began to realize that she could write about life on the farm itself—that she could make art out of her labors in the mountain dirt, fields, and forests. She turned to her typewriter and began crafting straightforward, funny stories inspired by her life in the mountains, narrated by "Mis' Dolly," Olive's literary alter ego. She sold the first story to *The Atlantic Monthly* in 1919. Over the next five years, her short stories appeared regularly in *The Atlantic Monthly* and *The Reviewer*. They were so popular that Olive's publisher collected them into a book, *Highland Annals*. Released in 1925, it established her as a well-known "regional" writer in addition to her previous success as a poet and playwright.

Her stories detailed life in the mountains, rich with character studies of Olive's neighbors—tenant farmers who worked and hunted on her land in North Carolina. Olive exercised a degree of literary license in the telling and changed all names—but the personal dynamics and geographic descriptions ring true. Educated writer Mis' Dolly is a "fish out of water" in the woods, a good foil for the practicality and wiles of the mountain folk. In "About Granpap and Trees" she describes how her cabin roof was in need of repair before winter, but she couldn't bear to be the cause of a beautiful tree being felled. *If tree-worship was ever the religion of any tribe, I know that I am ancestrally bound to that folk…[but] the oak boards of my cabin roof had to be reinforced. I could not spend another winter with the snows driving in on me. A "board-tree" had to be felled… I set out with granpap, the most skillful board-maker in the Unakas, to select a victim.* Each tree that Granpap considers, she talks him out of, until he grows suspicious of her company and makes a second tree-hunting excursion without her. In her absence, however, he manages to cut down her very favorite tree, only to find that while it looked perfect for board-making on the outside, its wood was thoroughly knotted and gnarled—rendering it useless as material for roof repair.

In "My Wild-Hog Claim: A Dubious Asset," she relays the adventures of a hunting party on the trail of a wild hog. Mis' Dolly decides to accompany the men on the hunt, as does elderly Granpap. In a moment of brashness, she promises that if Granpap catches the hog, he can have all of it. It was a long, rough day in the woods, and finally they spot the hog: *We saw the boar, on top of a lichen-covered boulder, sitting on his haunches, his eyes, like two little black stars, pouring vitriol that ought to have made the forest crumple. The rock itself, with its green, black and creamy spots, and veinlike roots climbing over it, seemed a part of the creature's body, making a monster as superior to attack as granite...* Shenanigans and chaos ensue, and who should end up casting the rope that catches him? Granpap. Although Dolly suspects she's somehow been tricked out of a hog, she honors her word.

These semi-autobiographical, regional stories were a departure from Olive's previous works inspired by mythology and other classical subjects. A few of the stories in *Highland Annals* touch on the lure of better wages and more modern housing for workers in cotton mills built in North and South Carolina in the 1920s. Mountain farming was hard work, and families were often hungry and very poor—it was hard to imagine that mill work, which theoretically paid better, wouldn't be an improvement. But the working conditions were often oppressive, with owners having little regard for human health or safety. The struggle between capitalism and workers' rights that Olive had been so keenly aware of in England was moving into her own backyard.

Additionally, as a member of the middle class who had been drawn to the mountains by their beauty, Olive could see the immense destruction that industrial logging was inflicting on the area's ancient forest, even as it provided well-paying work. She was never active in the national park movement, but saw it from conflicting viewpoints—by displacing mountaineers from their native land, it made them more likely to seek new work in the cotton mills; but some kind of preservation of the mountains' natural integrity was needed. Olive also struggled with her sense of moral obligation to help those less fortunate than she—her communist convictions—but couldn't commit the time away from her writing to be a dedicated social activist.

As the national park movement was gaining momentum—a crucial financial hurdle had been addressed with a five million dollar gift from John D. Rockefeller in March 1928, a pivotal moment in Olive's life was marked by a great and sudden loss. That July, William Crary Brownell, her editor at Scribner's, died unexpectedly. She missed his friendship and counsel deeply. Life in the mountains was lonely without his letters. But as the months passed, she began to discover a degree of literary freedom she'd never had before. Brownell had always discouraged her from writing fiction, preferring for her to focus on poetry and plays. Less than a year after his death, Olive began working on her first novel, *Call Home the Heart*, which was well received in 1932.

Call Home the Heart was inspired by the infamous Loray mill strike in Gastonia, North Carolina in 1929. The Loray mill was one of the first to enact policies that simultaneously doubled employees' work and reduced their wages. In response, 1,800 mill employees went on strike demanding fair wages and better working conditions. The Gastonia strike began on April 1, 1929 and by April 26th, Olive had traveled over 150 miles from Horizon Farm and arrived at the strikers' tent camp. Her friendship with Rose Pastor Stokes, who was then assistant secretary of the Worker's International Relief, came in handy in gaining her admission to the heavily guarded strike headquarters. Given her education and occupation, a friendly welcome was far from assured without the right connections. "I'm stamped 'middle-class' all over... but the strikers like me and make me feel like blood-kin. Bless their weary bones!" Olive wrote to Rose. The Gastonia mill strikes became notorious because of the ensuing violence—the chief of police and ballad singer Ella May Wiggins were murdered, and the conspiracy trial of several labor organizers left many people outraged, including Olive. She channeled the experience into her writing.

The protagonist of her first novel *Call Home the Heart* is a young mother named Ishma Waycaster, who struggles with her desire to learn about the world beyond her rural valley and leaves the mountains to work at a cotton mill. She becomes involved in union organizing, which leads to a strike that erupts into violence. The book explores questions of intellectual and political loyalty, and the ties of romantic love and family, as well as racial issues. By the time it was published in 1932, the American public had developed an unbridled enthusiasm for this kind of "proletarian novel." Olive published *Call Home the Heart* under the male pseudonym of Fielding Burke. No letters from Olive or her publisher remain to explain the decision—perhaps the most likely reason is that she already had an established reputation as a poet and playwright, and wanted the novel—a departure from her usual writing—to be judged on its own merit. Additionally, the main criticism of her work in general was its "sentimentality," which critics believed was typical of female writers. She may have been testing the stereotype by writing initially under a man's name. She was of course, "found out" but her identity didn't affect sales.

Her sequel to *Call Home the Heart, A Stone Came Rolling*, was published in 1935. In it, the protagonist Ishma Waycaster's adventures continue to be a lens for exploring the ways in which the working class submits to its own oppression—specifically, by conforming to the teachings of organized religion which praises poverty as a virtue. The *North American Review* considered it, "on the whole the best radical novel yet written in the United States." In an interview with the *Raleigh News & Observer*, Olive explained, "I am more interested in humanity than literature. My interest in literature is probably in my effort to put humanity into it."

But social justice novels concerned with workers' rights were beginning to lose appeal with readers as the specter of the Cold War loomed on the horizon. Olive herself felt intimidated by anti-communist sentiment. But she continued to work on her next novel, anticipating it would be her finest literary achievement.

As she labored over this third novel, she took time for a few less demanding writing projects as well. In 1941 the stories that had appeared in *The Atlantic Monthly* and *The Reviewer* were reprinted in a book titled *From My Highest Hill*, accompanied by photographs from Bayard Wootten, a pioneering female photographer who also took photos for Muriel Sheppard's *Cabins in the Laurel*. Olive personally accompanied Wootten on her photo shoots in North Carolina to make sure the portraits were realistic and honest—in short, that they matched the truthfulness of Olive's words.

In the early 1940s, life in the mountains around Olive's farm changed drastically. Although her property was outside the boundary line of the newly established Great Smoky Mountains National Park, the Tennessee Valley Authority made plans to dam the Little Tennessee River along the park's southwest edge. The new Fontana Dam—the fourth largest dam in the world at that time—provided much-needed electricity for the increased aluminum processing required to supply the war effort. Olive's farm was among the more than 10,000 acres that were inundated beneath the waters of Fontana Lake. She badly needed the money from the sale, but parting with the farm was bittersweet. She bought a house in Asheville, Bluebonnet Lodge, and earned a modest income by working as the book reviewer for the *Asheville Citizen*. And she continued to work on the final book in her trilogy that had begun with *Call Home the Heart*.

Her epic concluding novel, *Sons of the Stranger*, was finally published in 1947. Her publisher, Longmans, had insisted she cut the word count by at least a third, yet she ensured it remained a romantic epic and bold social protest. Her literary advisor Grant Knight told her that she had "written something magnificent—either a magnificent triumph or a magnificent failure." Despite Olive's unflagging hope of a revolution for the oppressed masses, the time for that hope, and books that fanned flames of discontent, was over. *Sons of the Stranger* sold poorly, although, to her publisher's credit, the burgeoning anti-communist hysteria made it possibly the worst time to promote a novel about the Industrial Workers of the World, no matter how well written.

Olive was disappointed that her monumental novels of human struggle, female independence and communist philosophy had faded so quickly into the vast shelves of literary obscurity. She kept writing, although she could sense that the interests of the reading public were shifting away from what she had to offer them. "I seem to have lived too long," she wrote to Grant Knight in June 1955, when she was eighty-six. "All of my old admirers of my verse that made it easy for me to publish are dead.... I've felt like a paralytic deprived all over of movement except the power to smile. I have built up an inner dignity that makes life bearable, but that is all. This is the first time I have made such a confession and it will be the only one. *I am not a whiner.*"

But not all of her admirers were gone. John F. Blair, a former editor at the University of North Carolina Press who started his own company in 1954, asked her for the privilege of publishing a new collection of her verse, titled *The Spotted Hawk*. Olive agreed, although she was worried he would lose money on the project. The book was published in 1958 and promptly won three prizes for poetry—giving her confidence a much-needed boost. Old friends and literary admirers sent her congratulatory letters. She began to feel encouraged about her writing again and kept working on her three unfinished books. Only one of those projects was published before her death—again by John F. Blair, in 1962. *Innocent Bigamy* was a collection of twelve short stories that evoked the mood of *Highland Annals*. Olive described them as "simple and realistic; nothing controversial...but entertainment, good enough I hope, to provide relaxation necessary for the weary reader without making him feel he is wasting his time."

Her humor and wit served her well. Even as she reached her late 90s, she stayed mentally sharp and largely independent. Unwilling to move into a nursing home, she sold her house to a younger couple, with the stipulation that she could live out her days on the top floor. She died of pneumonia shortly after her 99th birthday, on January 22, 1968, in Asheville and is buried in the Green Hills Cemetery in West Asheville.

Her life in the Smokies wasn't easy or comfortable by any means, but she still loved them, preferring to stay through difficulties rather than live anywhere else. During a time of hardship she wrote to her editor, "...Would you [sell the farm]? But do you know there are mountains on it? Peaks that catch the clouds and have flirtatious entanglements with the moon and stars—wear azalea scarves in the Spring and spread Persian carpets for me in the Autumn?"

Although her works are now obscure, *Call Home the Heart* was brought back into print by The Feminist Press in 1983, and *From My*

Highest Hill was reissued with a new foreword by the University of Tennessee Press in 1998.

Scholar of Appalachian culture Cratis Williams, in his exhaustive three-volume dissertation on the portrayal of the southern mountaineer in fiction, wrote in 1961 that "Dargan, although not a native mountain woman, perhaps caught more accurately the isolated Carolina mountaineer's dialect, essential character, and habits of mind than any other writer of fiction ever to attempt to interpret Carolina mountain folk." It is fitting then, that Olive found her most enduring literary inspiration as she shivered at her typewriter in her drafty cabin on Horizon Farm, a place where she too endured sorrow and struggle, yet found great joy, beauty, and life-long friendships.

Chapter 10

Lottie Queen Stamper

THE EXTENSIVE REVIVAL OF CONTEMPORARY EASTERN CHEROKEE BASKETRY IN CANE, OAK SPLINTS, AND HONEYSUCKLE, AND THE ATTAINMENT OF EXCELLENCE IN FORM AND PATTERN, IS A RESULT OF THE MANY EFFORTS AND ACCOMPLISHMENTS OF LOTTIE STAMPER.

LOTTIE QUEEN STAMPER · 1907–1987

—*Qualla Arts and Crafts Mutual survey, 1987*

Lottie Queen Stamper

On a warm spring day in 1937, Lottie Queen Stamper, a young Cherokee basket weaver, received two unusual visitors at her home in Soco Gap, a remote community nestled in the mountains about fifteen miles east of the main Indian town of Cherokee, North Carolina. Even though she was only thirty, Lottie already had a reputation as an exceptional artist. Her house was an informal store as well as her studio, and people made pilgrimages through the bumpy, winding mountain roads to see her, coming by unannounced to watch her work or to buy baskets. But Sam Gilliam and Gertrude Flanagan, the principal and home economics teacher of the Cherokee Training School, weren't looking for baskets—they were hoping to convince Lottie to join the boarding school's staff. They needed a teacher with unusual qualifications, and wanted to know if she would be willing to teach basketry to their high school students.

Gertrude Flanagan had moved to North Carolina from Oklahoma, and shortly thereafter received a letter from the school board asking her to develop courses in "arts and crafts," a phrase which she hadn't encountered in her work. Without her own ideas of what arts and crafts instruction should be, she and Sam Gilliam sought advice from the community, which led them to Lottie and the ancient tradition of Cherokee basket weaving. The conversation that began at Lottie's house that day in 1937 put into motion a transformation that changed what generations of young Cherokees would understand about their heritage.

Over the following four decades, Lottie would become the central figure in rekindling knowledge of, and enthusiasm for, traditional basket weaving in the Eastern Band of the Cherokee. Much of what's known about her influence in Cherokee basketry and life has been chronicled in Anna Fariello's book *Cherokee Basketry*, and Western Carolina University's Cherokee Traditions project. Lottie Stamper began to teach as an "Indian Assistant" at the Cherokee Training School in June 1937, earning a little over $1,000 a year. She spent the next three decades as an instructor, continuing to teach at the public high school and offer adult education classes long after the Cherokee Training School closed in the early 1950s.

For centuries, Cherokee women wove containers to hold every-thing from corn to fish. It was common for homes to have dozens of baskets since they were used to store, process, and transport many different kinds of goods. There were two distinct styles of weaving—single weave and double weave, the latter resulting in a basket that, in the hands of an expert weaver, would be waterproof.

Rivercane, which looks like a delicate type of bamboo, was the pri-mary material for making baskets. For centuries it grew abundantly along the banks of the mountain rivers that flowed through Cherokee territory. However, by the late 1700s, the arrival of white settlers and subsequent expansion of cattle grazing, farming, and settlement had begun to affect the sensitive canebrakes. The 1800s were filled with disruption and upheaval for the Cherokee people—they suffered from disease, war, loss of traditional land to white settlers, and the Indian Removal Act. The Cherokee population in North Carolina was re-duced to around 400 as thousands were marched to Oklahoma on the Trail of Tears. An incalculable amount of traditional knowledge was lost over these tumultuous decades.

By the time James Mooney, a Smithsonian researcher who studied the Eastern Cherokee extensively, arrived in the late 1800s, he found a culture greatly diminished from what it had been only a hundred years earlier. Regarding basket weaving, he reported in his book *Myths of the Cherokee*, that the "last old woman who preserved the art of making double-walled baskets," named Wadi-hayi, had died in 1897. Mooney was convinced that the knowledge of the intricate technique had vanished with her. He turned out to be wrong, but so few women knew the technique that it was justifiably classified as a "lost art."

On January 4, 1907, nearly ten years after the death of Wadi-hayi, Lottie Queen was born, the fifth of six Queen children. They lived on wooded land in the Soco Gap section of the North Carolina Smokies. Her mother, Mary, knew how to weave white oak baskets, and taught her children—as was the custom to pass artistic knowledge down through families. In an interview with researcher Tommy Jo Bookout, Lottie recalled, "The whole family of us learned basket weaving from our mother. But it took a good bit of practice to make a good basket.

When I did learn it meant new clothes and shoes to wear back to school each fall of the year. This was my very first experience to make and sell a basket."

Weaving a basket in the traditional Cherokee way is not for the faint of heart. First, the materials must be harvested, which requires heading out into the woods with a knife or axe. The weaver can choose between several plant species: with the decline in rivercane, baskets were also made from white oak, maple, or honeysuckle. Weavers often specialized in a certain material, and Lottie's mother wove from white oak. Although Lottie's father didn't weave, he helped with the initial step in basket making, collecting raw materials. Further elaborating for Bookout, Lottie said, "I remember very well when I was a child when he and my mother used to go to the hills to get white oak saplings. That was after the cultivation of the fields and garden was over. This was the beginning process of white oak basketry. He split the logs into lengthwise pieces."

After her father helped harvest the oak, removed the bark, and split and trimmed the wood, Lottie's mother would separate the pieces into smaller "splints": the pieces to be woven, which she would then scrape smooth with a knife. It was a difficult process, separating the stick into thinner, weaveable splints. It took great dexterity and skill to pull the ends of the stick apart just right, which Lottie learned by watching her mother closely and mastered through hours of practice.

If the weaver desired, the splints could then be dyed using natural materials, which also had to be gathered and prepared. Cherokee men sometimes helped with digging roots and collecting bark needed to make dyes, but the women oversaw the long process of boiling the raw material. Lottie would set up her seven-gallon tub by a stream bank and fill it with cold creek water. She explained that she would "Fill [the tub] half of roots and the rest water and when the water boils away you've got to add more water. That's what you have to watch. If it boils away you burn the cane. Just like cooking food. If it's strong enough and you don't put too much material in there you ought to color it in about six hours. [The dye bath creates a] deep brown and dark black according to how long it's been boiling."

Boiling bark from the butternut tree yielded black dye; black walnut resulted in dark brown; bloodroot created tan; and yellowroot lived up to its name as a golden dye. Still, some weavers, like Lottie's mother, didn't bother with dying their splints, and got right to work once the splints were sized for weaving.

Learning to weave as a child, under her mother's exacting gaze, Lottie sometimes worked on perfecting a basket with tears in her eyes; working and reworking the splints until her mother approved of the quality. This pursuit of perfection, instilled by her mother, helped Lottie establish her reputation as a talented weaver. Once they had completed as many baskets as they could carry, Lottie and her mother would take them—on foot— to either Waynesville or Junaluska to sell them, a round trip distance of about fifty miles. The tourism industry in the Smoky Mountains was in its infancy then and not many tourists were venturing into the isolated valleys where the Cherokee lived.

Lottie's reputation as a basket weaver in Cherokee society increased in her late 20s, with her marriage to Bill Stamper. Her new mother-in-law, Sally Ann Stamper, and sister-in-law Lizzie Youngbird were both accomplished weavers with a breadth of knowledge they were willing to share with her. Lottie moved from her family's farm in Soco to her husband's community, Painttown, and began to work with her in-laws. Although she was already proficient in white oak weaving, they taught her to weave rivercane, along with how to use native plants as dye. Lottie favored dyes made from butternut tree root and bloodroot because the "color never fades away."

The 1920s were a prosperous time in the mountains, and the Cherokee benefited from the timber boom in many of the same ways as the European-American settlers. But with the collapse of that industry and the Great Depression in the 1930s, times became difficult. Lottie's nephew, Edmund Youngbird recounted to interviewers Mollie Blankenship and Stephen Richmond how his family "just barely made a living by making crafts. I can remember vaguely, it was back in the Depression days, and I was ten or twelve years old. There were a lot of bodies to feed, and we didn't eat fancy. Back in those days there was no money." Baskets were part of the barter system, to be traded for food—Edmund recalled seeing his parents exchange their woven goods for chickens, beans, pumpkins, and eggs.

New Deal programs provided jobs for the Cherokee and others in the mountains, and with the coming of Great Smoky Mountains National Park, tourism began to increase. Outdoor and hiking enthusiasts, drawn to the high mountain peaks, began visiting the small Cherokee towns on their expeditions into the mountains. The national interest for handmade crafts was also growing. Only one year into Lottie's teaching, her crafts classes were so busy with Christmas orders that adult basket weavers were enlisted to meet the demand. Small rivercane wastebaskets were snapped up at $1.25 (equivalent to $20 today); a larger "market basket" was $2.25. Gertrude sent two white oak baskets to be shown at the 1939 San Francisco World's Fair, and they sold for $2 each. The Cherokee School superintendent observed, "The teaching of basketry has taken surprisingly well and quite a group of girls are planning to make it their major craft activity."

By the time the national park was officially dedicated by President Roosevelt in 1940, Lottie had been teaching basket weaving to Cherokee high school students for four years, and the local crafts industry was beginning to gain momentum. Perhaps remembering her difficulties learning from her mother, Lottie was an encouraging and patient teacher. She focused on techniques for weaving honeysuckle and rivercane, which required slightly less labor to gather the materials than white oak or maple.

Traditionally, weaving had been passed down through families in a watch-and-imitate manner. But Lottie found some adjustments were needed when teaching a class. She developed a method in which she would plot the weaving designs painstakingly on graph paper, then post the patterns onto the wall for students to copy. Many of the traditional designs didn't have names, even for the hundreds of years they'd been used. For ease of teaching in the 1940s, Lottie and her students bestowed them with descriptions: Fishbone, Cross on a Hill, Man in a Coffin, Peace Pipe, Flowing Water, Chief's Daughter, Big Diamond—which are still used today.

In 1940, Gertrude Flanagan pushed Lottie's skills further. She wanted Lottie to learn the intricate technique of doubleweave basketry, and had secured some funding to compensate for the time and effort it would take. This was the weaving technique that anthropologist Mooney had reported to be, for all practical purposes, lost forever in 1880. In 1920, anthropologist Frank Speck had also reported that doubleweave was "almost abandoned among the eastern Cherokee." Reviving this difficult "lost art" was a first rate challenge. Still, Lottie knew of two women born in the late 1800s who might be able to teach her: Rebecca Toineeta and Nancy Bradley.

She visited Nancy first and was rebuffed (although Nancy eventually passed her knowledge on to her daughter, Rowena Bradley). Lottie's last hope was Rebecca Toineeta who lived on Swimmer Branch, a remote part of the Soco community. Lottie recalled how she pestered the old lady: "She didn't much want to [teach me,] but I bothered her until she showed and told me a little bit about it. She said… 'Bring it back to check, and don't come back any more.'"

But Lottie still hadn't mastered the technique. The difficulty in figuring out the methodology was that the doubleweave basket is actually two baskets interlaced together to create one continuous form. The weaver begins at the base, as with most baskets, and weaves the sides upward. However, once the sides are finished, instead of binding the rim, the weaver turns the cane downward and continues weaving along the outside of the basket until she reaches the base once more. It is extremely intricate work, resulting in a basket woven so tightly that, if perfectly made, can hold water. It also allows the weaver to show off an additional layer of skill, since different patterns can be woven into the inside and outside layers of the basket.

As the story goes, Lottie's breakthrough came from a place quite far away from the North Carolina mountains: London's British Museum. Lottie was given a photograph of a pre-Removal basket—a double-woven basket and lid—collected by Francis Nicholson, the colonial Governor of South Carolina. He had taken the piece home with him at the end of his assignment in the New World in 1725. The basket set later ended up in the British Museum, tagged with a note that claims, "They will keep anything in them from being wetted by rain." Studying the photograph, Lottie began working out the patterns and charting them on graph paper, "counting the numbers." In two and a half days, she had worked out the pattern. Then she turned to weaving a basket—using five hundred splints, she created a successful replica. "This, indeed, was the happiest day of my life," she remembered. "Now it was my duty to teach it to my brightest students, and it was their happiest when they learned [how to do it]."

But it wasn't only the technique of doubleweave that needed to be revived and taught. Other styles of baskets were becoming rare as well, particularly the "burden basket" which had declined in use since the early 1900s, according to research by Anna Fariello at Western Carolina University. The baskets were traditionally used to carry and store heavy goods, like harvested potatoes and corn, and were being replaced by wooden crates which could be more easily stacked and hauled by trucks. The burden basket is distinctive: a three foot tall container that extends from a woman's shoulders to her hips, woven with a square base and flat sides so it lies snugly against her back. It tucks inward at the midsection to provide stability and support and flares at the top, giving the gatherer a wider target. It was traditionally held to the body with a tumpline, a loose cloth rope tied around the forehead or neck and shoulders.

Gertrude Flanagan gave a burden basket to one of Lottie's most promising students, Agnes Lossie Welch, who was only twelve. Together, Lottie and Agnes figured out how to weave the complex shape. Agnes only attended school for nine months total, spending two hours each day learning basket weaving. She later became a successful weaver, and the burden basket became her signature piece.

In addition to ensuring that the Cherokee girls grew up with some exposure to skills as craftswomen, Gertrude and Lottie were very involved in the beginnings of handicraft associations. These organizations promoted the work of professional Cherokee artists, particularly by giving them credibility and standardization—a stamp of superior quality, of sorts—that made the crafts more appealing to collectors. The momentum to turn the arts into a more economically secure business

venture faltered during World War II, but was revived by Superintendent of the Cherokee Indian Agency, Joe Jennings, who began holding
meetings to plan for the creation of an artisan cooperative.

Established in 1946, the co-op was juried into the Southern Highland Handicraft Guild, a more geographically widespread organization of artisans devoted to the "arts and crafts" movement, in 1949.
The co-op, today called the Qualla Arts and Crafts Mutual Inc., paid
up front for work and gave artists an opportunity to sell their arts
and crafts year-round, no longer confining sales to the distinct tourist seasons in the Smokies. Gertrude Flanagan managed the newly
opened store along the highway, no doubt proudly extolling the skills
of young Cherokees who had learned their trade under her auspices.
Profits were shared among members, divided into equity payments.
Annual Craftsmen's Fairs held throughout the mountains in Tennessee and North Carolina were another way that Lottie and other artists
were able to display their skills. Many artists with expertise in wood-
carving, basket weaving, pottery, and weaving would demonstrate
their skills while selling wares.

By 1952, after fifteen years of teaching, Lottie had trained hundreds of the younger generation of Cherokee weavers. In recognition
of this contribution to reviving the craft, her skill as a weaver and
her excellence as a teacher, the Southern Highland Handicraft Guild
honored her with a lifetime achievement award. She was the first Native American recipient. Her skill with weaving sometimes seemed
to her students to come from magic in her fingertips, but she taught
with the certainty that anyone could learn to weave with enough
patience. When, as a child, she was crying under her mother's exacting tutelage, she probably never dreamed she would devote her life
to preserving and reviving the art of Cherokee basket weaving. But
through her devotion to teaching the craft, the words of James Adair,
author of the 1775 *History of American Indians*, still ring true today:
the "baskets which the Cherokee made were…highly esteemed…for
domestic usefulness, beauty, and skillful variety."

By the time Lottie passed away in 1987, the days when a hand-woven basket could be purchased for less than today's equivalent of fifty

dollars were long past. Such baskets are now displayed in museums around the world, eagerly sought out by collectors, and are beautiful symbols of the revival of an ancient Cherokee tradition that flourishes again because of Lottie's artistry and devotion to teaching.

Lottie Stamper, standing, with basketry students, ca. 1950s.

Chapter 11

Wilma Dykeman

WHAT WOULD YOU NOMINATE AS THE MOST VALUABLE ASSET OUR COUNTRY WILL POSSESS DURING THE LAST DECADES OF THIS CENTURY? OUR VAST OIL RESOURCES... OUR RESERVES OF COAL... SOPHISTICATED COMPUTERS?... I BELIEVE THAT THE ASSET WE WILL SEARCH OUT MOST DILIGENTLY AND TREASURE MOST DEARLY DURING DECADES TO COME WILL BE A GREEN, GROWING UNCONTAMINATED PORTION OF THE EARTH.

WILMA DYKEMAN · 1920-2006

—*Wilma Dykeman*, Look to This Day (1968)

Wilma Dykeman

With the rounded blue silhouettes of the Great Smoky Mountains in the distance, Wilma Dykeman grew up in a house on the outskirts of Asheville, North Carolina. The 1920s were a time of industrial growth for Asheville, but the Dykeman home was surrounded by native forest, complemented by flower and vegetable gardens, which both of her parents cultivated. The gentle murmur of Beaverdam Creek often drifted in through the house's open windows, making a strong impression on baby Wilma, whose first words were said to be *"waddy coming down"* to describe the creek water.

Long after she'd established herself as an accomplished author, Wilma Dykeman wrote a tongue-in-cheek essay about how, by raising her in a happy, secure home instead of introducing her to tension and dysfunction, her parents didn't prepare her very well for her career as a writer. Her childhood memories centered around moments like watching her mother Bonnie skim fresh cream from pans of milk, mixing it with wild strawberries for a refreshing summer dessert. The family would spend winter evenings together in the living room, a crackling fire warming the hearth while Bonnie read aloud to Wilma and her father, Willard. Or Wilma would linger in Willard's tidy woodworking shop that adjoined the garage, watching him turn a block of black walnut into a graceful piece of furniture. He built Wilma a swing when she was five, suspending it from the stout limb of a maple tree in the yard: "its seat was cut and shaped by hand, and below it was the grass and leaves, and directly above, the thick green maple leaves….I have never known, before or since, a simple object which brought more real pleasure than that swing," she wrote.

Her parents were thoughtful, generous, and kind. They raised Wilma, their only child, to be a self-confident, well-adjusted young woman. But her childhood wasn't entirely without sadness or worry. The Great Depression shook their financial stability, and in 1934, Willard, who was nearly forty years older than Bonnie, died of a heart attack when Wilma was fourteen. Bonnie never remarried; she and Wilma were devoted to and supportive of each other for their entire lives. "My mother denied me an unhappy, selfish home… She denied me quarrels and invective and discord and self-pity. She made me go out and find these for myself, if I had need of them—or wanted to be a fashionable writer," Wilma later wrote. Although she was poking fun at the claim that writers somehow needed to be unhappy and insecure to fuel their genius, Wilma did find abundant challenging emotional material to work with in the misunderstood and complicated psyche of her native Appalachian Mountains, if not in her family. With her finely crafted sense of both history and artistry, and her ability to write fiction and nonfiction with equal mastery, Wilma embraced the challenge of writing honestly and fairly about her homeland—rising to become one of the region's most accomplished and celebrated authors. In the most personal details of life—her own, and others'—she found universal meaning. And in Appalachia, she found echoes of the entire world. Her career spanned more than fifty years and included almost twenty books of fiction and nonfiction, and hundreds of newspaper columns and magazine articles. She taught college courses and gave countless lectures that centered on the history and culture of the Tennessee and North Carolina mountains. She built on the legacy of earlier writers like Olive Tilford Dargan, but set her own writing apart by the depth of her historical understanding of the region.

All of that was still to come in the summer of 1940, when Wilma was a 20-year-old newly minted graduate from Northwestern University in Illinois. She had accepted a teaching position at Finch, the prestigious girls' finishing school on Manhattan's Upper East Side, and was planning to leave the North Carolina mountains she'd grown up in, possibly forever. Until the school year started in September, she was briefly back at home in Asheville with her mother before heading north to begin this new phase of her life. Had she not unexpectedly fallen in love that summer, Southern Appalachia might have lost one of its most insightful storytellers. But on a pleasant August morning as she was cutting flowers in the backyard garden, a friend and "a stranger" arrived. Mabel Wolfe, sister to literary icon Thomas, had matchmaking in mind as she introduced Wilma to James R. Stokely, Jr. James was a thoughtful, philosophical young man who had befriended Thomas Wolfe in New York City years earlier, and subsequently became one of Mabel's acquaintances, since they lived so close to each other in the Southern mountains.

James and Wilma began falling in love that very morning. Wilma later wrote, "We discovered that we were both interested in words and in woods, in theater and in thought, in being very social on some occasions and very much alone on other occasions. We were passionately fond of travel, and equally happy in staying at home.... Many of the things that made us perplexing to other people made us seem clear and right to each other." On one of their first dates, James took her to the Newfound Gap Overlook along the state lines of Tennessee and North Carolina to be part of the crowd listening to President Franklin Delano Roosevelt dedicate the new Great Smoky Mountains National Park on September 2, 1940. The next month, on October 12th, they were married in the same garden in which they'd met.

With the goal of "getting to know our native land," Wilma and James embarked on a ten-week honeymoon drive across America. The giddiness of their whirlwind romance began to deepen into a close partnership that would grow stronger over decades of marriage. James was not only supportive of Wilma's writing career, but integral to it. He himself was a poet, and although he never earned a living from his writing, he had respectful friendships with several giants of American poetry: Robinson Jeffers, Carl Sandburg, and Robert Frost.

Frost, during one of James and Wilma's visits to his Vermont farm, told them about good friends of his, both successful writers, who had divorced because of incompatibilities with their careers. "The separation of these two people had wounded Frost," Wilma wrote, "because he cherished both of them and he believed they belonged together. His shrewd, friendly eyes watched us closely. My husband and I were touched by his concern for our personal relationship." Robert Frost wasn't the only person who worried that Wilma's career might cause strife in their marriage—acquaintances often murmured at the fact that she chose to write under her *maiden name*, a highly unusual choice in the 1950s.

Instead of driving them apart, Wilma's writing seems to have brought her and James closer together, deepening their collaboration and support of each other. James helped with research, read her drafts, asked questions, and when necessary, opened doors that weren't accessible to most women in the mid 20th century. His father had been a founder of a successful canning company, and although James had only a minor interest in the business, it provided him with both a modest income and the respect of businessmen and political leaders throughout the South.

Upon returning from their honeymoon, Wilma and James bought a hundred acre apple orchard—partly inspired by Robert Frost. They began building a stone cottage in Tennessee, then purchased a second orchard in North Carolina. Wilma also began to establish her literary reputation with short stories, largely published in the *Southwest Review*, *Prairie Schooner*, and *American Magazine*. Even with her promising career, she and James agreed that they wanted a family. In 1949, their first son, Dykeman, was born. Two years later, they had a second son, James Stokely III. But the writing, children, and farming turned out to be a little too much of an undertaking at the same time. Of the three, the farming was the least dear. So in 1953, they sold their orchards and moved into James's family home in Newport, Tennessee—just across the mountain range from Asheville. The house sat on the crest of a hill, on four acres of lawn, gardens, and trees, which sloped down to the Pigeon River at the foot of the bluff.

The French Broad River on the outskirts of Newport, which the Pigeon River flows into not far from the Stokely home, was the subject of Wilma's first book-length literary success. Unsolicited, she pitched the idea of a book about the river to the New York publisher Rinehart & Company, which had issued a series of books on the "Rivers of America." This series, although nonfiction, was authored largely by novelists and literary figures so as to be more appealing than most historical writing of the time. It was a revolutionary idea—in perfect keeping with Wilma's style of narrative nonfiction.

Although Rinehart initially rejected her proposal, explaining they only published books on "important rivers," the rejection letter left the door for resubmittal open just enough: "'If [the book] is interestingly enough written,'" Wilma later recalled in an interview in *Southern Living*, "they said, 'we would publish the story of a river no bigger than a man's hand.'" Undaunted and convinced that the French Broad deserved a place among the "Rivers of America," Wilma researched and wrote several chapters for their consideration. She was promptly offered a contract and her first book, *The French Broad*, was published in 1955 as the 49th book in the series.

The French Broad was particularly notable for its controversial chapter on the effects of pollution and the ecological destruction of the river—published seven years before Rachel Carson's *Silent Spring*. Wilma's editor had tried to remove it and she resisted. "I hesitated, then replied that I had to have this chapter but I would try to make it interesting," she recalled at an awards ceremony in 2001. "I would call it 'Who killed the French Broad?' Perhaps people would think it was a murder mystery. (Of course, it was murder but not a mystery.) At publication, that chapter received more response, from Raleigh to California, than any other part of the book." Poet Carl Sandburg wrote her after finishing his copy, "Your blood and brain absorbed that tributary so completely in feel and imagination that the book would not have been misnamed, Hey feller, how does it feel to be a river?...I said a couple of times, Jesus, she can write!"

Her boys, Dykeman and James, were six and four when *The French Broad* was published to excellent reviews—but conscious of the central role her mother had played in her own life, Wilma made sure her writing didn't overshadow her family. She wrote about being a mother too—in her fiction, and in numerous essays. She was a "Southern Woman" and she thoroughly enjoyed it, celebrating her ability to wear flamboyant hats and high heels, and to bake pies whenever she desired. Her humor often shines through when mentioning raising two boys—did other families suffer from various afflictions like "nightly hydrophobia," she once asked in an essay: "children who have spent half an afternoon reveling in a pool of thousands of gallons of water are all at once repelled at the thought of a small tub of the stuff—coupled with a bar of soap. They resist all encounters with water that is not filled with ice cubes, fish, or other people."

As the boys grew up and attended grammar school, Wilma wrote while she had the house to herself. When they got home in the evening, she shifted her focus to them, although her eye for detail and sense of a good story were always with her. She watched them run across the lawn catching fireflies, struggled to get them into church clothes, called them in from playing baseball in rainstorms. Mothers everywhere must have empathized with her when she wrote of dropping them off at camp: "Suddenly, before she can say here's-the-poison-ivy-lotion or don't-forget-to-brush-your-teeth, the mother of the camper beholds a transfiguration…suddenly he is a total stranger…. He turns his shoulder, as indifferent and casual as a sturdy little boy's shoulder can be and pretends that the woman in the shirtwaist dress behind him is some unknown wanderer who hitchhiked a ride in the family car…."

Few women in the 1950s and '60s had the support from their husbands to both embrace a full family life and pursue a career, and Wilma and James were quite the odd couple in rural, conservative Newport, Tennessee. Wilma's second book, *Neither Black Nor White*, was coauthored with James and was a bold statement about their commitment to social justice. The book was catalyzed by the Supreme Court's 1954 ruling against separate but equal schools. Newspaper and magazine reporters traveled through the South to record reactions to the ruling but, Wilma observed, "They all talked to the same people; they all came with their own stereotype and they went back and they wrote about it. We didn't recognize this South; it was just their South…" So she and James spent a year and a half researching and writing a more realistic book of interviews and oral history about Southern racial attitudes after *Brown v. Board of Education*. Sometimes the research required overnight trips, which weren't safe for the boys. During those times, Wilma's mother Bonnie watched her grandsons while Wilma and James drove across the winding roads of thirteen Southern states and conducted over five hundred interviews. "We let the South speak for itself; it had a multitude of voices," Wilma told interviewer Richard Marius in 1989. "It was a strangely wonderful time," she remembered, "There was an openness about everybody. They thought if you went to talk with them that you agreed with them… What we wanted to know was what they believed in. And we wanted to listen."

Wilma had received a Guggenheim fellowship which helped cover some of their expenses as they worked on the project. They attended KKK gatherings and NAACP meetings, talked to ordinary people they met at gas stations, and made appointments to see politicians and leaders in cities and small towns. Read decades later, the book is startlingly raw—the sights, sounds, and smells of a familiar South, but the interviews sit uneasily:

> You watch a Klan meeting on a still summer night or under a chilly autumn wind, as it is directed from the bed of a battered truck backed up into a sedge field on the city's outskirts... the faithful few hear the ill-organized, defiant, familiar messages of impotent anger.
>
> In a small town in middle Mississippi a stranger informed us: "We got one of the highest gasoline taxes of any state in the country, and most of it's being used by the Governor to equalize the [Negro's] schools...it's something the government can't force on the people. Oughtn't to do it, can't do it."
>
> One North Carolinian sighs as he talks with you about some of the facts of Negro migration from the South. "'Oh, the Negroes are leaving by the wholesale,' some people tell you and they're glad. They've never noticed that it's the boy with the engineering degree who's leaving, and it's his idiot brother who's staying."

James's presence at interviews—a man—also helped Wilma gain access to places and people who wouldn't have taken her seriously as a woman, even if she did have an impressive writing career. Wilma's presence opened different doors—she was able to talk with women who had never discussed their feelings on civil rights with anyone other than their families.

Neither Black Nor White was published in 1957 by Rinehart & Company, the same publisher that had given Wilma her first book contract for *The French Broad*. The book won the Sidney Hillman Award in 1957 for being "the best book of the year on world peace, race relations, or civil liberties." This created more opportunities for Wilma and James, enabling them to write about 20 articles in the late 1950s and early 1960s for *The New York Times Magazine*, *The Nation*, *The Progressive*, and civil-rights focused magazines. Particularly in their role as stringers for *The New York Times Magazine*, they were often trailed by a sheriff's deputy out of concern for their safety. Asheville minister John Nelson recalled asking Wilma once, "Were you afraid?" She answered, "No. There are things you have to do. They must be done, even when it is uncomfortable to do so."

In complement to their travel, Wilma and James delighted in returning home, settling in to familiar and comfortable surroundings with their boys once more. Great Smoky Mountains National Park was slowly returning to wilderness as trees grew up through old fields and home sites, and the Park Service expanded the network of hiking trails. The rivers and streams of the mountains were especially resonant for Wilma. She, James, and their sons often hiked and explored the national park, favoring the secluded trails of the Cosby and Big Creek sections. Given her affinity for creeks and rivers, Wilma was particularly enthusiastic about Cosby Creek, "one of the swiftest, most picturesque streams in the park. It provides natural wading ponds and breathtaking swimming pools along several stretches," she wrote in an article for *The New York Times*. LeConte Lodge was another favorite family destination—they made sure to never hike up and down the same trail, often choosing the winding eight mile Boulevard Trail to reach the lodge, and the steeper, more direct five mile Alum Cave Trail for their descent.

For a writer so in touch with the cultural and natural history of the region, Wilma was remarkably never pigeon-holed as a travel writer. She composed a handful of articles encouraging people to visit the new national park in Eastern America, which touch on themes she explores in her books—a fascination with water and sensitivity to the native culture of the mountains. In her short article for *The New York Times*, "Secluded Smokies," she praises Little River, which flows beside the winding road that leads from park headquarters toward Townsend. "Little River rises at an altitude of 6,000 feet in the mountains; by the time it has reached this valley, it is pure and cold and forms dozens of pools large enough for swimming," she wrote.

"Large boulders also provide ideal spots for sunbathing. This road, then, is not for making time but for taking time. Every curve along the way reveals an inviting picnic area, swimming pool, or a spot to try one's luck for trout." In another article for *The New York Times*, "A Stage for Nature in the Smokies" she mentions a restored tub mill along the Junglebrook Trail, "passers-by not only can see this man-made structure in action but also can acquire a very real sense of the atmosphere of pioneer times, that until just quite recently, existed in some of the more remote hollows."

And always, whether after day trips into the Smokies, overnight camping trips, or long excursions through Europe, she returned faithfully to her desk and typewriter and kept writing. During the early '60s, writing while her sons were at grammar school, she completed her first novel, an epic tale of post-Civil War Appalachia. She dedicated *The Tall Woman* to her mother, Bonnie Cole.

Wilma wove themes from her nonfiction—reverence for water, societal prejudice, the importance of education—into the life of *The Tall Woman's* heroine, Lydia Moore. In the book, after the Civil War ends, tensions, mistrust, and ill will linger in a previously tight-knit Appalachian community. The novel follows Lydia's struggles to heal both her husband, a Union soldier emotionally wounded during the war, and her community, still divided by sympathies with the North and South; and her efforts to establish a school in the mountains so their children can have a better future. Importantly, it presented stereotypes of Appalachia—lack of education, rural poverty—in the context of universal struggles and ambitions. As Wilma later explained, she felt her novels allowed her to "probe to the quick of life. They stir us to laughter, rage, pity, horror, renewed awareness of the human condition—and they put us into closer touch with 'reality' than tons of statistics, reams of 'facts.'" *The Tall Woman* struck a chord with readers all over America; published by Holt-Rinehart-Winston in 1962, it has sold over 200,000 copies.

1962 was also the year Wilma began work as a columnist for the *Knoxville News-Sentinel*, sometimes writing up to three columns a week for "The Simple Life." These numerous short pieces explore how the local, personal, and familial echoed greater questions of literature and life and philosophy. Her speaking and lecturing career also began to develop into a robust traveling schedule. She gave fifty to seventy-five talks a year, which she prepared for meticulously. She had majored in speech at Northwestern, and once harbored dreams of being a star on Broadway, so she had little trepidation of appearing before crowds.

She was particularly beloved because of her sense of humor. "I believe that a sense of humor is necessary for any successful life," she once explained, "Humor provides perspective. Humor diminishes our ego while it nourishes our shared humanity. Humor allows us to be serious about the significant aspects of our life without being grim about the trivia..." In addition to her intelligence, insights, and humor, she began to be known for her penchant for flamboyant hats—broad brims and bright ribbons—which she started wearing early in her speaking career and quickly became "a Dykeman trademark."

Following the success of her fictional debut, her second novel, *The Far Family* was published in 1966. It takes place a generation after *The Tall Woman*, following the life of Ivy Thurston Cortland, the granddaughter of *The Tall Woman*'s protagonist Lydia Moore. The novel draws its conflict from the murder of an African-American, which is pinned on Clay Thurston, one of Ivy's brothers. Race, social justice, and stewardship of the land are resonant themes, as is the internal conflict about "being from Appalachia." Through her characters, Wilma explored how the deeply negative stereotyping of the region impacted pride and value in what the region's settlers accomplished in making a living from a harsh but beautiful land.

She also worked with James on two biographies about civil rights advocates in the southern Appalachians. They published *Seeds of Southern Change: The Life of Will Alexander* in 1962 and *Prophet of Plenty: The First Ninety Years of W. D. Weatherford* in 1966. Later she wrote a biography of Edna Rankin McKinnon, a pioneer in family planning from the 1930s to 1960s. *Too Many People, Too Little Love* was published in 1975. Although Wilma admitted being resistant to beginning nearly every biography she worked on, she later explained to Appalachian State Professor Sandra Ballard, "these were people who made me think 'if I don't write about their lives they probably won't have a biography, at least not now.' Each one of them really did have such a special contribution, and I guess my sense of mission has always been strong."

Her book-length works largely focused on Appalachia and the American South, but her newspaper columns for the *Knoxville News Sentinel* reveal a woman whose interests and involvements ranged broadly, impossible to categorize except that they were created by a bright and curious mind. Her "biography in brief," she once wrote, is a quote from William Hazlitt, an English critic: "I would like to spend the whole of my life in traveling...if I could anywhere borrow another life to spend afterwards at home."

In the 1950s through the 1970s, Wilma and James traveled through Canada, ranged across Europe—Greece, in particular, resonated with Wilma—and Wilma was part of a special delegation to China in 1976. They viewed traveling to foreign places as a way "to know more about this world and this adventure called life...When we know more about the corner of the world where we live, we know more about the green and fragile planet which is home to all humans. Our own little spark of curiosity is a part of the immense mystery which surrounds all life. To know! To seek to know! How dull and dead we are when we relinquish that right, that rapture in our lives."

As they traveled, sometimes accompanied by their sons and Wilma's mother Bonnie, they often noted similarities to the Smokies in the world's distant places. The craftspeople of Italy, Spain, and Scandinavia reminded them of weavers and woodworkers in the Appalachians; the Black Forest in Germany evoked reminiscences of George Vanderbilt's estate outside of Asheville, where German understanding of forestry was first applied to American lands; in the relationship of Bergen to the rest of Norway, they recognized the East Tennesseans' predilection for distinguishing themselves as separate—East—from the rest of the state. "What do an afternoon on the bluff [by her Tennessee house] and an evening at the Salzburg [Austria] festival have in common?" Wilma wrote. "My appreciation of them."

Her third novel, *Return the Innocent Earth,* published in 1973, was her least successful, but it was her favorite. It had "everything I care about...racial issues, powerful women, the ways people make choices," she explained in her interview with Sandra Ballard. She fictionalized a small family canning company in the Appalachians, effectively emulating the origins of James's family business. Concerned about her ability to write convincingly about corporate dynamics, she asked to attend company meetings and interview company officers. The novel examines the relationship between motivation for corporate profits, environmental responsibility, and local community; its plot tension comes from a worker dying from exposure to an incompletely vetted new chemical.

Her sense of the Southern Appalachians, from a cultural, historical, and ecological perspective, figured prominently in nearly all of her books. She embraced this, although often took issue with critics or reviewers who saw her as a "regional writer." She explained once to an interviewer, "I think the most frustrating thing that can happen to an author is to have regionalism equated with provincialism.... When really you are an American writer writing from place. Most great writing, I feel, has a sense of place. I hope this would make it more universal rather than limited."

She had firmly established her reputation as a writer of both fiction and nonfiction by 1974, when several Tennessee congressmen asked her to write a short history of Tennessee. They were confident she was the best regional writer to produce the blend of history and literature they wanted for the book, which would be published in 1976 as part of the national bicentennial celebration. Wilma admitted that she contemplated turning the project down, but "was afraid someone else would not write it with the knowledge and love for it that I have." In deference to the task she'd undertaken, she humbly explained in the preface that the reader should take the book to be a *portrait* of the state, not a definitive history. "Definitive history," she wrote, "must be inclusive. The page limitations determined that this book should be exclusive. The challenge and frustration of the task became one of choices. Through such choices, *Tennessee* became a personal interpretation. "

In the late 1970s, Wilma also made the "mistake" of pointing out to the head of the University of Tennessee's English Department, Dr. John Fisher, that despite UT's prominence as the largest university in the region, it didn't offer a single course in Appalachian Studies. "Now, I don't think it's regionalism," she said to an interviewer, "to know the place where you are. The arts have always, historically, had a great sense of place." Dr. Fisher agreed with her that it was a gap in the department's offerings—and asked if she would teach it. She demurred at first, saying she didn't have a Ph.D. "Then the next thing I said was I would do it until he found somebody else." She taught the course for over twenty years.

In addition to her enthusiasm for the region's history, she was ever-encouraging of anyone who mentioned wanting to be a writer to her. Sally Buckner relates in her anthology *Our Words, Our Ways* that: "Ms. Dykeman urges students to learn to listen and look at the world with keen eyes and ears, then apply themselves diligently. She also draws a keen distinction between aptitude and attitude. 'The talent comes from developing the aptitude,' she has said. 'The writer comes from developing the attitude.'" Wilma and James were also frequent lecturers at Berea College in Kentucky and the other regional universities. Wilma was the first woman to join Berea's Board of Trustees, in 1969, and she served for thirty years.

On a June day in 1977, when James was sixty-three, shortly after returning home from lecturing at Berea, he died of a heart attack in their garden. Wilma was deeply affected, for they had managed—despite many people's doubts—to be each other's partner in every sense of the word for nearly forty years. She wrote about her grief, quoting Dante's *Inferno—I woke to find myself in a dark wood/ where the right road was wholly lost and gone.* "Down, down into ourselves we go," she wrote, "like a lost wanderer knowing no path through the woods, finding no light to illuminate the lonely way. We discover a self and a suffering whose existence is stranger than far countries or lost rivers…. A week ago, [James] left on one of the few journeys we have not taken together. But he is not wholly away—and I am not wholly here. We are still together."

Her mother, Bonnie, was still alive; her sons had both graduated from Yale University, and they all supported each other in their grief.

Wilma kept writing her frequent newspaper columns, and traveling, although she never completed and published another book of fiction. She turned her attention to new projects, often collaborating with her sons. She co-wrote *Highland Homeland*, a history and portrait of the Great Smoky Mountains, with her son James Stokely III. James was the executive director of the Appalachian Experience section of the Children's Museum of Oak Ridge and asked her to consult on the project. Their work over the next four years resulted in meticulously researched and written teaching materials honoring the history of the region, as well as a book, *An Encyclopedia of East Tennessee*. Wilma also co-wrote *Appalachian Mountains* with her son Dykeman Stokely.

In 1981, Governor Lamar Alexander named Wilma the state historian of Tennessee. Although the role was initially a four-year term, she held the honorary position until 2002. Her attitude toward history, combined with her writing ability, enabled her to make it come alive like few other writers could do. This unusual sense of what history could be began to form when she was a little girl and met her great-grandfather at a family reunion: "He had served in the Civil War; through him I realized that history was people—and that it did not die but lived on in the consequences flowing from each event, every encounter..." This rare ability to tell good stories woven from the history of the southern Appalachians was one of the main distinguishing attributes of her fiction. In 1994, Governor Ned Ray McWherter gave her the Pride of Tennessee award because, as he explained, "she has managed to capture and truthfully portray the people, places, and events that make East Tennessee and Appalachia a unique place in world culture."

When she died from complications from hip surgery on December 22, 2006, Wilma was laid to rest in a simple wooden coffin with a spray of native plants—hemlock, laurel, and rhododendron—placed on top of it. She was buried in the cemetery of the Beaverdam Baptist Church in Asheville, the namesake of the creek that flowed past her childhood home. Her headstone has two phrases on it: "Precious above Rubies," a line from her first novel *The Tall Woman*, and the words "writer, speaker, educator, environmentalist."

Wilma once explained that her writing technique involved gathering "words, bits of speech, turns of phrase. My laboratory is without walls: It is anywhere I and other people happen to be passing or gathering. The various ways in which we use words reveal more than we might suspect: Our region, our race, our social affiliations and economic status, our personality, the immediate past that has shaped us and the future we shall be helping to shape." The words Wilma chose, in her countless lectures, articles, and eighteen published books, were expressions of her constant search for commonality and understanding among things that were often considered different and foreign—whether it was the stereotyped hillbillies of the southern Appalachians or peasants in inland China. The future she worked tirelessly to shape was one of greater sensitivity to nature, racial justice, and open-mindedness.

Dykeman with the Dalai Lama.

Wilma Dykeman with husband James Stokely.

Chapter 12

Amanda Swimmer

POTTERY MAKES THAT DIRECT CONNECTION OF MOTHER EARTH TO THE HANDS OF THE POTTER.

AMANDA SWIMMER • 1921–PRESENT

—Dr R. Michael Abram, Cherokee Cultural Historian.

Amanda Swimmer

"A man asked me 'will [the pots] break?' I said, 'that ain't no rock, that's just clay!"
—Amanda Swimmer, laughing.

The rows of schoolchildren at the Cherokee Elementary School watch quietly as Amanda Swimmer, her long, gray hair tucked under a bandanna, takes a small lump of wet clay and begins to knead it. She rolls it into a long, thin, tube—reminiscent of a snake—and begins to curl it upon itself to make a small pot. It's a technique that Cherokee potters have used for centuries to create thin waterproof vessels for storing food. The craft that Amanda teaches was traditionally a closely guarded family secret, passed down from parents to children and never shared with anyone outside the family. But in the past 200 years, traditions have been changed by visionary artists like Amanda, who pursue two goals: their own artistic expression, and teaching members of younger generations so the knowledge that remains will not be lost.

Enforcement of the Indian Removal Act of 1830 caused the deaths of thousands of Cherokee marched west to Oklahoma during the winter of 1838. Fewer than 500 people were able to remain in their mountain homeland, left with heartbreak for their decimated tribe and a painful awareness of how easy it is for centuries-old knowledge to be lost. Amanda Swimmer, born in October 1921, has devoted her life to reviving and strengthening traditions of Cherokee pottery. She represents a change in the tradition of passing methods of artistry down through families—usually, potters were descended from potters, or married into a family of them; however, Amanda's mother was a medicine woman, and her father was a farmer. Shortly after Amanda married, at age fifteen, she decided to dig some clay from the thick deposit near her house and see if she couldn't make a pot. Thousands of pots later, complemented by significant artistic recognition, Amanda's humble moment of "why not?" has changed not only Cherokee pottery, but the options available to younger Cherokee who want to become artists.

When Amanda was born, the Cherokee community was still

recovering from the Trail of Tears. Her grandmother was one of the few Eastern Cherokee who avoided being sent to Oklahoma by hiding in the mountains. Many old traditions had been shaken by the Removal, and much of the traditional knowledge continued to be lost as the older generation died. Amanda grew up in the Big Cove community on the Qualla Indian Reservation, in a household not so different from those of the European-American settlers in the North Carolina mountains. She was the youngest of Molly and Running Wolf Sequoyah's twelve children. Somehow they all managed to fit into a one-room log cabin, although it did have a sleeping loft where most of the kids slept together. Molly cooked for her large family with a Dutch oven over the fireplace; there was no stove. Amanda's brothers were required to chop wood and stack it neatly on the porch to dry. All the children helped carry water from the spring for washing and cooking.

Running Wolf farmed acres of corn. The view from the covered porch of the cabin was of narrow rows of corn winding across steep hillsides. Instead of buying sugar, Running Wolf grew sugarcane, which they boiled to make a sweetener. Tobacco, potatoes, beans, and cabbage rounded out the family's main crops, complemented by a milk cow and a bevy of hogs which were their main source of protein. They would kill a hog when the signs were right in summertime, and boil the meat in a big wash pot, then put it in jars. To supplement the hogs, her father would hunt wild game, using handmade blowguns or bows and arrows, in the traditional Cherokee way.

Once the crops were grown, the family had to harvest and preserve them. Molly canned most of the beans and cabbage; the family preserved their potatoes and remaining cabbage by loosely covering them with dirt in a shallow trench outside. Amanda and her siblings would help with the potato harvest. Bean bread sustained many Cherokee families, including the Sequoyahs. Molly would boil pinto beans "real good," then stir in cornmeal and a little "sody." This mixture would make a dough which she rolled into balls. These she dropped in boiling water, scooping them out when they floated to the top. They also made a similar dish from wild-harvested hickory nuts, and ate lots of grits, corn kernels ground by hand with a mortar and pestle. Between all their efforts, the family of fourteen was mostly self-sufficient. Molly also wove baskets for storing food, quilted, crocheted, and sewed the family's clothes.

The woods provided everything Amanda and her siblings needed to play with too—they would climb trees and swing on the thick grapevines that hung from the tallest branches. Higher up in the mountains, large timber operations were stripping the old-growth timber, but the lands around the Sequoyah's farm stayed largely untouched. She and her siblings would explore and play tag, and when they tired of that, would visit the family up the road that had a hand-wound record player. The music fascinated them, but Amanda admitted they were too bashful to actually dance to the music.

The twelve Sequoyah children attended school in a one-room building four miles away. They'd walk along the railroad tracks to get there, and as the youngest and shortest, Amanda was frequently dragged along by her siblings. "They's hard to walk on, railroad tracks," she remembered. Although first through eighth grade lessons were taught at the school, Amanda attended only through fourth grade. She learned basic geography, arithmetic, and English. Lessons were taught in English, but all of the children spoke Cherokee fluently at home with their parents.

On Wednesdays and Sunday evenings, the entire family would walk a good distance "over the mountain," no matter the weather, to go to the Baptist church in the Towstring community. They carried oil lamps to light their way back home after service, along the dark mountain paths. Although the Baptist faith was important to the family, her parents participated in traditional Cherokee ceremonies as well. Amanda would tag along to the events, hosted by neighbors, where her parents wore traditional costumes and danced.

As much as her life resembled that of non-Cherokees in the mountains, in one particular respect, things were very different for Amanda and her siblings. Their mother was a respected medicine woman. Most healers in Cherokee culture were men, but Molly gained a reputation as a skillful midwife and herbalist. Their lives were constantly interrupted by someone fetching Molly to be a midwife, or wanting treatment to cure an illness. Although medicine men and women jealously guarded their knowledge—as Amanda explains "sharing the medicine makes it less powerful"—Molly taught her children some of the more straightforward herbal concoctions such as using ginseng root and snakeroot teas to treat high fever and measles. Amanda drew on her mother's knowledge when she was raising her own children, using simple herbal remedies to help cure their colds, infections, and toothaches, but her hands were better suited to artistic endeavors.

In 1936, when she was fifteen, she married Luke Swimmer, whom she met while attending the Baptist church. Luke was ten years older than she was, and his first wife and a baby had died a few years earlier. He had one surviving daughter who was four when he married Amanda. She gave birth to their first child the following year, but the baby was too premature and died after four months. Although another son would die when he was four, Amanda and Luke raised six surviving children in a tiny house. Their kitchen was so small, the stove had to sit on the porch. The kids shared a single room and two beds—very little personal space. They were able to afford a larger house after one of their sons signed up to join the Army in 11th grade—he regularly sent money home, which paid for building a bigger frame house with five bedrooms.

As they looked for opportunities beyond subsistence farming to support their family, Amanda and Luke became active in the changing Cherokee culture, influenced by growing tourism in the Great Smoky Mountains. The economic shift had begun about a decade before Amanda was born, when Pullman trains began bringing wealthy tourists to Asheville, about fifty miles to the east. The luxurious Grove Park Inn had opened in 1913 as the city began to prosper. Adventurous tourists would make the trip out to Cherokee to look for unique souvenirs and gifts. In response to this growing market, Cherokee craftsmen and women had begun making their baskets and pottery more decorative, shifting the emphasis of their work from functionality to beauty. Maude Welch, a Cherokee potter who had family in South Carolina, was instrumental in bringing the attractive "Catawba" style of decorating pots back to the Great Smoky Mountains. This showier style of pottery was distinguished by modern standards of beauty rather than traditional function—incorporating new shapes, fancy handles, more intricate design work—and gained traction as Cherokee artisans tried to earn a living from their work.

Amanda began her pottery career by teaching herself—a nontraditional approach. Artisan skills had been passed down through families as a "generational legacy," but Amanda discovered a clay deposit on the land behind her house and told her husband she was going to figure out how to make pottery. She recalled in an interview printed in *Foxfire 12*, "After I got married, I decided to hunt that clay right above where I lived. I made some small bowls and I told my husband, I said, 'Let me try to burn them. Just make a hole right there in the yard.' We just piled wood in there and burned my pottery. And that came out pretty good. And I just kept on playing with that wood, off and on." She had no inkling as she began experimenting in those early days that the impact of her work would expand beyond the beauty of her pots—and make her a significant contributor to the revitalization of Cherokee culture.

Amanda used the traditional fingerpot method, never a potter's wheel. For small bowls, she would begin by hollowing out a lump of clay using her thumbs; for larger pots she would roll the clay into a long coil, then wind it around and upwards from a base of clay. To finish, she would blend the edges of the coils together to make a smooth surface of a pot, dipping her fingers in water occasionally to keep the clay moist and workable. One of her dearest friends, Jerry Coleman, remembers sitting beside her on countless evenings while she had "that ol' piece of board across her lap and a big ol' clump of clay, and [she'd] just make something gorgeous out of it."

After forming the pot, Amanda let it dry and then shaped it with carving tools. To get rid of any knife marks, she massaged the clay with a damp cloth. To finish it, she burnished the pot with a river stone, a "shinin' rock," Amanda called it. In pottery families, the rocks were handed down through generations. Next a design would be pressed into the still-wet clay, often with a carefully honed wooden tool. Although she and other potters have names for their designs, she explains that the "designs you put on there don't have no meaning. The meaning of the designs has been lost in the years."

Traditionally, Cherokee pots were left to dry in the sun—for two weeks, until they were "chalky white," as Amanda says. The next phase involves burning the pots in two steps: first they're "preheated" until they're bluish, then Amanda builds the fire larger and burns the pots for about 24 hours to add color and help waterproof them. Amanda, with her husband's help, experimented with this too. Through the years she honed her techniques and her tools, eventually discovering that a metal garbage can makes a perfect, affordable kiln for firing pots. "You have to leave 'em in there 'til the fire goes plumb out," she says. "You get 'em out when they're cold...you get them out too soon then they'll crack."

With young kids to take care of, Amanda didn't try to earn a living from her pottery immediately. She worked at a nearby factory, earning $3.50 an hour making "cap and bonnets and scarves and lacy caps, and stuff like that. Rollers, all kinds of hair rollers... and hair bobs" for four and a half years. She was one of the foreman's most reliable workers; she never missed a day in her entire employment at the factory. Luke worked on crews that were building Fontana Dam, and other hard-labor jobs that required him to be away from home for long stretches of time. He helped build the Blue Ridge Parkway road above Cherokee—he would walk up the mountain to work in the morning and back down to home in the evening. "He was always walking somewhere," Amanda remembers.

But two main tourist developments in Cherokee affected her family's life, and those of many other Cherokees: in 1950, "Unto These Hills," an outdoor drama that attempted to explain the story of the Cherokee Removal in 1838, opened in an amphitheater-style performance space in the town. Luke built all of the wooden seating for the amphitheater, which is still used today. He would work construction jobs during the winter and as a janitor at the Drama during the heat of the summer.

The Drama explored the effects of Andrew Jackson's betrayal of the Cherokees, and told of the efforts of the white man William Holland Thomas, who'd been raised by the Cherokee, to help his tribe stay in the mountains. Six years after Unto These Hills was first performed, the "Oconaluftee Indian Village" opened just outside of the main town of Cherokee. It featured a recreated Cherokee Village from the mid 1700s. Guides escorted visitors through the grounds and introduced them to native Cherokees who demonstrated a variety of traditional crafts—finger weaving, pottery, basketry, blowgun construction, hunting, and more. Amanda left her job at the factory in 1957 to join the Village as a fingerweaver, demonstrating an elaborate weaving technique. But she quickly gravitated to the pottery demonstrators, taking a spot at the pottery table while other potters were on their lunch break. Eventually she convinced the supervisor to make her a full-time pottery demonstrator. Through this work at the Village, she became an informal apprentice to the Cherokee women Cora Wahnetah and Mabel Bigmeat, who came from traditional pottery making families and were renowned for their artistry.

Pottery and basketry are two skills traditionally acquired by Cherokee women because pots and baskets were vessels for storing and preparing food—women's chores. Therefore the task of creating objects to hold the food belonged to women. But pottery is a labor-intensive art. Clay is heavy, and collecting it is difficult work. Entire families would go on clay digging trips, and certain clay locations were vigilantly kept secrets. Once harvested, the clay had to be worked into a useable consistency; sometimes sand was mixed in to prevent the pot from shattering during firing. The knowledge of how to make a pot waterproof had been lost during the decades around the Indian Removal, but Amanda and her mentors rediscovered the firing techniques that would facilitate a waterproof seal. Cherokee pots traditionally aren't glazed, but are given color by the different kinds of wood used in firing the pots. As Amanda explained in Foxfire, "I use poplar, dried poplar mostly, and maple. Then if I want to make a light color, I just use hardwood. That's oak and locust. If you use locust, it gives you an orange color. Hardwood uses more flame and less smoke, and the soft wood makes more smoke than flame." The more smoke you have, the blacker the final pot will be. The entire process of making and finishing a pot takes about two weeks.

With her children mostly grown, Amanda was able to focus purely on her pottery. She worked as a demonstrator at the Oconaluftee Indian Village for thirty-five years. One busy summer, she made over 1,000 pots—cups, bowls, two-pronged "wedding vases," and more. She sold most of her work through the Qualla Arts and Crafts Mutual, a Cherokee artist co-op founded in 1946, as well as to tourists that park rangers and friends would bring to her house. As her reputation grew—both for her fidelity to traditional methods and her skill at creating lovely pieces—her work was sought out by collectors and museums. In the early 1980s, her contributions to Cherokee art over the past several decades were honored by an exhibition at the Qualla Arts and Crafts Mutual in Cherokee.

She received a North Carolina Heritage Award, one of the state's highest honors, in 1994. In 2000, with the opening of the National Museum of the American Indian, one of her pieces, initially owned by the Department of Interior, was added to the Smithsonian's collection. Five years later, the University of North Carolina-Asheville awarded her an honorary doctorate for "her skills as an artist, as an inspiration to other artists and for her work with the Qualla community."

Although she didn't enjoy leaving the mountains, her fame as a potter gave her the opportunity to travel throughout the Southeast and Northeastern United States. In 2002, she was part of a small, select group of potters invited to study ancient Cherokee pots. Two research institutions, the Museum of the Cherokee Indian and the Research Laboratories of Archaeology at UNC-Chapel Hill, gave the Cherokee potters an unprecedented opportunity to examine ancient pottery specimens that were in the museum's collections. This interaction with objects from their people's history inspired the potters to establish a new guild that would honor and recognize the works of their ancestors. The Cherokee Potters Guild highlighted the main attributes of historical Cherokee pottery: "stamped, hand-built, thin-walled [and] waterproof." Most of the potters were a generation younger than Amanda, but she remained active in encouraging interest in pottery-making as a career for young Cherokees.

In the pottery classes she taught for decades at the Cherokee Elementary

School, the children would watch as she deftly blended the lines of the coils into a smooth wall of the pot and the clay took shape into a delicately rounded container. Her engagement with the children was her way of ensuring this part of their heritage is nurtured for generations to come. She watched with pride as they shaped their own pots. "They really want to learn," she explained in an interview. "They can make some things I can't make!"

The challenges of Amanda's generation were to rediscover the techniques of the past, and to build a market for selling Cherokee pottery so that there would be a reason other than nostalgia to share traditional methods. It seems she has largely succeeded. She has a quiet sense of humor, with deep smile wrinkles around her eyes, and a warm presence that draws children to her. Perhaps it's the experience gained from raising seven children of her own that makes her love teaching. Her own life has bridged so many changes that she can sense how generations easily forget or lose knowledge that no longer seems relevant to their lives. But her pottery stands as a testament to the enduring power of art, and functionality, that the early Cherokee prized. She has fused the past with the future, and has created an extensive body of work to inspire generations of artists that come after her.

Chapter 13

Dolly Rebecca Parton

I REMEMBER AS A LITTLE CHILD THOSE (MOUNTAIN) SONGS WERE SO HEAVY AND SO SAD, AND THE WAY THEY SANG THEM WAS SO MOURNFUL THAT IT JUST MADE SUCH AN IMPRESSION ON ME — IT JUST KIND OF IMPRINTED MY WHOLE PSYCHE WITH THOSE SONGS. AND TO THIS DAY I WRITE SO MANY OF THOSE SONGS... I STILL LOVE THAT MUSIC.

DOLLY REBECCA PARTON · 1946-PRESENT

—Dolly Parton, in an interview with the author at Dollywood, May 2014

Dolly Rebecca Parton

During cold winter evenings in the 1950s, Avie Lee Parton would quilt by the light of a kerosene lamp, her husband and eleven children crowded into the small log cabin on Locust Ridge, about ten miles from Great Smoky Mountains National Park. While she quilted, Avie Lee would tell Bible stories or sing traditional mountain ballads passed down through her family. "It was like our movies," her daughter, Dolly, would later remember. Before singing, Avie Lee would explain a little of the backstory to the kids. "And so it was like 'Okay, we're going to watch a movie now and the announcer's told us what it's going to be,'" Dolly explains. And then Avie Lee would lift her voice in a high, nasal tone as she recited the verses of "Barbara Allen" and "Pretty Polly."

Mountain families had spent evenings this way for over a hundred years—children listening as their mothers, keepers of the settlers' cultural heritage, recited folk ballads brought over by ancestors from the British Isles. The ballads were also a way for women to bring creative release—fantasy and escape—to the never-ending, difficult work of survival in the mountains.

Avie Lee came from a family known for its musical talent, and her fourth child, Dolly Rebecca Parton, inherited her mother's affinity for music. However, Dolly's insatiable love of performing was all her own. As a child, Dolly would listen intently, drawn to anything musical, absorbing traditional Appalachian music deep into her psyche. Her great-grandmother was still alive and Dolly later reminisced about her musical influence. "We called her Mammy but her name was Melinda Messer Owens. And she used to play all these old-timey instruments. She used to make a lot of instruments (which I used to do when I was little too). And she just had this incredible old voice. She used to write and make up a lot of songs, but she also used to sing all those old songs like my mother—those old British ballads, Welsh and Scottish."

In the decades since she lived in that one room log cabin and listened to her mother sing, Dolly Parton has traveled the world, acted in blockbuster movies, and become one of the most successful musical entertainers of all time. But her emotional connection to the Great Smoky Mountains didn't fade with her rising stardom; the experiences of her life in the mountains are woven throughout her work and art. She holds tightly to her childhood memories and the young woman she was in the mountains. Remembering that the mountains are always home keeps her centered, and as she likes to say, "real."

For much of her early childhood, Dolly's life resembled the experiences and challenges of generations of mountain women before her. Avie Lee and her husband Lee married young, had little education, and even less money. When Dolly was born on January 19, 1946, they lived in a remote, one-room log cabin without electricity. Her father was a sharecropper who worked tobacco fields owned by Martha Williams. As Dolly wrote in her autobiography, "In a hard land that is stingy about giving up much of a crop, that share doesn't come to a whole lot." This was a reality for generations of mountain families, some of whom had been forced to leave their communities and relocate outside of the boundaries of the national park in the 1930s and farm land they didn't own.

Lee Parton, too poor to pay the doctor who made the house call on horseback to see Avie Lee through the difficult birth of her fourth child, gave Dr. Robert F. Thomas a sack of cornmeal as compensation. Dr. Thomas was famous for his willingness to care for mountain families in the remotest mountain valleys, the poorest people in a very poor society.

But Lee Parton was a hard worker and had a respectful relationship with the land-owning Williams family, who treated him fairly and looked after his family. Around 1950, Lee had finally saved enough money to buy his own land. The place was called Locust Ridge, and comprised several hundred acres and a log cabin, purchased for $5,000 dollars. As was common of settlements in the Smokies, they kept the yard—which was hard packed dirt, not grass—swept clean. The cabin walls were lined with newspaper as wallpaper, an old mountain trick for trying to keep out winter drafts, "...but to us kids they were something new to read and new pictures to look at," Dolly recalled. "Some things got overlapped, so I can remember having to peel part of the paper off the wall to see how a 'Snuffy Smith' [comic] turned out." Dolly was fond of saying the house had "two rooms and a path, and running water, if you were willing to run to get it."

Lee Parton planted tobacco and potatoes, and as mountain children always had, his twelve kids helped work the fields, sometimes missing school during harvest time. They had a cow, which provided their milk and butter, and Avie Lee tended a bountiful garden. They supplemented what they could grow with wild plants foraged from the mountains, like "poke sallett," traditional mountain fare made from boiling the bitter greens of the pokeberry plant, and "ramps," a type of wild onion that grows in early spring. The family also raised hogs, the main protein for many mountain families. "When you grow up in the country," Dolly remembers, "you know every wild green you can eat, you know every berry, root, every animal that's edible. That's what you do—that's country life."

Green's Rolling Store provided anything they might have needed to buy. It was an old school bus converted into a mobile grocery store by a man often simply called "the peddler." People bought or bartered for things they needed whenever it made its run by their house. Everything from frying pans to needle and thread to candy was available for purchase, or if you had no money, you could trade chickens or eggs or butter for other goods. Dolly wrote in her autobiography, "I can remember the chickens, tied by their feet to the outside of the old bus, looking quizzical but seeming to accept their part in the overall scheme of things."

With so many children and such meager income, Avie Lee and Lee could rarely afford to buy clothes for Dolly and her siblings. Instead, they repurposed flour sacks, a time-honored custom of resourceful mountaineers. Lucky for Dolly, her grandmother favored her, and would make sure she got "the prettiest" sacks. Toys too, were most often homemade. Avie Lee could craft dolls out of corncob and cornshucks, with cornsilk for hair. Dolly named one of hers Tiny Tassletop and wrote her first song about the doll. Lee Parton was a talented woodcarver and also made toys for the kids. But every Christmas, the parents made sure each child recieved one store-bought item, which the kids treasured.

Mostly, their entertainment came free, from the wild mountains around them. They would dye their feet with purple pokeberry juice to make "Jesus sandals" and pretend to be disciples romping through the hills with staffs made from discarded tobacco stakes. Dolly later remembered, "One thing I enjoyed a lot with my sisters was playing house with moss. There was a kind of thick, green, luxurious moss that grew in the shady places up in the hills… even today I would be hard-pressed to find carpet that beautiful. I have never ceased to be amazed by nature."

Owens family gatherings, on Avie Lee's side of the family, were always filled with singing and guitar playing in addition to visiting and eating. "Those old songs were so singable…" Dolly recalls, "but they say that's how they used to carry the news before there was radio. Somebody'd write a song about something happening, somebody'd take it to the next town, tell about the story, and then they'd sing the song.…" These tales of murder and heartbreak, early death or abandonment, while beautiful, were also sad. "My momma would sing, and she would cry, and we would cry," Dolly remembered. "It was part of our life—we knew Momma wasn't singing sad because she was sad," it was just the songs.

While Avie Lee and her sisters still sang the ballads their ancestors brought from Europe—long, mournful tunes sung unaccompanied in a minor key, the family had embraced newer styles as well. Banjo music grew in popularity after the end of the Civil War, and guitar playing became widespread in the mountains around 1910. Recorded music and radio also contributed to the growing popularity of "white Country gospel," which had its roots in the religious revival circuit started in Kentucky in the 1800s. Dolly's extended family knew and loved all of these old and new traditions, and were happy to teach the younger generation, much to Dolly's delight.

After Dolly learned how to play guitar and banjo, it was nearly impossible for her father to get her to help with the tobacco and potato crops. She went to desperate measures to avoid the work—like trying to hit herself in the face so hard she'd get a nosebleed to get out of helping. She later admitted she was never quite successful at that, but she became very good at making up other excuses to spend as much time as possible picking away at the guitar and writing songs. She struck up a friendship with a loner mountain man everyone called Sawdust, who showed her a few tricks on the banjo—a camaraderie she later memorialized in her hit song "Applejack." "I was writing serious songs when I was very young," she explains. "Just these sad stories because that was what I heard."

Dolly wasn't the only Parton child who was musically gifted, and she shared her earliest performances with siblings. Lee would drive Dolly and two of her sisters to various mountain churches to sing religious songs, variations on the revival music that became popular in the Appalachians in the 1800s. One church was particularly memorable, as Dolly recalled the preacher began his snake-handling performance while the girls were singing. He held the snake by the back of the head "and it was twisting and coiling all around his forearm...." Dolly and her sisters didn't know what to do, so they kept on singing as if nothing was happening. On that particular evening, her father decided to step back inside the church (he usually waited outside for the girls), and he became frantic as soon as he saw the snake. He sprinted to the front of the church, snatched Dolly and her sisters, and they headed for the car.

Like many professional musicians before her, church singing only whetted Dolly's desire to perform. She was eager for attention, obsessed with singing and songwriting. She would take a discarded tobacco stake, put it in the ground, and balance a tin can on top, as if it were a fancy microphone. Then she'd scatter some corn nearby so that the chickens would hang around and be her audience. Or she'd agree to babysit, but would use the younger kids as a forced audience for her homespun concerts, retrieving them when they crawled too far away.

When she was ten, in 1956, she got her first lucky break, her first taste of local celebrity. Cas Walker, an eccentric man who had begun selling groceries out of a wheelbarrow and built the business into a multimillion dollar grocery empire in three states, had ventured into entertainment-as-advertising in 1929 with his own radio show, "Farm and Home Hour," in Knoxville, Tennessee. The show, and his business, Cas Walker's Cash Stores, were immensely popular. In 1953, he added a television component which featured an impressive array of country musicians, including Roy Acuff and Chet Atkins. Dolly's Uncle Bill Owens, one of her mother's brothers, was determined to get her a spot performing on it. She impressed Cas Walker with her voice, but also by her pronouncement, "I want to work for you"— instead of the usual request "for a job." The difference in attitude struck Cas, a self-made millionaire who'd quit school at fourteen, as significant, and he soon hired her as a regular performer.

Even as she became locally famous in rural East Tennessee, her sights were set on the Grand Ole Opry in Nashville, the pinnacle for country music performers. The mountain music she was singing had become commercially successful in the 1920s—"Eck" Robertson, Charlie Poole, and Gid Tanner and the Skillet Lickers popularized Appalachian singing and string bands. Radio stations began broadcasting "barn dances" that featured 'old-timey' string bands. But the Great Depression in the 1930s had fundamentally changed the music industry, ushering in the era of an "individual star system" with lead singers like Hank Williams, or groups of brothers like the Delmores and Stanleys, accompanied by horns, swing, and bluegrass—a sound that heralded the rise of modern country-western music.

The Grand Ole Opry, which had started as a Barn Dance show in 1925, had become enormously popular. The studio couldn't accommodate the huge numbers of fans who wanted to watch the live show, and switched several venues before settling at the Ryman Auditorium in 1943. The Ryman, known as the "Mother Church of Country Music," is where Dolly got her second big break as a child performer.

During the summer of 1960, when she was fourteen, she and her Uncle Bill drove to Nashville. They talked to anyone they thought might help her get on Opry, and spent hours hanging around side doors of music venues, waiting to pester any country music producer or star who emerged.

One evening Johnny Cash himself stepped into the parking lot where they were waiting. Fast-talking Bill introduced Dolly and she, finding her voice, told the star, "Oh Mr. Cash, I've just got to sing on the Grand Ole Opry." Something in their dedication or desperation touched Cash, and he talked to the night's scheduled performers. Since every performance was carefully slotted and confined to the hour-long radio broadcast, Dolly needed someone to give up his spot for her. Jimmy C. Newman generously agreed to let her take his place, and like a dream come true, Johnny Cash himself introduced her: "We've got a little girl here from up in East Tennessee. Her daddy's listening to the radio at home, and she's gonna be in real trouble if she doesn't sing tonight, so let's bring her out here!"

Despite her sparkling Opry performance, no recording offers materialized. She and her uncle stayed in Nashville for the summer, continuing to pester people who worked in country music, spending long nights waiting in parking lots to ambush just the right person and pass along a demo tape. The rest of the summer looked like it was destined to be a disappointment. But through sheer stubbornness—mostly a refusal to leave his office—they won over Buddy Killen, a record exec at Tree Publishing in Nashville. He offered Dolly and Bill a deal as songwriters, and arranged for Dolly to have a demo recording session at Mercury Records. Although "It May Not Kill Me (But It's Sure Gonna Hurt)" got some airplay in Sevierville and Knoxville, the demo songs didn't catch on enough for Mercury to continue working with her.

On the heels of that setback, with the summer over, Dolly went back to East Tennessee and started high school. It was the beginning of four years she wouldn't remember too fondly. She was different than the other kids—she wanted something other than a normal life, and had already achieved enough fame to invite jealousy which led to rumors and vicious gossip. She was regarded as a tramp, and often called worse things behind her back. She kept singing for Cas Walker, but was really just "waiting to be eighteen, waiting to be free, waiting to follow my dream" back to Nashville.

The day after her high school graduation in 1964, she moved to Nashville. She signed a contract as a songwriter for Combine Publishing and, often collaborating with her Uncle Bill, wrote a handful of successful songs for country artists like Skeeter Davis and Bill Phillips. She got a recording deal of her own with Monument Records in late

1965 but was groomed as a "bubblegum pop" singer despite her eagerness to pursue country music. The label executives initially felt that
her strong vibrato wasn't a good match for country. But they changed
their minds in 1966 when Bill Phillips' "Put It Off Until Tomorrow"
went to #6 on the country music charts. Dolly had co-written the
song with Uncle Bill, and (uncredited) she sang the harmony vocals
for Phillips. After a couple of years of low-level success in the pop
music genre, her first country single, "Dumb Blonde" reached #24 on
the country music charts in 1967. Although the song tells the story
of a woman chastising her cheating man—"just because I'm blond
doesn't mean I'm dumb"—Dolly might as well have been talking to
the record executives. Country music was where she was meant to be,
and she knew it. That same year, she accepted the offer to be country music entertainer Porter Wagoner's new duet partner, performing
with him on his traveling show and weekly syndicated radio show.
She and Porter worked together for nearly eight years.

When Dolly first arrived in Nashville, the country music industry
was still very much an "old boys club," run by men who saw women
only as bit performers to liven things up a little; there was generally
only room for one female performer on a show. A full-fledged female
star in her own right was a very rare thing, but Dolly looked to Kitty
Wells and Loretta Lynn for inspiration, believing that she too could
have a leading role. She was used to it being difficult to get the things
she wanted. And while she smiled and sang sweetly, she drew inspiration from a long line of fiercely determined mountain women.

Alanna Nash, who wrote the biography *Dolly* in the 1970s, observed, "A study of Dolly's life reveals that despite her protest that she
knows nothing about the women's movement, liberation is the word
that best sums up what Dolly has been seeking from the day she was
born. With an active imagination, Dolly, the child, was able to tran-
scend her desolate surroundings… that imagination and unyielding
faith provided a way to spare her the bleak future that seemed so certain to be hers as a woman of the mountains. Freedom from poverty
and isolation was only the first hurdle, however, with the long battle
ahead for creative expression.…"

For years, Dolly and Porter were a successful team. They released duets together, and Porter oversaw her writing, singing, and production. While working with Porter during the late 60s and early 70s, she wrote and recorded some of her most iconic songs, songs that drew on her childhood in the mountains. "My Blue Ridge Mountain Boy" reached #6 in 1969, which she followed with "In the Good Old Days (When Times were Hard)," about her childhood. She also wrote and recorded "Down from Dover" a ballad song from the point of view of a pregnant teenager hoping her lover will return; he doesn't, and the baby is stillborn. Porter Wagoner told her she'd never get played on the radio with songs like that.

There was truth to his comment, but Dolly incorporated elements of her musical heritage into her music as often as she could—it set her apart from other performers, and was the music she always felt she was born to sing. And sometimes her mountain-storytelling songs were big hits. "It was always about the men breaking hearts, because they always do," she says with a twinkle in her eye. "But the girls are breaking the boys' hearts and the women and the children are dying—and you either write about that, or songs about old crazy people that we knew...the mountain angel.... I can write some of the most pitiful songs in the world!" She laughs. Even some of her songs that don't seem to be influenced by old world traditions have the soul of ballads. One of her most iconic songs, "Coat of Many Colors," about a patchwork coat her mother sewed since they couldn't afford new clothes, reached #4 in 1971. It is a modern variation of the old English folk tunes her mother sang to her, with a more subtle rendition of the accompanying rhythmic aberrations of Elizabethan ballads.

In 1973, Dolly released a concept album about her childhood in the Smokies. My Tennessee Mountain Home featured a stark photo of the Locust Ridge log cabin on the album cover, and songs included a recitation of the first letter she wrote to her parents after moving to Nashville from the mountains. She also wrote and recorded a song named after the mountain doctor who delivered her, "Dr. Robert F. Thomas," and a slower, more meditative cover of her earlier hit "In the Good Old Days (When Times were Bad)." The album wasn't a commercial success, although its autobiographical sentiment resonated with die-hard Dolly fans. "I wish I could've made a living doing just pure country, doing those mountain songs, doing bluegrass," Dolly told NPR interviewer David Greene in 2014, "But you can't, really. You know, as the years went by, I saw that I was going to have to expand, get into movies, do some more business things. Because I knew I had the desire to sing and had the ability to sing and to write. But I thought, well, I know a lot of people that do that. And they starve to death, or they never get anywhere. So I started trying to focus on all the ways to make it more of a business, and to accomplish all that one can. You know, I've got to do a whole lot of things, and I'm grateful. But when I'm at my best, I think my voice is best suited, you know, for the old mountain style and the bluegrass. I guess it's just because I feel that so much."

Dolly followed *My Tennessee Mountain Home* with the release of one of her most enduring songs. "Jolene" was a simple and profound execution of an irresistible, haunting riff and pleading vocals that hearkened back to the folk songs of her youth but lacked the old-timey flavor of much of the traditional mountain music. The song reached #1 on the country music charts in February 1974 and has been covered by myriad international artists since. The album *Jolene* also included the song "I Will Always Love You," written to express Dolly's feelings about ending her professional partnership with Porter Wagoner.

Dolly and Porter had worked together very successfully for seven years, but Dolly was ready to leave the Porter Wagoner Show and take more control of her music. She was becoming a star, as she always knew she would—big blonde hair, sparkly dresses, and her sassy sense of humor mixed with business acumen destined her for greatness. She began experimenting with her singing and songwriting, figuring out how to cultivate elusive "crossover" appeal into the pop market. And she landed roles in a variety of movies—the hugely successful *9 to 5*, *Best Little Whorehouse in Texas*, *Rhinestone*, *Straight Talk*, and *Steel Magnolias*. But no matter how many times she saw her name in lights, Dolly never forgot the mountains of East Tennessee.

In 1985, she partnered with the Silver Dollar City amusement park in Pigeon Forge, Tennessee, just down the road from where she was born. Acutely aware of the lack of economic opportunity that had so greatly influenced her childhood, she saw revitalizing Silver Dollar City as a chance to create jobs for people in the mountains. Of course, she couldn't resist changing the name: Dollywood opened in 1986. She recalled in her autobiography, "The first time I saw that Hollywood sign in LA, I wanted that H changed to a D." Her theme park celebrates mountain culture and gives musically talented locals a chance to perform in Dollywood's many shows. When she took over the park, she explained in an interview in Ms. *Magazine* which had named her one of its Women of the Year, "It's a dream that I have long cherished. I love the Smoky Mountains and I love the hearts and minds and souls of the people there. I wanted to create a prestigious place and jobs in the area where I grew up. I just felt it was a great thing—a Smoky Mountain fantasy to preserve the mountain heritage." In the nearly thirty years since Dollywood opened, it has grown to nearly ten times its original size and has over 3,000 staff members, making it the biggest local employer.

The theme park incorporates a couple of nonprofit efforts into its acreage too. In 1991, Dolly partnered with the American Eagle Foundation to provide facilities and financial support for the rehabilitation of eagles, owls, hawks, and other birds of prey. Twelve years later, in recognition of her contributions to wildlife research and rehabilitation, the U.S. Fish and Wildlife Service gave her the 2003 Partnership Award. In 2009, she and Uncle Bill recorded an original song to raise awareness of the restoration efforts of the American Chestnut Foundation, and provided land around Dollywood and financial support to the foundation's restoration efforts. American chestnut trees were once a prominent part of the Smokies forests, until an Asian blight completely eliminated them in the U.S. by 1950.

However, Dolly's philanthropic activities range much farther than the Dollywood campus. She has never forgotten how important her ability to dream and imagine a different future was to her success. Consequently another of her major initiatives ensures that children, regardless of family income, have access to books that will inspire and educate them. In 1996, she launched Dolly's Imagination Library. Organized via the Dollywood Foundation, the Imagination Library sends a free book each month to registered children, from birth until their fifth birthday. The program began in Dolly's hometown, and is now established throughout the U.S., England, Canada, and Australia. Over a million children are registered in the United States alone, and over 70 million books have been mailed since the beginning of the program.

In 1994, Dolly recorded an album live at Dollywood, the same year her autobiography, *Dolly: My Life and Other Unfinished Business*, was published. The album *Heartsong: Live from Home* featured a mix of new songs she'd written and traditional folk songs. "I've been waiting all my life to do an acoustic album of the songs I grew up lovin' and singin'... It's the album I hope and believe I will be most remembered for..." she wrote in her autobiography. She included the famous traditional ballad "Barbara Allen" on the album, and rereleased old favorites "Coat of Many Colors" and "My Tennessee Mountain Home." The single "To Daddy" peaked at #3 on the country charts.

But even with the strength of *Heartsong*, when Dolly's record label Decca was consolidated into MCA, record company executives were ambivalent about her future prospects. The music business is ruthless, and they felt Lee Ann Womack was the same kind of singer—and much younger. So in 1997, having spun off a pop career, movies, films and more, Dolly later explained she found herself "not knowing exactly what I should be doing in my musical career." She went back to her childhood cabin in the Smokies for inspiration.

The album *Hungry Again* "returns her to the mountain soul of her seminal work," music critic Alanna Nash wrote in her biography of Dolly. "Her real strength as a lyricist lies in her novelist's eye for setting and detail, in her poetic imagery, and in her unfaltering realism. When she combines all that with her considerable gift for feeling, the effect is often chilling, particularly in her songs about poverty in the mountains of East Tennessee...her songs with the greatest depth have for the most part been those culled from her storehouse of memories of her native region." The album received favorable reviews, but didn't set any sales records. Its far-reaching influence would take a few more years to realize, for it laid a strong foundation for Dolly's return to more traditional Appalachian music in the early 2000s.

In June 1999, she was approached by North Carolina based bluegrass label Sugar Hill. The label's president, Barry Poss had taken a poll of bluegrass fans and professionals to see which artist outside the genre they'd most like to see do a bluegrass record. Dolly was the clear favorite. She was interested and excited by the offer, although she later told *Billboard*, "I've always done bluegrass music. It's not like I came in the back door with this music. I've been doing it on my front porch for years." Sugar Hill lined up the best bluegrass musicians for her to work with on *The Grass is Blue*, her 35th studio album. The album was a resounding success, surprising even the self-confident Dolly, who garnered Bluegrass Album of the Year and a Grammy in 2001. It was the perfect time to release a bluegrass album—the Coen Brother's blockbuster movie *O Brother Where Art Thou* and rise of groups like Alison Krauss and Union Station were recasting bluegrass in a newer, hipper light for the mainstream American public.

Building on the success of *The Grass is Blue*, Dolly began work on her next album, *Little Sparrow*. Her father Lee, who had always called her his little songbird, passed away on November 14, 2000, and she dedicated the album to him. It reportedly took her three days to get the project together, drawing largely on the musicians who had contributed to *The Grass is Blue*. But *Little Sparrow* was a conscious expansion on the bluegrass genre, with stronger influences of mountain, folk, and Irish music.

The title song of *Little Sparrow* is Dolly's version of a traditional Appalachian song, like the ones her mother would sing, which begins with her voice unaccompanied, then gives way to a lonesome fiddle and lyrics that evoke the mournfulness of classic Irish ballads. "Mountain Angel" also draws on the common traditional theme of a pregnant women, abandoned by her lover, who loses her baby and goes insane from grief. The album reached #12 on the U.S. Country charts, her highest solo album in nearly 10 years. Tucked in with the mountain music were some covers of songs by Frank Sinatra ("I Get a Kick Out of You") and "Shine," by rock group Collective Soul—to Dolly's great surprise, "Shine" won a Grammy for best female country vocal performance in 2001. She completed her trio of bluegrass and folk albums with *Halos & Horns* in 2002, a little more folksy and less mournful than *Little Sparrow*. With this body of work, she had proven Porter Wagoner wrong beyond a shadow of a doubt: she could be a star and sing music that hearkened back to her Appalachian heritage. "When I'm by myself, or when I don't have a real project, or just left to my own, just thinkin'," she explains, "I'll just find myself singing some old song—or writing a song of my own that has that old timey flavor...I still love that music to this day."

In 2009, Dolly graciously accepted the title of official ambassador for Great Smoky Mountains National Park's 75th Anniversary celebration. National Park Superintendent Dale Ditmanson explained, "When we first sat down with our park partners and began brainstorming about how the park's anniversary could best gain national stature we asked ourselves; 'If we could pick one person who is the most recognized and personifies the love of the Smokies, who would it be?' The answer was a resounding 'Dolly Parton!'"

Dolly's great-grandparents and their relatives had once lived in the Greenbrier area of the national park, and had been relocated in the 1920s and '30s, leaving their farms to be reclaimed by the forest. The Old Settlers Trail leads past their former farmlands, winding through valleys occasionally punctuated by mossy rock walls and small cemeteries. Dolly recalled in her autobiography: "Once, years and years ago, I went with my daddy up to Greenbrier where most of his people were born and lived and died. We were walking through a little graveyard way back in the mountains and looking at the tombstones. Daddy was telling me about all of the people and how they were related to me. We turned down a row of graves and I saw something that took my breath. There was a small grave with the name Dolly Parton on it. That was the strangest sensation I have ever had...you can't really imagine how that feels unless you've seen your own name on a grave."

As the anniversary celebration's official ambassador, she was inspired to write an original musical production for Dollywood. She drew on her family's history in the mountains as she penned eight original songs for *Sha-Kon-O-Hey!: Land of Blue Smoke*, which depicts the story of the last family living within the land that would become Great Smoky Mountains National Park. The profits from the musical's soundtrack were donated to the nonprofit Friends of the Smokies and raised over $225,000; the musical also garnered the Heartbeat Award for Entertainment Excellence from the International Association of Amusement Parks and Attractions.

On September 2, 2009, seventy-five years to the day after President Franklin Delano Roosevelt officially dedicated Great Smoky Mountains National Park, Dolly Parton and her support crew emerged from her comfy tour bus at Clingmans Dome, near the highest point in the national park, to enjoy a spectacular sunrise over the rows of blue mountains stretching out to the horizon around them. That afternoon, Dolly would perform at the Park Service's rededication ceremony at Newfound Gap celebrating the 75th anniversary. "When we were up on the mountain, I thought of my childhood," she recalls. "I think of my childhood a lot…when I'm out on stage, even overseas, I think how I used to dream about doing that, traveling all over the world…. I reflect back so often on my childhood and my early dreams and that early music." She adds with a songwriter's flair, "That early music and the mountains, and the birds, and the bees, and the songs—they were just a natural part of it all. [We were] just ragged kids being part of that natural music and love and nature."

Ceremony attendees were shuttled up the mountain in busses, disembarking at Newfound Gap which provided breathtaking views of the surrounding mountains. Dolly took the stage at the rededication ceremony dressed in a tight, colorful patchwork dress that evoked her iconic song "Coat of Many Colors." She began a heartfelt rendition of her new song from the *Sha-Kon-O-Hey!* musical, "My Mountains, My Home." Her focus was on performing, but she would later remember, "I could feel the mist," that was enveloping the stage and the crowd, "that spirit that lives in these mountains—that blue smoke that we talk about, that the Cherokee call Shaconage—and they were saying it was just mountain mist, like a mountain ghost almost. And so I thought, well perfect. That's perfect for me because I embody being part of these beautiful mountains and just a pure mountain girl." She pauses half a beat and adds, "You know, from my childhood, I mean. I look so phony now, but I am really a true mountain person."

Dolly brought traditional mountain music out of the rural churches and front porches of Appalachia and gave it airplay around the world, turning herself into one of the music industry's most successful artists. Although her childhood steeped in mountain poverty wasn't easy, she embraced her rags-to-riches story. In interview after interview, she remains ever thankful for her musical upbringing in the Great Smoky Mountains, and that she has been able to earn a good living singing with the same bittersweet joy that buoyed her ancestors through hard, challenging lives amidst the stark beauty around them. "I call it my Smoky Mountain DNA," she says, "this music, I live it, I feel it, I grew up with that. These are the songs I came out of the mountains singing...."

Dolly Parton circa 1950.

Dolly Rebecca Parton

Part 3: Boots in the Wilderness

Women and
Great Smoky Mountains
National Park

Chapter 14

Laura Thornburgh

WHAT OTHER MOUNTAINS HAVE THE NAME, GREAT, THUS GIVEN THEM? THE HAZE THAT HANGS OVER THEM CHANGES FROM SMOKE GRAY TO HEAVEN'S BLUE, MORE RARELY TO A MYSTIC PURPLE, WITH CHANGING LIGHTS AND SHADOWS...THE CONCEALING HAZE MAY VANISH FOR A FLEETING MOMENT, DISCLOSING COVES AND VALLEYS, TREES IN BOLD RELIEF ON SLOPES TIMBERED TO THE TOP; A FLASH OF SILVER— A MOUNTAIN STREAM CASCADING DOWN THE HILLSIDE. THEN AGAIN THE HAZE, ENVELOPING, SOFTENING, CONCEALING, VEILING, MYSTIFYING.

LAURA THORNBURGH · 1882-1973

—From Chapter 1, The Great Smoky Mountains, *Laura Thornborough 1937*

Laura Thornburgh

September 2, 1940 was a sunny, perfect day in the Great Smoky Mountains. Clouds floated in a clear blue sky as gentle breezes cooled the happy crowd picnicking and relaxing at the scenic overlook at Newfound Gap. The people, mostly locals from Tennessee and North Carolina, had assembled to listen as President Franklin D. Roosevelt took the stage to officially dedicate Great Smoky Mountains National Park. One petite woman among the multitude listened with personal pride: Laura Thornburgh had been a dedicated advocate of a national park in the Smokies for the past 20 years, although she was too humble to make much of her efforts. A journalist for the *Chattanooga Times* reported that "Miss Thornburgh is as modest as one of the very violets that grow on the sides of her beloved mountains."

It is difficult to appreciate now how unrealistic the dream of creating a park from privately owned property in the Smokies actually was. The National Park Service itself had existed for less than a decade, created in August 1916 by President Woodrow Wilson. Although there were over twenty national parks by the mid 1920s, Acadia National Park on the coast of Maine was the only one in the Eastern United States. National park boundaries in the West had been tremendously difficult to establish and enforce, even on land already owned by the federal government. So the utter improbability of creating a national park from privately owned properties in the Smokies, from both a political and financial standpoint, would have paralyzed all but the most fervent believers. Although Laura Thornburgh valued practicality and frugality in most aspects of her life, her heart was captured by the romantic, idealistic notion.

Her pursuits early in her career led her away from the mountains, to New York City and Washington, D.C. as she took part in some of the earliest attempts to use filmmaking for educational purposes, not just entertainment. While the Smokies were too rugged for 1920s-era filmmaking equipment, her understanding of how to combine storytelling and visual media would shape her contributions to the national park movement. With her combined talents in photography and journalism, she became one of the most widely known "voices of the new national park," writing a column for the *Knoxville Journal* and publishing the park's first guidebook. She chronicled the mountains' return to wildness from decades of logging, and introduced thousands of readers to the natural and cultural beauty of the region.

Born on February 8, 1885, Laura grew up in Knoxville, Tennessee just beyond the shadow of the Great Smoky Mountains. Her family was prominent in Tennessee's political circles—her grandfather Montgomery Thornburgh had served as a state senator and state attorney general. Her father Jacob Montgomery Thornburgh, after fighting for the Union in the Civil War, returned to Tennessee and was elected to the U.S. House of Representatives for six years, before settling in Knoxville with his wife Emma to practice law and raise their family. Laura had a sister, Elizabeth, and a brother, John Minnis, who became a well-respected judge in Knoxville. Jacob and Emma Thornburgh fostered a love of books and reading in their children, and were committed to developing and expanding Knoxville's public education resources as well. When Laura was four, her father donated a significant number of books to the city's public library. The McGhee Library had been established only a few years before, and the Thornburghs' generosity boosted its offerings considerably.

Laura was a voracious reader, and her eagerness for knowledge was a hallmark of her life. Louisa May Alcott's *Little Women* had a powerful early influence on her as she later explained, "I realized then that one's own life or the everyday life about you is material for a book. The determination borne then [to write my own book] never left me." She loved poetry, too, and in high school, began a tradition of buying a new book of poems each spring. In a journal entry from May 1918, against a backdrop of anxiety about World War I, she wrote, "And in order to forget it all just a little, I'm reading—poetry, my annual spring orgy." She kept up this tradition for decades, explaining in a 1940 interview about the books that had had the greatest influence on her, "Reading poetry in the springtime has been my custom for years... and I recommend all young people to read poetry in the springtime. It may keep them, too, from doing something much more foolish!"

After completing high school, Laura enrolled at the University of Tennessee to continue her studies of the literary arts. She began keeping a journal in college, in 1903, titled *Notes from a Student,* which she wrote intermittently for the next fifteen years. In it she reflects on the writings of Kant and Plato, as well as lesser-known writers whose works influenced her thinking, including her thoughts on life, love, family, and her aspirations.

Laura began working as a journalist even before she'd received her bachelor's degree. In addition to writing book reviews, she was asked to cover the Summer School of the South for the *Knoxville News Sentinel.* The Summer School, credited with being one of the major contributors to the improvement of teaching quality in the region, was founded in 1902 to increase the skills of Southern professors and teachers, and nurture supporters for more state budget allocations for education. Its goals must have made an impression on Laura because she, too, spent much of her early professional life trying to improve teaching methods in higher education.

She graduated from UT in 1904 and after a spending several months in Geneva, Switzerland, returned to the United States to continue her studies. She became involved in a somewhat controversial form of media, at least in the education field: the motion picture. Movie technology was expanding rapidly in the years leading up to World War I, and Columbia University and its affiliated Teacher's College offered some of the first classes on the subject in their programs on visual aids and motion picture production. Laura moved from Knoxville to New York City to study at Columbia. She was a natural at analyzing film style and composition—an ability that she used to excel at film editing, and later at photography when she returned to the Smokies.

After completing her studies at Columbia, Laura was hired as an educational film editor for National Non-Theatrical Motion Pictures, Inc. and also worked as a scenario editor for the United States Department of Agriculture's educational film service, based in Washington, D.C.

Through the long years of World War I, she always managed to find employment—it helped that she understood cinematography at a time when the government was interested in using the new medium to share information. She also began developing her own theories about how to apply motion pictures to a classroom learning environment. These ideas led to her first book, Motion Pictures in Education, which was co-written with the director of the USDA film unit, Don Carlos Ellis. Published in 1923, Motion Pictures in Education was the first written work for which Laura used a pen name: Laura Thornborough, the Old English spelling of her last name.

Motion Pictures in Education established her as an expert in using film as a teaching tool and boosted her reputation as an innovator in the teaching profession. Soon after its publication, she was invited to join the faculty of the University of Tennessee's summer school program. She was also active in the League of American Pen Women and served as chairman of their National Motion Picture Committee in 1924, working to facilitate discussions between film writers and producers, and particularly to further the job prospects for women in this new form of media.

Her second book, Etiquette for Everybody, was published in 1923, followed by The Etiquette of Letter Writing in 1924. A fourth book, Interior Decorating for Everybody, followed in 1925. Despite these wide-ranging earlier books, her return to Tennessee in the mid-1920s firmly shifted her interests to the Great Smoky Mountains and the emerging possibility of establishing a national park. A scrap of notebook paper labeled "Reading. Summer of 1925" from her personal notes, now kept in the Special Collections at the University of Tennessee, gives a glimpse into how completely Laura had fallen under the Smokies' spell. In a single summer, she endeavored to read a sizable collection of local history: The Southern Highlander and His Homeland (John C. Campbell), In the Tennessee Mountains (C.E. Craddock), The Carolina Mountains (Margaret Morley), and a dozen other local classics covering topics from folk plays to the ecology of the Cherokee National Forest.

The national park movement was gaining support under the direction of Col. David Chapman and the Great Smoky Mountains Conservation Association. But it was never an easy undertaking. The southern Appalachians were better known as a place of rural poverty than scenic beauty, so early park boosters knew that photographs were essential to building support: breathtaking vistas of mountain

peaks disappearing into the horizon; lush rhododendron overhang-
ing cascading waterfalls; towering old-growth hemlock trees and tulip
poplars.

Although other photographers like Dutch Roth and Jim Thompson would become more famous for their stunning images of Smokies'
backcountry, Laura too hauled her heavy photo gear into the mountains and along rough trails. Especially in the days when they were
devoting their energies to convincing politicians that the Smokies
should be protected as a national park, Laura and Jim Thompson
hiked together, swapping photo tips and commiserating about the
weight of their 8 and 12 pound cameras. For petite, 5'2" Laura, it
was often useful to have a horse along to bear the extra weight of the
camera gear.

Jim Thompson is well-known for portraying the beautiful vistas and
natural majesty of the mountains, but most of Laura's subjects were
the local people: well-known hiking guide Wiley Oakley dwarfed by
ancient tuliptrees on Ramsey Cascade Trail; a grizzled Civil War vet-
eran playing a handmade fife for his grandchildren; a family tending to their sorghum molasses mill. Laura's warm, curious personality
put people at ease, whether they were mountain folk or visitors from
Washington, D.C.

Given her affinity for socializing, she was active in reaching out
to the politicians who could help create a national park. The initial political momentum around the idea of a national park in the
Smokies began to gain traction during 1923. The timing of the original park advocates, including Laura, was fortuitous—National Park
Service Director Stephen T. Mather had written in his 1923 annual
report that he was interested in "additional national parks established
east of the Mississippi, but just how this can be accomplished is not
clear." Laura and other active members of the newly-formed Great
Smoky Mountains Conservation Association began working to show
the National Park Service that such parks were indeed an attainable
goal. In 1925 Laura was part of the hiking party that included Assistant Director of the National Park Service Arno B. Cammerer and a
special commission dispatched to inspect the potential for creating

a national park in the Smokies. The small group climbed to Gregory Bald, an unusual grass-topped mountain that offered breathtaking views in every direction of the valleys below and mountains beyond. Cammerer was surprised and intrigued by what he saw—despite the ravages of logging, the mountains were still wild and beautiful. Five years later, after the highs and lows of countless more victories and setbacks for the park movement, Laura was part of a small group that convened in Washington, D.C. to witness Secretary of the Interior Ray Lyman Wilbur accept the deeds to over 150,000 hard-won acres that would become part of the new national park.

In 1926, a year after she purchased some property on the lower slopes of Mount Le Conte, Laura sold part of the land to Mr. C.P. Biddle—but with a significant condition: if the Great Smoky Mountains Conservation Association raised the funds to pay Laura the original cost of the land, Biddle would forfeit his ownership rights, Laura would return his money, and the land would be deeded to the federal government for the national park. After some energetic fundraising, the Association came up with the money, and despite the ensuing lawsuit disputing the legality of the clause, Laura was credited with a generous land donation to the national park effort.

In 1927, her photograph of a Smokies vista was selected as the cover image of the magazine *American Forests and Forest Life*. She also wrote stories about the Smokies for *American Forests* as well as *Travel*, the most widely-read travel magazine of the 1920s. She enticed readers with descriptions of her adventures in the mountains, whetting their appetites for a national park. Of a camping trip to Silers Bald, she wrote: "*As I stood at the apex of this mountain top meadow…fringed with a grove of beach and birch…there were nothing but mountains and sky, more mountains than the eye could see or the mind could comprehend.*" Her awe of the Smokies prevailed despite visits to other famous mountain ranges. She once compared the Smokies to the Alps, the Apennines, and the Sierras, and concluded, "I have stood on other high peaks…but never have I been so stirred as watching that first sunrise from Mount Le Conte."

After hikes, overnight camping trips, or excursions on horseback, she would relax at the "Cottage," her small, seasonal cabin in Gatlinburg which was built in the late 1920s. The famous mountain guide Wiley Oakley made her a wooden sign, "Thorn Borough," which she hung near her front steps. Three large, covered porches ensured that she could enjoy being outdoors even from the comfort of home: there was a front porch complete with swinging chair, an eating porch with table and chairs, and a sleeping porch with hammock. The interior reflected Laura's love of reading and writing, dominated by books spilling out of built-in bookcases, a writing desk, and a hefty stone double-fireplace to keep off the chill of early autumn nights. Practical and frugal, Laura put nails in the wall and then slipped large wooden thread-spools over them to make coat hooks. The cabin kitchen was designed for simple, wholesome cooking, and Laura was adept at creative meals, as she explained in a newspaper interview in 1938: "I like cooking with leftovers so much that I really think the best things I do are with these." She was well-known for her spaghetti and meatballs, and hearty salads of local summer produce, topped with French dressing and mayonnaise.

The Cottage wasn't winterized, so she would spend the colder months in Knoxville with her brother John and his family, before returning to Gatlinburg for the spring wildflower season and the lush warmth of summer. Although she found her place in the mountains, Laura delighted in trips to the cultural cacophony of New Orleans, and had many happy memories of dancing and Broadway shows in New York City in her younger days.

Laura developed stronger friendships with the native people of the Smokies than many of her hiking and conservation-minded friends. She had written her college senior thesis on Scotland's famous poet, Robert Burns, and perhaps when she began venturing in earnest into the backwoods of the Smokies, almost two decades after she graduated from UT, she recognized the thick brogue evoked in Burns's poetry—*And there's a hand, my trusty fiere! And gie's a hand o' thine! And we'll tak a right gude-willy waught, For auld lang syne*— echoed in the language of the mountain people. She carefully recorded the inflections of her local hiking companions and friends, and even typed up a handwritten note that one of her guides, Sam Cook, had written to her. *"Miss Laura thorn Burgh, I got your letter... The Co. has Built a fine Hotell at treemont and a nice Store. You can come on trail too treemont Hotell. You can get some nice tramps Hear. Your friend, Sam Cook"*

Typing his letter to preserve it, and the note she added at the bottom: *"[I] have copied according to spelling and capitalization. There was NO punctuation and I have added the periods"* might be mistakenly construed as poking fun at these uneducated mountain folk, but Laura clearly loved the people of the Smokies and many of them considered her a friend.

In her most well known book, *The Great Smoky Mountains,* she recounts one of her visits with "Aunt" Lydia Whaley, offering readers one of the first glimpses into the elderly mountain woman's exceptional life. In the days before this particular visit, Aunt Lydia had been sick. But she carefully explained to her guest how she'd brewed up some strong medicine and cured herself: *Git ye some star root. A grasp o' sourwood sprouts. Rosemary weed. Sawdust offen a piece of rich pine. And anvil dust. Add water and vinegar, and bile it down to a pint.* Unfortunately for Laura, when Aunt Lydia had finished explaining, she fetched the bottle and told her visitor to taste it. "It was not an invitation but a command," Laura wrote. "I tasted it and choked...."

Despite the scenery and pleasant company in the mountains, Gatlinburg remained only a seasonal getaway for Laura. She was still editing films for the Department of Agriculture, and in 1930, she published her fifth book—again, on a distinctly different topic than her previous works. It was called *The Psychologist Keeps House,* co-written with Dr. Edwina Abbott Cowan, one of the foremothers of modern psychology. In 1933, Laura produced her most publicized film, the government-sponsored *Historic Scenes along the Mount Vernon Memorial Highway,* to celebrate the completion of the highway that led from Washington, D.C. to George Washington's plantation in Northern Virginia.

1933 was also the year that President Franklin Delano Roosevelt announced that the federal government would contribute $1,550,000 "to complete the project" of buying land for the new national park in the Smokies. There were still many acres left to purchase, lawsuits to settle, and details to work out, but momentum was now on the side of those in favor of the national park. Laura began to focus her writing and photography on the place she loved most. As many business people who supported the idea had hoped, the publicity around the park was beginning to draw tourists to the area. To help educate the public about the allure of the coming national park, the *Knoxville Journal* hired Laura as a "special writer," focused on producing columns about the flora, fauna, and recreational opportunities in the Smokies.

Laura was a member of the Smoky Mountains Hiking Club of Knoxville, founded in 1924. The club's goal was to gather for a hike on a monthly basis, and applications for membership were reviewed by a committee to ensure all members were reputable citizens. Of her fellow hikers, Laura wrote, "What a jolly crowd...all united by their love of the outdoors. And around the campfire at night the songs, the kindly laughter which followed initiation of new members into the gay 'order of the barnyard....' No one complained. It just wasn't done, no matter what the discomforts, rain, snow, or hail, hoot-owls or gnats."

When she couldn't join them on the trail, members of the Hiking Club kept her informed of important happenings so she could report them in the Knoxville newspaper. Park rangers also called to let her know when they'd completed trail improvement projects like building bridges over streams, or when there'd been a particularly fierce windstorm and they wanted people to come into the park and avail themselves of free firewood. She also interviewed Civilian Conservation Corps boys and local personalities like Jack Huff, who built LeConte Lodge. She and Art Stupka, the national park's first naturalist, spent hours strolling along trails together, discussing the biology and geology of the Smokies. Laura reported on the annual spring "Wildflower Pilgrimage" of organized hikes and talks, which was started in 1950. Readers of her column learned to expect Laura to share insights from everyone from fishermen to ornithologists (she often hosted visiting scientists at the Cottage). On one notable hike, Laura and Wiley Oakley accompanied a biologist from the American

Museum of Natural History in New York, who was looking for new salamander species. The scientist's findings (and amusement at Oakley's squeamishness about the amphibians) were later reported in *The New York Times*.

Laura often wrote about the new trails that were being constructed; the Boulevard Trail to the top of Mount Le Conte, the Deep Creek Trail in North Carolina, and an ambitious thoroughfare that skirted the highest ridges in the Smokies, the Appalachian Trail. Several years later, she recounted one of her first hikes along the AT, in the western part of the park:

> *For three days we saw not a human being other than members of our party…but the infinite variety [of mountains] made us forget tired feet and muscles and packs that grew heavier as the days wore to a close. It was on the third day on the narrows between Silers and Clingmans that I looked down into a thunderstorm held between high ridges on the Tennessee side, and holding tight to a laurel bush I leaned over and played in that thunder-cloud as one plays in the watery spray at the bow of a boat.*

Although she describes most of her trips in the Smokies with delight, her first trip to the top of Mount Guyot, the second tallest peak in the Smokies, was distinctly unpleasant. "It was the hardest, roughest, and most exhausting of all the trips I have ever made in the Great Smokies… Memories of the journey back to camp are nightmarish. I recall sliding and hurtling down the mountain side; slipping on the round, mossy rocks; stumbling, falling, rising only to skid and slip and fall again…" she wrote.

After such hikes and adventures, she was happy to settle into a chair on the Cottage's porch with a glass of white wine and some vanilla wafers, to spend evenings chatting with friends, neighbors, and visitors. She kept good company in Gatlinburg. Her neighbors included Jeanette Greve, who wrote and published the first history of Gatlinburg, and Anna Porter, who started the town's library. In later years, Laura would sit and discuss philosophy with her nephew John and his wife, while her grandnieces and nephews played cards and tried not to be directly underfoot. She shared her delight of the mountains with the kids too, often taking them to the Greenbrier area of the park and inducting them into the "rock-hopping club" in the icy waters of the Middle Prong of the Little Pigeon River.

A short letter from May 1935, however, shows that Laura's life was not without economic concerns—she had been corresponding with a small book publisher in London, England, The Mitre Press, about a manuscript she was working on titled *Tales and Trails of the Tennessee Smokies*. Mitre published an "American Folklore Series" and Laura thought her book would be a good fit. In the end, however, Mitre wanted her to invest upfront in the cost of the book and she wrote that since she was currently "hard up financially" the arrangement wouldn't work. Luckily, Thomas Y. Crowell Company, a publisher in New York that had worked with her on earlier books, agreed to publish the completed manuscript, re-titled *The Great Smoky Mountains*, in 1937.

The book was a great success—published at exactly the time when tourists were eager for information about the new national park, the first in the southeastern United States. Laura's clear, engaging prose described the great appeal of visiting the mountains, from meeting mountaineers, to hiking and horseback riding, to the park's native flowers, trees, and animals, and the comforts that could be found in Gatlinburg. Her photographs, too, enticed readers to see the new national park. *The New York Times Review of Books* praised *The Great Smoky Mountains* as notable for Laura's ability to "do justice to the interesting features of these mountain people's old, deep-rooted lives... she writes with full appreciation, too, of the beauty and richness of nature in these misty hills." *The Great Smoky Mountains*, now in its ninth edition, is one of the most popular books ever written on the Smokies. It made Laura a regional celebrity and established her reputation as an authority on the Smokies.

Her book explained the history of the national park and its unique ecology as well as the cultural traditions of the mountain people, but readers loved it for Laura's insights into how they might best enjoy the park when planning to visit. "[T]he waters of these mountain streams are cold, even on a hot summer day," she wrote, "and unless you enjoy a cold plunge do not venture in. Personally, I have found nothing so invigorating as a dip in a mountain stream after a strenuous hike."

She devoted an entire chapter to "Some of my Favorite Trips" because she had been asked for recommendations so often. She suggested the long trail up Brushy Mountain, generally on horseback, for its "lessons in plant geography and ecology" and the "very fine" views from the mountaintop. Mount Le Conte was another favorite destination, particularly the Alum Cave Bluff Trail during June, when the purple rhododendrons bloom. And, she explained, the vistas from Mount Le Conte always reward the weary hiker:

"I burrowed down in the mountain rosebay and myrtle and from my warm nest looked out over a scene that held me silent. The petty annoyances of life seemed far away. I sat awed, spellbound, lost in the beauty unfolded before me…enthralled by the spell of the Great Smokies. Even the guides, who had seen it all many times, sat silent under the same spell."

Through *The Great Smoky Mountains*, Laura became a guide to the Smokies for people eager to hop in their new cars and "go motoring," to explore this national park in the eastern United States. She began a new career as a lecturer and authority on the Great Smoky Mountains, leaving behind her previous work as a motion picture editor. She received fan letters from people in Pasadena and Charleston and Conwith, Iowa; Toronto, Canada; Marfa, Texas; and Maplewood, New Jersey. Residents of Illinois, Arizona, and Ohio sent cards and letters too, and President Franklin D. Roosevelt's secretary thanked her for sending the president a copy.

And there were always updates and revisions to make to the book. The park boundary was frequently changing, there were new trails and new policies, so that expanding her knowledge of the area became both her consuming occupation and avocation. Gatlinburg was becoming a bustling town as two million visitors came through the

Great Smoky Mountains National Park in 1960. As busy as Laura was with lectures and writing newspaper articles, though, she never forgot how to also relax—a newspaper clipping from a 1962 *Knoxville News Sentinel* contains one of Wilma Dykeman's editorials concerning the fact that "Hammocks Have Become Obsolete." In the margin, Thornburgh scrawled "not at the Cottage" and she underlined "not" three times.

A journalist once asked Laura what the most influential book she'd ever read was. Her answer was "The Holy Bible." A devout Catholic, she had offered her Gatlinburg cottage as a place where mass could be held until a proper church was built. She delighted in taking her grandnieces and nephews to the downtown tourist attraction Christus Gardens, which opened in August 1960 and featured dioramas of the life of Christ—she went so often that the owners waived her admission fee. Her writing, too, has gentle references to her faith: "there is a stillness that descends upon us like a benediction…a settlement of cabins [along Baskins Creek], strung like beads upon a rosary…." In the mountains, she told her readers,

> "…the trails into wilderness areas, through cathedral-cool mountain top forests, encourage prayer and meditation. Here one may temporarily forget the woes of a war-torn world, or think things through, get a better perspective, a truer sense of values, gain inner peace and fortitude to meet tomorrow's problems and the tasks ahead. The Great Smokies, accessible and friendly, have much to offer."

In 1973, the year Laura Thornburgh passed away, over seven and a half million tourists came to hike, ride, and enjoy the beauty of Great Smoky Mountains National Park. Protecting the mountains that had so deeply touched her soul and her life became Laura's most fulfilling undertaking as she spent "part of every year rambling with her camera among the peaks and valleys and rounded woodlands…" reported *The New York Times*. A life-long learner and teacher, she left a rich legacy of information about the early years of the national park and the heritage of the mountain people, a foundation of knowledge for those who shared her interests in the cultural and natural aspects of the Great Smoky Mountains. "Whenever I discover new trails and find new beauties," she wrote, "I feel an intense desire to share this knowledge with others and shout this discovery to the whole world."

Laura Thornburgh

Chapter 15

Anne Broome

ANNE BROOME IS NOW, OF COURSE, PART OF OUR WILDERNESS HERITAGE... ANNE AND HARVEY WERE THERE AT THE BEGINNING OF THE WILDERNESS MOVEMENT AND THEY'VE BEEN THERE AND HELPED US AND LED US THROUGHOUT THAT MOVEMENT TO TODAY...

ANNE BROOME • 1904–1983

—Will Skelton, President of Harvey Broome chapter of the Sierra Club

Anne Broome

The thermometer outside registered eight degrees on January 18, 1959, and four inches of snow blanketed the mountains. Anne Pursel Broome and her husband Harvey had planned to go hiking. The weather did not deter them as they got out of the car at the Chimney Tops trailhead in Great Smoky Mountains National Park. The sun shone brightly but offered no warmth as they set off down the trail, snow squeaking under their boots.

As they crossed the footbridge over Road Prong Creek, they noticed the water in the usually vivacious stream was flowing: "not over its customary bed of boulders and gravel, but over buttresses and boulders of green-tinted ice!" Harvey would later write.

> "The air gnawed at our faces.... Snow lay on the ground, on the trees, on the twigs, on every leaf, on every bit of vegetation—light and bright in the searching sun....This was living!...January, with beauty clean, pristine, and very cold. The bitter temperature that slashed our faces had also produced these fantasies in ice and snow. We turned away. We could stand just so much of the beauty and cold. But we had lived profoundly for a couple of hours in the bitter-sweet of a mid-January day."

Anne Broome moved to the Great Smokies from Cambridge, Massachusetts in 1937, three years after Great Smoky Mountains National Park was officially established by Congress, and three years before President Franklin Delano Roosevelt would stand at Newfound Gap for the belated official dedication ceremony. Her husband Harvey, who'd grown up in the shadow of the Smokies, had been a strong advocate for the national park, and was a significant figure in the national conservation movement. Over the next forty years, Anne and Harvey would relish the reemergence of the Smokies' forests as the mountain ecosystems recovered from logging and farming, and flourished under new protections. They would also travel extensively across the country, seeking to protect other wild lands through political advocacy work with The Wilderness Society, which Harvey had co-founded in 1935.

No Place for the Weary Kind

By the end of her life, Anne Broome would come to know the Great Smoky Mountains—the trails, the diversity of plants and animals, the way a day spent in nature could lift spirits—with a familiarity and passion matched by few other people. She would also leave a legacy as a powerful, behind-the-scenes contributor to wilderness protection across America. She was a friend of, and collaborator with, many of the country's most passionate environmentalists, from Appalachian Trail founder Benton MacKaye to Wilderness Act author Howard Zahniser, to author and conservationist Aldo Leopold. Perhaps because of her Quaker upbringing, she avoided the limelight herself, preferring the arduous tasks of connecting inspiration with action, and the necessary but unglamorous work of taming logistics, an essential foundation for the political and social change that the environmental movement aspired to. In her later years, she also collected, organized, and published her husband Harvey's writing in several books. Without her efforts, Harvey's meditative, insightful prose about the mountains, and the human relationship with nature, would never have been shared outside of a few lucky friends and family.

As the head secretary of the University of Tennessee's Botany Department for fifteen years, Anne worked with brilliant professors who studied plants in the Smokies and around the world. Her typing skills and finely honed sense of order and organization, from her training at the Katherine Gibbs Secretarial School in New York City, boosted the department's effectiveness immensely. And in return, Anne learned a substantial amount about the mountain flora and fauna from the faculty, sometimes remembering facts and figures better than the professors themselves. Her friend Bob Howe later recalled, "She acquired a depth of knowledge of the wealth and variety of plant life in the Smokies. And I, who had studied horticulture, learned to look to Anne as an authority for identification of various plants that I should have known, but I had forgotten...."

When tragedy struck, Anne's talents became even more invaluable. The building where the botany department was located burned in 1934, and Anne's boss, Dr. Lexemuel Hesler, the head of the botany department and Dean of Liberal Arts at the university,

lost everything—his extensive fungi collections, notes, book manuscripts. He was forced to rewrite his books and reassemble his collections, and relied heavily on Anne to help him and other staff as they
reconstructed what had been destroyed.

Although her position was officially to assist only Dr. Hesler, she was
remembered by Professor Jack Sharp as "a bulwark for younger people,
as well as our protector...more than willing to help other members of
the Department, and [she] spent hours doing chores for us." In 1946,
Sharp returned from a two-year collecting trip in Mexico to find that
she'd typed and organized all of his letters. "I was, naturally, very tick-
led," he said. In due time, Professor Sharp would become head of the
UT Botany Department as well as an internationally renowned researcher and moss expert, and he never forgot Anne's kindnesses.

Her work in academia, driven by intellectual curiosity, provided
balance with Anne's other pursuits, mainly the fraught and thorny
issues of political advocacy for wilderness preservation. For decades,
she and Harvey spent their vacations on Wilderness Society business,
assessing threats to wilderness across America. As part of the Society's
annual leadership council meetings, Anne, Harvey, and other members would ride packhorses or hike into some of the most remote—
and threatened—lands in America: deep canyons, primeval forests,
and snowy tundras that were targeted for mining, oil extraction,
road-building, or dams.

This was, perhaps, an unexpected path for a young woman who
grew up among the Northeast's biggest cities. Anna Waller Pursel—
who never officially changed her name to 'Anne' but might as well
have—was born in the small town of Bloomsburg, Pennsylvania in
June 1904. Orphaned when she was very young, she was raised by
aunts and uncles, many of whom were Quakers, in Philadelphia, New
York City, and Brookline, Massachusetts, just outside of Boston. She
was promptly offered a job as the secretary to the head of Harvard
University's School of Education, Fred Smith, after graduating from
the Katherine Gibbs Secretarial School in New York City, a progressive institution that had expanded to train more women to fill the gap
in men's work during World War I.

She was happy in Cambridge: she had a great working relationship with Dean Smith and enjoyed the intellectual community around the university. But one day in February 1926, making her way through the piles of snow left by a particularly intense winter storm, Anne met a friendly group of students at the Methodist Church near Harvard Square. One of the young men was Harvey Broome, a charming Southerner studying at Harvard Law School. They fell in love, and kept up a flurry of written correspondence after Harvey graduated and moved back to Knoxville in 1927. They wrote so frequently that daily notations were too formal—instead they'd write *Thursday* or *Saturday morning* on their letters. Whenever he could, Harvey would make the multi-day train trip up from Knoxville to Boston to visit her and see other dear friends, like his longtime mentor Benton MacKaye who had been working to establish a hiking trail through the Appalachian Mountains that would run from Georgia to Maine.

To a Quaker from the North, Knoxville must have seemed like a different planet: provincial, segregated, with fewer opportunities for women to have careers. But after ten years of letter writing, they decided to get married, and that Anne would join Harvey in the Southern mountains. True to her Quaker upbringing, Anne hoped for an electric sweeper or washing machine as wedding presents—practical, useful things—instead of china sets, crystal goblets, or silver flatware. Befitting those sentiments, their July 1937 wedding ceremony was simple and small, hosted in the living room of Benton MacKaye's house in quaint, rural Shirley Center, Massachusetts.

Still, there was no getting around the fact that Anne was an unconventional woman in the South. Despite having a devoted beau, she hadn't rushed to get married, and at thirty-three, felt she was too old to have children. She and Harvey would instead dote on their dogs, particularly Shadow, a Gordon setter whose "impetuous forays," as Anne described them, kept the neighbors always on alert. Her main concessions to the Southern traditions around her were a delight in the large, boisterous extended Broome family, and her love of cooking. She brought her sense of adventure into the kitchen, often urging friends and family to "try a recipe for the experience." But she could be quiet and reserved, with a gravitas about her that she knew sometimes intimidated people who didn't know her well, and she kept a small file of newspaper clippings about the art of being a conversationalist and a good hostess.

Anne arrived in Knoxville at a time of significant change for the land and people of the Great Smoky Mountains. The national park had been officially established for only three years, and Harvey and other conservationists were eager for more victories in their quest for the preservation of America's still wild places. Anne embraced this calling as well, falling in love with the Smokies as if they had been her home for her entire life.

She developed a ritual of taking a solitary, semiannual hike to the summit of Mount Le Conte, which she continued into her 70s. On one memorable solo hike in 1961, she hurt her knee. "She was alone and crippled in one of the rugged and remote areas in the Smokies," Harvey stated. "She was lucky to get out, but it was a luck bolstered by years of experience and stamina developed in the wildest and roughest places." She and Harvey often eschewed the trail for the untamed forest, although occasionally his sense of adventure—or perhaps abandon—exceeded hers. During one ten-degree day in January 1961 they climbed Mount Le Conte despite the two feet of snow. Anne snow-shoed along the trail; Harvey climbed directly up the mountain slope. It was one of the highlights of their year.

But it wasn't the adrenaline rush of danger that lured them off trail in the Smokies, or deep into other wild lands. They hiked to be a part of nature, to appreciate places minimally impacted by humans. Harvey wrote of a hike with Anne to Silers Bald in 1945, "The winds were restless, and late in the afternoon the fog swept in as we toiled up a grassy slope on the west shoulder of Clingmans. I felt that we were surrounded by all the sadness and loneliness in the universe... The soughing of the wind through the evergreens went on interminably. When we were watching the ravens sporting and hovering and soaring in the winds, Anne said: 'Think what goes on up here when we are not here.'"

To be able to enjoy as much time hiking as possible, Anne and

Harvey bought a rustic cabin in Emert's Cove, just outside the Greenbrier area of the national park, as a base camp for long hikes into the mountains. The cabin was primitive: it had only one room, with a separate lean-to for cooking, and no electricity or running water. They called it Cobbles Hollow. On one typical morning in 1942, Anne and Harvey woke up before dawn to make a quick breakfast before setting out on a long hike. Harvey wrote that the "setting moon gleamed like a jewel through the branches of the trees, and moments later tiny streaks of clouds were touched with rose. This was the day we hiked fifteen miles, traversing Porters Mountain, obtaining incomparable views of Charlie's Bunion, the Jumpoff, and Porters Valley."

Anne kept a journal of visits to the cabin as well, recording, in the tradition of the best naturalists, the yearly cycles of nature: snakeskins left, or not, by a reptile they nicknamed "Samuel the Serpent," whether the bubbling spring was gushing, dry, or trickling somewhere in between, encounters with bears, and the constant need for the small patch of grass around the cabin—the one nod to cultivation— to be trimmed (which Harvey was apparently ever-forgetful about). One year, Anne "with gentle patience" coaxed titmice into taking seeds from her outstretched hand, as Harvey wrote in their Christmas letter. Bluebird sightings were always recorded as happy occasions, because the pretty songbirds preferred more open environments than the encroaching forest of Cobbles Hollow; the deep hoot of barn owls or trill of screech owls also delivered a thrill. One of Anne's few indulgences in non-essential objects was her collection of owl figurines and other objects with owl motifs.

Her writing about her encounters and adventures in the Smokies was guided by the ethos of what she called, "cosmic consciousness," which she once wrote to a friend was the understanding that "There are two different approaches to life: the one which takes note only of the fact itself; the other which sees behind the fact a significance, a beauty, a suggested meaning that transforms it, a wonder that infuses the common with the spiritual." Her journal entries are pithy, but infused with meaningful detail:

Cobbles Hollow, April 21, 1962: Arrived about noon, with Harvey and Helen Wells. (No dogs.) We bought six flame azaleas at Proffitt's nursery. It is warm in the sun, cool inside. Le Conte is in its accustomed place. Ice shows in a ravine, but we do not see snow. The mountain iris surprised us in bloom. The narcissus is just arriving. How quiet.

October 5-6, 1963: Emert's Cove Party of Smoky Mountain Hiking Club...Harvey and I slept outdoors on Willie V's porch, with gibbous moon shining in our faces. I had drunk several cups of coffee on purpose to stay awake. It was worth it to see Orion's pale diadem... twinkling in the moonlight.

May 8, 1965: I had planned to stop here very briefly and then hike to Rainbow Falls. Now that I am here on this mild day that makes a body expand with its perfection, I do not want to leave... My mind and heart and eyes are almost overcome with "the fullness of the earth" to borrow Harvey's phrase."

As hiking companions, Anne and Harvey were perfectly suited for one another, but they also went on many organized excursions with other members of the Smoky Mountain Hiking Club. The Club, founded in 1924, had a robust membership of enthusiastic hikers and conservationists. Harvey had served as the club's president in 1932 and was always involved with the club's park/conservation committee. Anne dabbled in a variety of different groups, from the social committee to photographic committee. In 1954, she was one of the club's senior officers, fulfilling the duties of recording secretary. She and Harvey helped build the club's rustic log cabin in Porters Creek, a shelter available to members as a convenient starting point for hikes in the national park.

They spent many memorable hours on the trail with SMHC friends, making the annual June pilgrimage to see the vibrant azalea bloom on Gregory Bald, and enjoying views from the famous rock outcropping called Charlies Bunion along the Appalachian Trail, among other memorable destinations. Passages from Harvey's hiking journal, *Out Under the Sky of the Great Smokies*, give a glimpse into their adventures, and the spiritual nourishment he and Anne found in the outdoors. They hiked in all weather, finding storms as exhilarating as days of luxuriant sunlight. Adventures in the Smokies could draw forth Anne's exuberant and adventurous spirit. Harvey recounted a memorable hike in 1953:

> "We parked at Forney Ridge in a wind which blasted at us from the North Carolina side. It was not raining but the fog was thick....On the open slopes we were embattled, leaning into the wind as though it were a solid thing...Anne went ahead at Double Springs. We were in the beeches—stubby, limby, and many-twigged. The wind became a wild, deep-throated roar.... At the first grassy bald we looked out into sheer, gray space. Anne appeared like a wraith at the first opening, shouting "Hurry, hurry before the wind dies down." It was a scene of wild, ungoverned riot.... Anne took off in a wild run down the steep slope toward the woods, the wind ripping at her plastic raincoat, until in the dimness she seemed more spirit than body. I have heard of a sunstroke, but as I watched her mad dash, I thought this is the first time I have seen a wind-stroke. Almost like a bird she was buffeted back by an up-draft and joined us on top. We shouted our excitement and our words were torn from us and lost in that great roaring...."

Anne and Harvey devoted much of their lives to advocating for the preservation of nature so that others might experience the physical and spiritual restoration that they and their friends found on adventures in the Smokies. As Harvey wrote in *Out Under the Sky of the Great Smokies*:

> "On trips into the mountains [with Anne and many others], there came a disturbing awareness of the rift between the untrammeled wilds and the rifled countryside.... It was not enough to enjoy wild country; one felt compelled to try to conserve and defend the land against further spoliation."

Indeed, the early 1950s were a time of shifting land management priorities. The U.S. Forest Service had become more involved in timber production after World War II and more than doubled national production—from 3.5 billion board feet to 9.3 billion. Federal and state governments were also interested in building dams and expanding roads. But at the same time, organizations for wildlife enthusiasts and sportsmans' associations were expanding rapidly, meaning that more people were using national forests for recreation; parks and wilderness were increasingly becoming a commodity. The Wilderness Society leadership, including Anne and Harvey, were squarely at the center of the power struggles between those who valued environmental integrity and those who looked to exploit previously undeveloped natural resources.

Anne and Harvey's dear friend Howard Zahniser ("Zahnie"), the executive secretary of The Wilderness Society, first broached the subject of national legislation to protect undeveloped wild areas in 1947. But he would have to wait nearly ten years for political momentum to shift his way. In the intervening years, there were plenty of land issues to weigh in on. The Broomes, along with Zahnie and other members of The Wilderness Society's leadership council, convened each August at a location close to places in need of protection. They readied themselves for the long and vicious political fights by taking "field trips" into the lands they were working to protect, to bolster their convictions that these places were still wild, beautiful, and valuable to America in their present untrammeled condition. Following the council meetings, the Wilderness Society would issue official stances on national policy, and encourage members to write to their congressmen, the President, and others in political leadership in support of protection for wild places.

One pivotal battle took five years: in August 1950, Anne, Harvey, and others rode horses down into Echo Park, a breathtaking open glade hidden among towering cliffs and canyons of Dinosaur National Monument on the Colorado-Utah border. The Bureau of Reclamation had decided a dam at the confluence of the Green and Yampa rivers within the monument—therefore flooding Echo Park—would be an ideal location for generating power. Proponents of the dam, including Secretary of the Interior Oscar Chapman and the Truman administration, argued that dams were needed as part of national security during the Cold War. The Wilderness Society opposed the dam on the grounds that it weakened the protective legislation of the National Park Service Organic Act, which stated parks must be preserved "unimpaired." The political battle would last longer than the Truman administration, and linger into the early days of the Eisenhower administration. Ultimately, in November 1955, Zahnie won over the Western congressmen to defeat the Echo Park Dam. This victory gave a glimmer of hope to his idea of a national bill for wilderness protection.

In this atmosphere of cautious optimism, Harvey was elected President of The Wilderness Society in 1957. But his private law practice didn't allow him enough time to focus on wilderness issues, so he and Anne decided that he should close his practice. He took a lower paying, lower time-commitment position as a clerk for a federal judge in Knoxville, accepting the job on the condition that he would be able to devote appropriate time to his wilderness advocacy work. Together, Zahnie and Harvey, with consultation and support from Anne, began drafting a bill that would establish a system of wilderness preserves to be managed under strict guidelines: no roads, no motorized vehicles, no resource development of any kind. Although he frequently consulted with Harvey and Anne, among others, Howard Zahniser was the driving force behind the legislation. He became so adept at advocating for the bill that Wilderness Society Council members—including Harvey and others with legal backgrounds—began to worry that the Society's tax-exempt status might be revoked and they would need to register as a lobbyist. This was particularly worrisome because it would jeopardize a great deal of the Society's funding—and therefore the organization's existence. Harvey cautioned Zahnie, reminding him of how much he disliked fundraising and asking if Zahnie had a plan to replace the Society's income if it was classified as a lobbying entity.

Although it sometimes seemed that political fights took all their time and effort, Anne and Harvey were determined to avoid being swept up in or overwhelmed by the vagaries and whims of politics and power struggles. Their Christmas letter of 1962 explained that "Harvey is cutting more wood (no power saw) and is learning simple cabinetry. Anne is weaving more. Each knows the misadventures of learning new skills, and senses in these experiences the slow—infinitely slow—growth of human culture. Each thinks it best to do some things with his hands...."

Through the years, weaving became more than a hobby for Anne. She owned a spinning wheel as well as a loom, and taught herself to card wool, spin it into thread, and then mastered intricate weaving patterns. She even experimented with different materials, occasionally harvesting grass from around Cobbles Hollow to make placemats. She became so skilled that she was admitted to the Southern Highland Handicraft Guild, which maintains strict standards and requires being approved by a jury of member artisans. Weaving everything from bedspreads to placemats as gifts for family and friends became a great pleasure for her.

The Cobbles Hollow cabin and hikes into the Smokies were also welcome respites from the fraught phone calls and letter writing over The Wilderness Act, which had still not come to fruition. In fact, it had some powerful opponents—in addition to the timber, ranching, and mining interests, the Director of the National Park Service, Horace Albright, believed that giving Congress oversight into management of national parks would hinder his agency's effectiveness. But in 1963, after over sixty drafts of the bill and eighteen committee meetings, Zahnie could see the light at the end of the tunnel: The Senate passed The Wilderness Act in a bipartisan vote of 78-8, and it was endorsed by President John Kennedy, setting the stage for a vote in the House in 1964.

Anne and Harvey would mourn the untimely death of two significant men in between the Senate vote and the official signing of the legislation: President Kennedy was assassinated on November 22; and Howard Zahniser, perhaps exhausted by his efforts to ensure the passing of the bill, died of heart failure in May 1964. Harvey, still

President of The Wilderness Society, was part of a small, somber but victorious group that gathered in the Rose Garden to watch President Lyndon Johnson sign The Wilderness Act into law on September 3, 1964. The President observed, "If future generations are to remember us with gratitude rather than contempt, we must leave them a glimpse of the world as it was in the beginning, not just after we got through with it." The bill created a legal definition of "wilderness" in the United States and designated an initial 9.1 million acres of federal land as a National Wilderness Preservation System.

That immense political victory was followed by a new threat close to home for Anne and Harvey: in 1965, the National Park Service proposed a new 35-mile road through Great Smoky Mountains National Park to connect Bryson City, North Carolina with Townsend, Tennessee. Decades-old government promises and economic development struggles were tangled up in the road proposal, but Anne, Harvey, and other conservationists strongly objected to a new road through pristine park land. As Harvey wrote in late 1966, "It was the first confrontation in the country between those who would use National Parks for gain and convenience, and those who would protect the vitality, complex ecology, and solitude of wilderness."

Anne and Harvey were part of the organizing group for a "Save Our Smokies" hike to protest the plans for the road on October 23rd 1966, spearheaded by their dear friend Ernest Dickerman. Although the protest was peaceful, plenty of law enforcement officials were stationed near Clingmans Dome just in case something happened. Five hundred and seventy-six people signed the roster at the high point in the Smokies, Clingmans Dome; nearly 500 hiked four miles to Silers Bald, part of the crest of the Great Smoky Mountains. And two hundred and thirty five people continued with Harvey for the full seventeen miles from Clingmans to Elkmont—Anne hiked the route in reverse. "Many Americans do care for their wild places," Harvey mused, reflecting on the turnout. The media attention garnered by the protest helped raise public awareness of the issue and as disapproval spread, the road project was eventually dropped.

But the consequences of road planning and building on places dear to Anne and Harvey wasn't over. Harvey had written in their 1965 Christmas letter, "The cloud of the motor age has thrown its shadow equally over our national preserves and our own sequestered valley." For several years they had known Cobbles Hollow would be acquired as right of way for the Foothills Parkway, a two-lane scenic road that was planned to encircle the national park. On August 6, 1967, Anne began recording the end of an era in her cabin journal:

> *Well, sad to say Cobbles Hollow is on its way—Harvey and I arrived a little before 3, he to meet Bill Curtis, an appraiser. It is all a part of the drawn out episode of building a Foothills Parkway. Surveyors have been on our land 18 months or 2 years ago, maybe, but this is the first time we have been approached in person.*

They began slowly removing things from the cabin and surrounding land—special plants that they wanted to save were dug up and replanted in Knoxville, including several hemlock trees that had been planted over four years earlier "as a kind of antidote to the unspeakable tragedies at Dallas" after President Kennedy's death. Anne, "under Harvey's careful supervision," dug up the hemlocks in late February 1968, to relocate them to their Knoxville house. The trees had not yet been replanted, due to a variety of other obligations, when a second, more personal tragedy shook the Broome family. On the pleasant morning of March 8, 1968, Harvey was sawing a log to make a birdhouse for a wren. He died of a sudden heart attack in the yard, gone so quickly there was no reason for an ambulance. He'd had some health troubles as a young boy, and a chronic 'weak heart,' which his fervor for hiking often masked.

Anne found support among members of Harvey's large extended family, Smoky Mountain Hiking Club friends, and members of the Sierra Club. A few weeks after Harvey's death, on March 21, 1968, Congress approved the first new Wilderness Area since the passage of the Wilderness Act in 1964, protecting nearly 150,000 acres between California's San Rafael and Sierra Madre mountain ranges—a sign that his life's work would have long-lasting impact. Anne stayed involved in wilderness preservation advocacy, and would regularly call William Skelton, the president of what came to be known as the Harvey Broome chapter of the Sierra Club, to talk. He said, "I've gotten lots of calls from her, starting with the phrase, 'Did you know that…?' And you can fill in the rest of it. In fact, that's one of my best memories, I suppose, of Anne—was talking to her on the telephone about what's going on in environmental issues…. And she was always willing to write a letter. Always willing to get involved. Always aware of the issues of what was going on in the environmental wilderness preservation movement—ranging from the Smokies to Alaska."

She continued hiking, with friends and sometimes alone, as had always been part of her life. She wrote to a friend in 1975, recounting her birthday hike… "I left the house before the Carolina wren had left its roost on a post near the front door…. What is as pleasant as a June day in East Tennessee, and what is better than being able to hike in the Great Smoky Mountains…? You like to tease me about organizing and planning my time. Well, it paid off. I was ready to start hiking east from Newfound Gap at 9 am, reminiscent of past custom (before the days of four lane and divided highways.)"

She was an unassuming, motherly presence at meetings of the Smoky Mountain Hiking Club, always concerned with making sure that newer members felt at ease and welcome among the tight-knit camaraderie of old timers. And occasionally at hiking club or Sierra Club meetings, she would agree to read from Harvey's hiking journals. His heartfelt musings on wilderness, and descriptions of the joys of hiking and exploring America's natural lands, resonated with her listeners, many of whom had known Harvey and still missed him. Before his death, Anne had been helping Harvey organize his prolific writing into publishable form, typing and sorting his notes and offering editorial input. As the years passed, she began to contemplate finishing the project and publishing a book of his writings herself.

With the guidance of Paul Oehser, who directed publications at the Smithsonian Institution and had served with Harvey on the board of The Wilderness Society, Anne began to compile some of Harvey's writings into a book, and perhaps soon realized there was enough for several. The first was published in 1970, a slender collection of essays called *Harvey Broome: Earth Man*. That same year Congress approved the first new wilderness area within national park boundaries—in Arizona's Petrified Forest National Park. Two years later, Anne published *Faces of the Wilderness*, Harvey's personal accounts of trips affiliated with The Wilderness Society from 1941 to 1965. In 1975, she published a small print run of *Out Under the Sky of the Great Smokies*, an intimate journal of Harvey's explorations in the Smokies and thoughts on wilderness and conservation. Noted conservationist Michael Frome wrote an endorsement of the book that highlighted what made the Broomes' conservation writing resonate: "The focus may be on the Smokies, but [it] expresses a sense of universality that should appeal to lovers of nature the world over." This was the book that Harvey and Anne had been working on together before he died—the Acknowledgments, which he wrote in 1967, begin, "Anne Broome has for thirty years shared fully my enthusiasms. She assumed the enormous burden of transcribing my Journals and that of the retyping; and her counsel has borne fruit in tightening the text." In 1978 Anne proudly noted another major victory for Harvey and Howard Zahniser's legacy: President Jimmy Carter signed the Endangered American Wilderness Act, establishing 1.3 million acres of new wilderness lands. The Secretary of the Interior Bruce Babbitt also recommended that parts of Great Smoky Mountains National Park be given a wilderness designation, but the legislation faced fierce opposition, mostly from supporters of another mountain road through the park. The wilderness legislation in the Smokies was eventually defeated, but the park is still required to manage land as if it had the designation—at least until altered by some future proposal.

As she reached her early eighties, Anne became a devoted swimmer, which was less physically demanding than hiking. She volunteered at the public library, helping keep the bookshelves organized, and became a sponsor of the local broadcast of Garrison Keillor's Prairie Home Companion. Although the natural beauty of the mountains had always captivated her, she became increasingly interested in the area's cultural traditions. She would venture down winding mountain roads to find rural mountain churches, eager to learn more about the Appalachian tradition of old harp singing. She discovered how interesting baseball could be when two of her grandnephews took up the sport in school. But a strong sense of mission simmered under these pleasant undertakings: her determination that the richness of Harvey's writing wouldn't be lost when she too passed away.

She became a one-woman publisher of Harvey's works—trying to figure out the best way to market the books, taking care of payment of printing copies, and dealing with the frustration when stores returned unsold inventory. "She elevated him with her persistence," her friends Bill and Alice Hart would later remember. "She put so much energy and passion into making sure the richness of his writing would last." In the fall of 1983, she had the satisfaction of arranging for booksellers to begin offering more of Harvey's books for sale—moving them out of "the warehouse," which was a bedroom in her house, to local stores.

Shortly after this accomplishment, she became very ill and was diagnosed with pancreatic cancer. On October 12, 1983, the night she died, her niece, Marian Broome, was sitting in the hospital with her. It was the second night of the World Series, and Anne encouraged Marian to turn the game on, both of them interested in the showdown between the Baltimore Orioles and Philadelphia Phillies. At her funeral service on October 18th, family members, environmentalists, hiking friends, and church and library friends gathered to remember Anne as a generous, talented, humble woman who had contributed so much energy to the conservation movement in America.

In the spring of 1999, long after Anne had passed away, as copies of Harvey's books became harder to find, conservationist and author Michael Frome took on Anne's role of advocate for them. He mentioned Out Under the Sky of the Great Smokies to Scot Danforth, the publisher of the University of Tennessee Press. Impressed by Harvey's writing style and his stature in the conservation movement, Danforth agreed it would be a good project to reprint and received permission from The Wilderness Society to do so. Frome wrote a new foreword, offering context and praise for both Broomes' work and their passion for wilderness preservation. Today, the book continues to be discovered by readers who recognize the timelessness in Anne and Harvey's adventures in the Smokies and their reflections on the human relationship to the wild.

For Anne, the birdsong and flower bloom, weather patterns and serpent skins in the Smokies made her feel connected to a greater, more mysterious and beautiful pulse of all life on earth. She created a deep relationship with the earth in its infinite biological glory that few have achieved. But in her partnership with Harvey, Anne worked tirelessly to ensure that the opportunity to create a meaningful connection with nature was available to all those who follow.

Top: Anne Broome (second from left) with members of the Smoky Mountains Hiking Club.

Left: Anne with William Hart, III and Alice Hart.

Chapter 16

Margaret Stevenson

SHE'S A LITTLE BIT MOTHER
AND WHEN THE GOING GETS ROUGH,
A LITTLE BIT DRILL SERGEANT.
YOU NEVER DOUBT SHE CAN DO WHAT
SHE SETS OUT TO DO.

Le Conte Lodge
DINING ROOM

MARGARET STEVENSON • 1912–2006

—*Jon Stiles*, Blount County News Sentinel, *on Margaret Stevenson*

Gracie McNicol

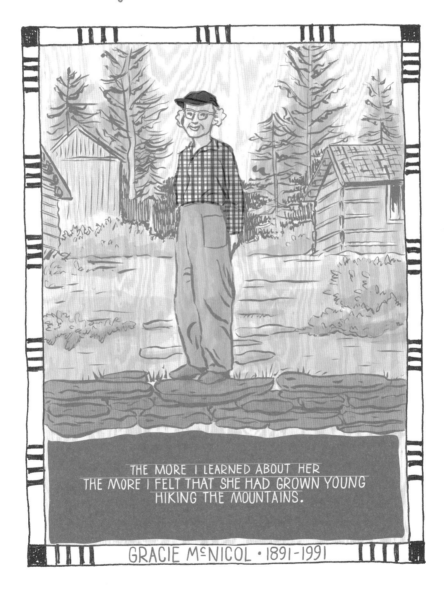

THE MORE I LEARNED ABOUT HER
THE MORE I FELT THAT SHE HAD GROWN YOUNG
HIKING THE MOUNTAINS.

GRACIE McNICOL · 1891–1991

—*Anita Crabtree, hiking companion, on Gracie McNicol,
quoted in* Gracie and the Mountain *by Emilie Powell*

After hours of hiking, backpack straps pull heavy on shoulders, boots clatter over loose shale on the trail. The hikers are sweaty, but the air holds a heavy scent of fir trees, a promise that the top of the mountain is close. A red squirrel trills from the limb of a tall spruce. Then, through the trees, small cabins appear, their wooden walls a weather-beaten gray. LeConte Lodge, established on the mountain of the same name in 1926, is a welcoming sight for aching backs and weary feet. Hikers make their way to the main office to let the staff know they've arrived, get keys to their cabins, sign the official guest log.

The main office is a large, cozy room with rocking chairs, an old-fashioned loom for weaving, and shelves overflowing with decades of magazines and books. Framed photographs along the walls give a glimpse into the history of this rustic outpost, the only overnight accommodations in the national park other than camp sites. The lodge itself has grown from a single cabin with a dirt floor and tarpaper roof to a small enclave of cabins, a mess hall, and the office. Other photographs highlight a few significant people whose lives were uniquely shaped by Mount Le Conte and the lodge. There is Jack Huff and his wife Pauline, who founded the lodge; Paul Adams who hiked up in 1925 and began to build it. And, more recently, there are two trim, white-haired ladies: hiking legends Margaret Stevenson and Grace Viola McNicol.

Margaret and Gracie separately hiked hundreds of miles each year in Great Smoky Mountains National Park, setting records and inspiring hardened outdoorsy folk and non-hikers alike. Each woman began hiking the Smokies seriously only later in life; Gracie McNicol was sixty-two in 1954 when she first set foot on a hiking trail in the Smokies. Margaret was fifty-two when she first began hiking regularly in 1960. Their extensive hiking records would be notable enough even without the fact that each woman had overcome significant physical challenges prior to becoming a dedicated hiker. Gracie had struggled through several severe bouts of sickness in her life—even having to learn to walk again after a debilitating illness during her thirties. Margaret's constant cheerfulness masked decades of back pain and memories of a childhood haunted by her mother's time in and out of mental hospitals as she struggled with severe bipolar disease. They both found solace, joy, and ease in hiking the mountains, but there was something magical about Le Conte that drew each woman to hike it devotedly, until she'd reached the summit many hundreds of times.

Le Conte is the third highest mountain in the Great Smoky Mountains, and it is no small feat to reach its summit. Five trails lead from lower valleys and ridges to the top of the mountain, allowing a variety of approaches—but all are difficult. The most popular, Alum Cave Trail, is the shortest, at five miles, but it's plenty steep and rocky. Cables have been attached to the side of the mountain so hikers can hang onto them and lessen their chances of tripping over the edge of the sheer slope. The more leisurely Boulevard Trail offers the opposite approach: the climb is relatively gentle, but requires walking a total of eight miles to get from the Newfound Gap parking lot to the lodge. The Trillium Gap, Rainbow Falls, and Bullhead trails offer varying combinations of steepness and length in between those two. In short, your feet will be aching by the time you get to the lodge, no matter how young or old you are. Both Gracie and Margaret kept hiking the mountain well into their eighties, spending thousands of hours getting to know the slopes of Le Conte. The staff at the lodge became extended family to them, and the combination of exercise, friendship, and glorious natural beauty seemed to keep them both younger than their years.

They occasionally met each other on the Le Conte trails, but never hiked together. Gracie liked to walk alone to better appreciate the wilderness around her; Margaret was a social hiker—anyone who cared to show up at the trail was welcome to hike with her, and she was regularly joined by up to twenty people. As she became more famous, her hikes were sometimes announced in the newspaper. Her warm personality and cheerfulness drew people to her, and made it easy for them to forget aching feet, scraped knees, or profuse sweating which so often comes with hiking. She particularly loved being on the trail in the spring because of the immense variety of wildflowers, and in the fall because of the spectacular autumn color. But she really just loved to hike anytime.

"According to her, it never got hot in the Smokies," Lois Costanza, one of Margaret's most constant hiking companions recalled. "I once turned to her and said, 'I've got news for you Margaret. It DOES get hot!'" In October 1983, Margaret headed out for a memorable hike with Knoxville newspaperman Carson Brewer, who wrote, "Fifteen yards up the trail, Margaret Stevenson looked like a blue ghost in her sky-blue poncho amid the fog...sometimes fog predominated, at other times it was the rain.... Margaret kept saying the sun would come out. Only time she was ever wrong."

But Margaret's refusal to complain about the weather was one of the many things that made her a good hiking companion. She was also quite astute at sensing when tired hikers could be urged a little further. "Oh, it's just around the corner," she'd say in her booming voice, never out of breath. "Where we were going was *always* just around the corner," her companions remembered. Sue Jenkins, a member of Margaret's Thursday Hiking Group and author of *My Feet Hurt & When Can We Hike Again?*, explained that "She touched so many people. She never met a stranger. She could talk to a fence post. She would tell some of the funniest, dumbest jokes!...she said, 'A mama skunk and her babies marched into church and sat down in their own 'pews.' That's a typical Margaret joke."

And sometimes Margaret herself was the punch line for a good, clean joke: she generally put her boots on with a shoehorn, and once after a long hike, was unable to find the shoehorn and had a terrible pain in her foot. With help, she removed her boot only to discover she'd hiked miles with the shoehorn inside her shoe. Everyone had a good laugh at that—two of her problems, solved at once!

Margaret had relished being outdoors as a young girl—she was fond of saying one of her first memories as a small child, born in Kuling, China in 1912, was riding in a sedan chair, "carried on the shoulders of stout coolies" through the mountains overlooking the Yangtze River. Her father Harvey Roys was a physics teacher at the University of Nanking, and a colleague of Pearl S. Buck's husband. The family moved back to the United States in 1921 and Dr. Roys began teaching at the University of Oklahoma. Margaret became an enthusiastic member of the Camp Fire Girls, an organization that encourages young women to acquire outdoor skills. She attended summer camps in Oklahoma and Michigan, and spent a couple of her college summers working as a camp instructor in hiking, outdoor cooking, and tennis.

She graduated Phi Beta Kappa from the University of Oklahoma in 1934, and decided to pursue an advanced degree in social work at the University of Pittsburgh. There, at a church gathering, she met William Robert Stevenson, a student at the Pittsburgh-Xenia Presbyterian Seminary. Three weeks after they met, Bob asked her to marry him. The wedding took place in Pittsburg shortly after he graduated from seminary school, and then they moved to their first church in tiny, remote Zenith, Kansas, in 1936. Margaret loved going with her husband to visit families. Bob would talk with the farmer, while Margaret chatted with his wife, usually in the kitchen, while the woman plucked a freshly killed chicken, baked a cake, and cooked a feast in honor of the pastor. The dust storms were memorable too. The effects of the Dustbowl reached the Kansas wheat fields in the '30s, and she would constantly sweep the pile of dust that snuck in under the crack of the door.

Social pressures in a small town in the 1930s—people expected certain things of a minister's wife—may have frustrated the brilliant, high-achieving young Margaret. She gave up her own studies and began helping with Sunday school instruction; getting a job wasn't socially acceptable. She had begun having intense episodes of lower back pain when she was twenty-three, and as she explained later, "had several periods of difficulty" with her back and other joint pain for the next twenty years.

The Stevensons began to move frequently as Bob pursued graduate studies, church pastorates, and became a Navy chaplain. Margaret raised their children: Judith, who had been born in Zenith; Margaret, born in Ithaca; and Bill, born in Jacksonville, Florida. They were living in Twinsburg, Ohio when Bill started attending elementary school and Margaret found herself with more free time. She began to go for long walks by herself. She later recalled, "I was doing this for pleasure, with no thought of possible physical benefits. I soon realized that I was feeling much better, that my energy output had increased enormously, and that my physical difficulties were disappearing. Also rewarding was a sharpened interest in and identity with nature's gifts…forests, running water, the flowers and birds."

When Bob accepted a position in southwestern North Carolina in 1959, Margaret found kindred spirits in a group called the Trail Trotters, hiking enthusiasts in the little town of Tryon, North Carolina. The Trotters went on frequent day hikes, and also planned longer trips throughout the Great Smoky Mountains, a couple hour's drive to the west. In October 1960, Margaret first set foot on Mount Le Conte. She couldn't possibly have known, but it was the beginning of the 718 total trips up the mountain she would make over the course of her life. "Hiking was her own thing," her daughter Margie recalled. Most of her life had been dictated by the demands of her husband's career, but on the trail, Margaret was fully in charge.

In 1973 when Bob retired, the Stevensons moved to Maryville, Tennessee, in the shadow of Great Smoky Mountains National Park. Margaret decided she would devote herself to hiking and anyone who wanted to come along was welcome. She developed a routine: she'd wake up around four thirty without an alarm clock, eat some homemade granola, and wait for a hiking friend to come pick her up and head to the trail, leaving bright and early. She never locked the front door when she left—after locking herself out once, she decided to ensure that never happened again; what did it matter if thieves took her earthly possessions? (She was never robbed.) She generally liked to be back home by 1 p.m. to listen to the afternoon opera programs on the radio. (In her sixties, she would still hike up Le Conte, relax a bit and visit with the lodge staff, then head back down, covering a minimum of ten strenuous miles in a single day.) Although she could drive and owned a car, she preferred not to; it was understood among her hiking companions that Margaret would work out the logistics of the hike, and catch a ride with one of them, in exchange for planning the excursion.

She hiked with anyone—from earnest Boy Scouts, to tenderfeet in boots squeaking with newness, to Olympic runner and local TV personality Missy Kane. When Margaret was on the trail, she was the leader. And to Margaret, being a leader meant being a thoughtful companion to those hiking with her. "She had that amazing ability to listen, to share burdens, to walk in silence if need be," a friend recalled at her funeral. Hiking with Margaret was occasionally referred to as "Therapy on the Trail." Diana Eriksson, who first heard about Margaret from a friend when she was living in Indiana and later became a regular hiker, remembered, "Margaret's group was supportive. If you were alone or single—if your spouse didn't like hiking or was busy—you had a group to be with." Although Margaret had hiking companions for every day of the week, the "Wednesday Hiking Group" became the most robust and enthusiastic, and continued to flourish even after Margaret passed away. Many people who didn't consider themselves the "outdoors type" were encouraged to walk with the group, and gradually fell in love with hiking.

And together, they had adventures. Once, observing that a couple of the teenagers on a hike seemed bored, Margaret suggested they do a little off-trail exploring and plunged into the woods. "I was terrified," one of her companions recalled, but the boys got a little more interested in what was going on, and in who this crazy white-haired lady was who seemed to be both fearless and inexhaustible. "She's a little bit mother, and when the going gets rough, a little bit drill sergeant," journalist Jon Stiles wrote, "You never doubt she can do what she sets out to do."

Another time the group arrived at Metcalf Bottoms to start a hike and saw some heavy construction equipment near the trailhead. One of the workers warned Margaret that when they came back, the bridge over the river would be gone. "Okay," she said, and didn't hesitate as she led the group up the trail. But sure enough, when they got back hours later, the bridge was gone. They made it over the water by climbing into the mouth of a humungous bulldozer and being ferried across Little River. Another legendary story of Margaret involves a grueling hike up to one of the park fire towers—"and look at the view!" Margaret announced, throwing her arms wide, before she noticed two naked people who clearly hadn't been expecting company.

Margaret also got a good laugh when watching a friend fight a bear for his backpack. He'd been collecting blueberries and blackberries at Spence Field. His pack was still open when a mother bear and two cubs "came through the bushes, grabbed his knapsack and started off with it. Both of us went after the bear…" who defended the backpack and Margaret backed off. "I thought, this is Les's problem," she said. So she watched as Les most foolishly challenged the bear. "The thing he said was he didn't want the bear to get his wallet in his knapsack because it had all his credit cards in it. And he didn't want that bear using his credit cards."

The more she hiked, the stronger she felt and the happier she was. In 1976, she became the first woman to hike all 150 trails in the park. She and Dr. Elgin Kintner, a pathologist at Blount Memorial Hospital in Maryville, began the challenging undertaking in 1973 and averaged 300 miles a year. Some stretches of trail required hiking twenty-five to thirty-five miles in a day. For sustenance on those longer-than-a-marathon hikes, Margaret would make "Citadel Spread": peanut butter, butter, honey, and "all the powdered milk you can get into it," fashioned into patties. The only time she and Elgin sat down on their hikes was to eat: "I think on that thirty mile one… we just ate at lunchtime. We did fifteen miles and ate lunch and then did the other fifteen," she recalled.

Her preference for day trips—which weren't always so brutally long—also made her hiking style more inclusive; her companions didn't need to have special camping equipment to come with her. Comfortable hiking boots were the only requirement. Elgin, in fact, often hiked with an umbrella—to keep both the sun and rain off his face. On one sunny day they passed some hikers who laughed at the old folks with an umbrella—mistaking them for neophytes. But that didn't bother Margaret.

"I have always loved to walk and the process of walking," she told a newspaper reporter. "I don't have to get anywhere." One year, she hiked up to Gregory Bald five times in five days (forty-four miles total). "It was the week of the azaleas, and it was a gorgeous week," she explained. "The weather was gorgeous every single day." As the years passed, she was logging a lot of miles. She famously walked 3,000 miles one year and drove 500. She hiked so much that she developed carpal tunnel syndrome in her right arm from the repetitive motion of swinging her walking stick. And her most frequent destination was the top of Mount Le Conte. She hiked Le Conte so many times that she literally memorized the trail—and it became a source of strength for her to draw from during difficult times. After a multi-hour, post-cataract retina surgery for which she couldn't be completely sedated, she later explained she spent the operation "hiking Le Conte in my mind."

Her favorite route to Le Conte Lodge began along the meandering Boulevard Trail that passed exposed gray rocks of Anakeesta shale, wound beneath the ripe red berries of mountain ash trees in the fall, and offered breathtaking views of countless lower mountains in the Greenbrier section of the national park in all seasons. At the lodge, she would chat with staff and guests, sign the guestbook, and admire the view at Cliff Top. Then she would hike down the Alum Cave Trail, a round-trip of over thirteen miles. Once, she hiked up with Bill Landry—host of a Knoxville TV station's culture segment "The Heartland Series" that ran for over twenty-five years— and a couple of his cameramen. They were having so much fun at the lodge that Margaret forgot to insist they leave in time to make it down the trail before nightfall. The four of them ended up stumbling along in the dark, with the two cameramen steadying Margaret on the rough trail.

As she began to become a local celebrity for her accomplishments, she would sometimes incorporate fundraising into her hikes. On one occasion, nearly fifty people contributed $250 each to the American Lung Association for the fun of hiking with her. When Margaret was preparing for her 200th trip to Le Conte, the newspaper issued an invitation, fitting of her welcoming style of hiking: "Everyone who has ever hiked with her was invited to share the trek." That day, the Alum Cave Trail became the world's most difficult parade route; seventy people hiked "with" her, a crowd full of enthusiasm to be out in the Smokies with Margaret.

On her 80th birthday, she made her 602nd hike up Le Conte. The Maryville *Daily Times* announced "Anyone who would like to try and keep up with the octogenarian should be at Alum Bluff

Trailhead at 8:30 a.m., Saturday. Wear good walking clothes and expect to cover about 2 miles/hour." Yet again, people came out in droves; sixty people showed up to celebrate with her on the top of the mountain.

Margaret recorded every single one of her hundreds of hikes to Le Conte in a journal, notable for its pithy entries that consistently listed who was with her, which of the five trails up Le Conte they hiked, how long it took, and a few brief, important details:

020. July 19, 1973 via Alum Bluff with Lois and Claire Stevenson, my nieces. 9:00 to 11:30 to Cliff Top. Down the same way from 12:30 to 2:30. We met a bear.

025. September 28. 1974 via Alum Bluff to Lodge, Cliff Top, and Myrtle Point with Griff Kinsinger. Beautiful Day!

300. July 18,1987 The most exciting day of my life! About eighty friends went up the Alum Bluff Trail with me to the Lodge for a gourmet luncheon. Some of my family members were along, Margie, Mark, Sarah, Judy, and Virginia. 9.10 to 3. Channel 10 had two television spots on the occasion. Carson Brewer wrote for the Knoxville News Sentinel. Nancy Cain had articles for The Daily Times.

500. October 19. 1991 via Alum Bluff with fifty-five friends. Lunch in dining room. A great day! 8:50 to 3:10.

594. June 14, 1993 via Alum Bluff with Nancy Cain. Hard rain. We had to wade in places. 7:20 to 1:00.

As the decades passed and her reputation grew, she began to slow down a little bit, relying more on her hiking companions for safety in addition to company. Hikes that had taken her four and a half hours were beginning to stretch to over eight hours. But she kept going, regularly hiking Alum Cave Trail to the top of Le Conte, a tough climb even for hikers with younger, stronger legs. Still, she was recognizing that she needed to change her approach to hiking. Her companions would later remember that she "aged gracefully, aware of what she could and could not reasonably do." Her journal entry from 1997 reflects this consciousness in one of her last entries:

> 717. May 5, 1997 Monday sunny and cool 10 miles. Lois Costanza and I hiked the Alum Cave Bluff Trail to LeConte Lodge. Trip 717 for me. It was her first. We met Tom Morgan, Wayne Jones and Ed Wright as they came down the mountain. We talked with Tim Line and Melanie Mansfield at the Lodge, and saw Jeff and the llamas, and Brandon. Workers were putting a new roof on the office building. On the return trip a delightful couple from Switzerland took our picture. Lois was a great help to me. I couldn't have made the trip without her. 8:15 to 4:35.

There was only one other woman besides Margaret who had hiked Mount Le Conte so frequently, and with a similar devotion. Gracie McNicol was the first woman, other than staff at LeConte Lodge, to hike the mountain over two hundred times. Occasionally, Margaret and Gracie stayed at the lodge at the same time, noted in Margaret's hiking journal.

> 128. October 2, 1980 Alum Bluff to Cliff Top with Lynn Lutgens and Myrna Frasier. Met John and Anita Crabtree and Gracie McNicol, who is eighty-nine years old. 9:15 to 3:00.

A few years later Margaret was present at the lodge to celebrate Gracie's ninety-second birthday, writing:

> 187. October 1, 1983 Overnight trip to the Lodge, as a guest, for the celebration of Gracie McNicol's ninety-second birthday. Via Alum Bluff. Trips to Cliff Top and Myrtle Point. I went alone, but walked down with new friends from Spartanburg. Carson Brewer was there. Up 8:20 to 10: 20. Down 9:20 to 11:40.

Alum Cave Trail was the first trail in the Smokies that Gracie McNicol ever set foot on, in 1954, when she was 62. Over the next thirty years, she reached the top of Le Conte 244 times, a record before Margaret broke it. She later told her friend and biographer Emilie Powell, who wrote *Gracie and the Mountain*: "People would say, 'Don't you get tired of going to the same place over and over and seeing the same things?' But I told them that it's different every trip.... Going down Bullhead [trail] on a May day you can see more than 60 wildflowers and trees blooming. On that same trail in August you'd see at least half that number of different flowers in bloom along with mushrooms of many colors, if the humidity is right."

When she stayed overnight at the lodge on Le Conte, Gracie loved waking up before sunrise. She would hike in the dark along a narrow, rocky trail winding through thick myrtle and fir trees, usually alone, until she reached the flat outcropping on the eastern tip of the mountain, called Myrtle Point. Few guests at LeConte Lodge make this journey to see sunrise—the mountain is so high that it's usually chilly in the morning, and it takes a hardy soul to leave the warmth of wool blankets and get back out on the trail before dawn. But Gracie loved to greet the new day as the sun rose brilliant red above the far-off mountain peaks to the east. "Being out on Myrtle Point was a spiritual experience for Gracie," Lisa Line, a LeConte Lodge manager, remembers. "She was nourished by being out in nature."

That Gracie would become something of a celebrity for her dedication to hiking was a miracle in and of itself—or perhaps a combination of miracle and fierceness of will. She was an invalid from her youth into her thirties, and spent much of that time at her parents' house in the flatlands of Lost Springs, Kansas. She recovered briefly in 1924, when she was thirty-two, and entered nursing school. But she became bedridden again at thirty-five suffering complications from a ruptured appendix. Because doctors thought the fresh air would be good for her, she slept on her parents' screened-in porch year-round, even when the temperature dropped below zero. It took her two years to recover, and after being bedridden for so long, she had to relearn how to walk. With great determination and perseverance, she began her career as a nurse when she was forty, working in Dodge City, Kansas; Long Beach, California; and Sitka, Alaska, before arriving in Knoxville, Tennessee where her youngest sister Ruth lived.

Gracie had been an army nurse stationed on the Aleutian Islands during World War II, escaping on the final boat to leave before Japanese occupation. After the war ended, she remained in Alaska, working for seven years as a nurse at the Old Pioneers Home hospital. The Old Pioneers Home was just that, a place for men who'd come to Alaska for the Gold Rush in the late 1890s and hadn't struck it rich. After her hiking partner, a nurse named Carl, moved to Sweden, she couldn't walk alone for fear of bear attacks, and came down with cabin fever. She gave notice and began traveling across the country on a Greyhound bus, visiting friends and family. By the time she reached Knoxville, and her sister Ruth, she was tired of traveling and felt drawn to the lush ruggedness of the Great Smoky Mountains.

A few months after she arrived in Tennessee in 1954, she went on her first hike in the Smokies. She was generally a trim woman, and felt conscious of the weight she'd gained eating good home-cooked meals and spending hours riding on buses. She was eager for some exercise and to learn about the vast number of native plants in the Smokies, her interest in botany inherited from her parents who owned a plant nursery.

Like Margaret Stevenson, Gracie avoided driving, preferring to take the bus or ride with a friend. On this first venture into the mountains, she planned to take part in a guided hike up the Alum Cave Trail. She caught the bus from Knoxville to the national park, over an hour's ride one way. But she missed the stop at the trailhead and only realized her mistake a mile beyond the group's meeting point. Undaunted, she got off, walked back down the road, and found that the group had left without her. So she started up the trail alone, comforted by her knowledge that there were no grizzly bears in the Smokies.

Even as clouds darkened the sky, she felt happy and a sense of belonging. She recalled in a conversation with Emilie Powell, "I guess it was the trees, and plants and flowers…so many…so green and beautiful everywhere you looked from the tiny partridge berry to the giant trees." By the time Gracie reached the Alum Cave Bluff, where the ranger and his group of fifteen hikers had taken shelter, it was pouring. "All I could see was the top of your head, soaking wet, coming up the steps," the ranger later remembered. As they chatted, waiting for the rain to let up before heading back down the trail, the ranger mentioned he was leading an overnight hike to the LeConte Lodge on the mountaintop the next weekend. Gracie asked to join the group.

On June 14, 1954 with twenty-four other people, Gracie hiked to the lodge for an overnight stay. The sense of belonging that she'd felt on the trail was magnified at the lodge itself, with its delightfully Spartan cabins and friendly staff. She loved the colorful wool Hudson Bay blankets on the bunk beds, and the fact that it was chilly enough at night that they were needed, even in summer. It reminded her of Alaska. The camaraderie in the mess hall at dinner and breakfast was another fun part of the trip, as different hiking parties shared large tables and passed food family-style while swapping trail adventure stories. Gracie, with her extensive travel and nursing work, found it easy to talk to almost anyone.

After a few months of staying with Ruth, Gracie decided to end her cross-country pilgrimage and settle in Tennessee. She began to look for work as a nurse. After several rounds of interviews, she was hired in the obstetrics ward at Maryville's Blount Memorial Hospital—the mothers and babies a pleasant change from the old men at Old Pioneer Home. On her days off, she went hiking.

When she was new to the Smokies, she only went on organized outings led by rangers to learn what they knew about the plant and animal life in the mountains, and to study the way they walked the trail. "I could see there was a knack to it," she explains in *Gracie and the Mountain*. "You don't have to have much energy...just relax your whole self and walk in rhythm. When I realized I was tense, I would count 'one-two, one-two' until I got the rhythm." She would often swing her arms vigorously as well, to keep her pace up.

As she became more comfortable with hiking, and more familiar with the biodiversity of the Smokies, she felt that companions on the trail distracted her from savoring her surroundings. "When [I'm] around people, I talk too much and miss too much of nature," she said. To have the best of both worlds, she began hiking up to Le Conte with the ranger-led group, staying overnight, then hiking down alone. The lodge crew eventually got to know the quirky older lady who came so frequently, and she would get up and have breakfast with them before 7 a.m. Sometimes she would even cook breakfast for them and the trail crews.

After breakfast, she'd use the lodge telephone to let Gatlinburg taxi driver Bob Ogle know she was on her way down the trail, then descend the mountain before most other guests were out of bed. She generally chose the seven-mile Bullhead Trail down the northwest side of the mountain. Bob would be waiting for her in Cherokee Orchard just inside the national park boundary, a few miles from Gatlinburg, and would take her to the bus stop.

Through the years, she kept a wildflower notebook, extensively recording the plants she saw on each hike, with the particular trail she was on listed as well. Excerpts were published in the revised edition of Emilie Powell's biography of Gracie, *Gracie and the Mountain*. They reveal Gracie's keen interest in nature.

> *April 14, 1973: saw sunrise at Myrtle Point, day clear and sunny; down Bullhead Trail; dogwood, serviceberry, buckeye...spring beauty, bishop's cap, dutchmans-britches...pink lady's slippers (once counted over 200 in this spot of pine trees, less than half that today)....*

> *May 17, 1973: up by Trillium Gap Trail, weather warm, humid and hazy; dog-hobble, bluets...galax, foamflower, chickweed...; walked down Boulevard Trail with Anita Crabtree finding 179 painted trillium....*

> *September 13, 1973: up Rainbow Falls trail; weather turbulent, rain more than one hour during ride* [on horseback], *strong winds would open "windows" in clouds showing mountains in distance... sand myrtle blooming on spur, grass of Parnassus, red bee balm, yellow jewel weed.*

If there was a plant she couldn't identify with her wildflower book, she would write a letter to the botany department at the University of Tennessee. She was careful to include elevation and location of the plant, in addition to a full physical description. For over twenty years, she kept up a correspondence with personnel at the university.

The experience of being on the trail without human company was transformative for Gracie. She took her time, and relished sightings of birds and other forest critters. "I'd stand perfectly still, and the birds would gradually come to me, sometimes trying to see their reflections in my glasses," she recalled. "I have a pretty good conversation that way when I meet up with chickadees." She had loved watching the black-birds from her parents' porch in Kansas during her bedridden years—her fondness for winged creatures remained, although she delighted in being able to greet them as she too moved along the trail. Juncos, little gray and white birds, would flit from one side of the trail to the other in front of her. Often the strident call of a red squirrel, called "boomers" by locals, would ring out from the treetops. Even without human compa-ny, she was never really alone—and maybe she was less alone.

When Gracie first began regularly hiking to LeConte Lodge, she generally came on Mondays, and hiked back down on Tuesdays. She started hiking up about twice a month, and quickly became friends with all of the lodge staff. At that time, the only other person regular-ly hiking Le Conte was Reverend Rufus Morgan, an Episcopal priest who lived in Franklin, North Carolina, about an hour's drive from the national park. Reverend Morgan was six years older than Gracie, and nearly blind, but parishioners from the Church of St. Francis would accompany him into the Smokies and up the trails. He was affection-ately called "The Moses of the Mountains."

Herrick and Myrtle Brown had taken over running the lodge at the beginning of the 1960 season, and the staff watched as these two old-er, devoted hikers always seemed to miss each other during their pil-grimages. A fun sense of competition began to develop as Gracie and Reverend Morgan realized they were the two people other than lodge staff to have made so many hikes to the top of Le Conte. That year, Gracie climbed the mountain fifty-two times and the Reverend hiked up thirty-nine times—Gracie was sixty-nine and Reverend Morgan was seventy-five.

Gracie couldn't remember what year it happened, but at one point the Reverend hiked up on a Monday, and the two became instant friends, deeply connected by their love of Le Conte, hiking, and strong spiritual convictions. The competition to see who would hike Le Conte the most was friendly, but earnest. They each began writing their total number of hikes up the mountain each time they signed the register; by the end of 1965, Gracie totaled 122, the Reverend sixty-six. Their friendly rivalry would continue for almost the next twenty years.

For her entire working life, whether in California, Alaska, or Tennessee, Gracie had rented furnished rooms near the hospitals where she worked. She acquired no furniture, didn't own a car. Buying a fan for $17 seemed like a luxury purchase to her, although many folks living in un-air-conditioned rooms would have thought it a necessity. "She had a real independent streak," Lisa Line recalled. "She wanted adventure—not to be tied to a hearth." But after two years working at the hospital in Maryville, she wanted a place of her own, finally ready to put down roots. She bought a mobile home in the Shady Grove Trailer Park, a small community nestled between railroad tracks and a small mountain stream. Shady Grove was still within walking distance of the hospital, but with more space in her trailer than rented rooms, she began to acquire potted plants—different kinds of plant specimens soon crowded nearly every surface. She would tend them and listen to the radio when she wasn't out hiking.

Besides being a fearless traveler and mountain climber, Gracie was also an avid river runner. Nearly every summer she signed up for white water rafting trips out West. She found it thrilling: "The rapids will toss you up and then down and then maybe you'll go into a wave and it'll souse you and you'll be soaking wet…only to dry out in the next stretch of smooth water…. Each rapid is different so that you don't know exactly what to expect. The downward draw of the river is irresistible," Gracie explained in *Gracie and the Mountain*. Over the years she rafted down the Colorado River five times (twice in the Grand Canyon), the Green River, and the Salmon River.

Her trip down the Colorado in May 1962, a few months before her 71st birthday, was her last western river trip. She arrived exhausted from working double shifts, covering for a sick coworker for the previous three weeks. But it was her last chance to raft the wild river; by the next summer the construction of Glen Canyon Dam would impact the most scenic 350 miles of the trip. As her boat shot through the Lava Rapids, it hung seven to ten feet above the water, then slammed down. Gracie remembered in her biography, "When we hit, it seemed like a sharp knife was cutting through my back.... The pain was so great I had to lie down flat in the bottom of the boat."

She flew back to Knoxville, where her sister picked her up, and finally went to the hospital three days after the accident. X-rays showed she had broken her back, with fractured and compressed vertebra. She stayed in the hospital for six weeks, lying on a board as her back healed. It was inconceivable that she would be able to keep her tradition of hiking up to Le Conte for her October 1 birthday celebrations, but she vowed she'd be there when she turned seventy-two. Even after she was released from the hospital, she had to wear a brace that ran from her neck to her hips when she wasn't lying down. Slowly, with the encouragement of her dear friend Eula Fry, she began taking slow walks around the trailer park to maintain her sanity, as much as for any physical exercise.

Gracie used up all of her sick leave at Blount Memorial Hospital, and then was put on unpaid leave. She decided it was a sign from God that she should retire. After thirty years of nursing, she had some savings, but her income would largely come from Social Security payments. She lived frugally, keeping a couple of nice dresses for church and buying hiking clothes secondhand. She found ways to reuse a lot of things that came with what she bought—plastic bread bags instead of saran-wrap, for example. Plants and overnight stays at Le Conte were her only indulgences; when she retired, she owned ninety-two plants and had hiked Le Conte 141 times. As her back healed, she once again turned her eyes to the mountains.

By April 1963, eleven months after her final, fateful rafting trip, Gracie was out of her back brace and hiking again. She spent the next four years adventuring on the mountain as if to make up for lost time. Once again she became a devoted bus rider, taking the bus via Knoxville to the Smokies, a sixty-five mile trip. Retirement gave her time to learn more about the plant life in the Smokies and to seek it out as she hiked. She climbed Le Conte two or three times a month, as many times as she could afford to stay overnight. Although reservations for the lodge are generally booked months to a year in advance, the lodge managers, Herrick and Myrtle Brown, knew Gracie well and managed to accommodate her with only a few days notice since she would sleep just about anywhere—including, once, on a cot in the dining room.

But January 1967 added a new physical obstacle to the many she had already overcome. Finishing a Sunday school class at the Tabernacle Baptist Church in Knoxville, Gracie suffered a stroke. She didn't recognize the symptoms, only that she felt "smothery"—and woke up in the hospital in severe pain. The church's assistant pastor and a neighbor took over the main duties of caring for her, running errands and checking in on her at the Shady Grove Trailer Park. "It was the longest February of my life since the two years that I was bedridden," she remembered in her biography.

She forced herself to walk frequently, confined yet again to the trailer park instead of the trail—but getting a few steps further each day. She was trying to recover by April, when spring returns to the mountains in a stunning display of wildflowers. The Wildflower Pilgrimage, a week of hikes and lectures, coincides with the early spring blooms, and Gracie wanted to be healthy enough to participate. She still didn't feel back to normal by the time the Pilgrimage took place that year, but friends drove her into the mountains so she could admire the flowers near parking lots and pull-offs. The Browns, once again taking charge of the lodge, had called her to say they would expect her at some point during the '67 season. Gracie was careful not to over exert herself, but was determined to be there too.

In May she began making shorter hikes up the Alum Cave Bluff Trail. "Having my feet on Le Conte soil was like magic," she told her biographer Emilie Powell, "but I had to stop every ten steps or so to rest." She repeated this pilgrimage to the mountain throughout May, going farther each time, always alone. But in late May, her sister Ruth and a niece, nephew, and four grandnieces and nephews agreed to hike with her. Gracie started before them; the plan was for them to catch up with her eventually. On that hike she made it halfway to Le Conte, despite light rain and stopping to rest every ten feet or so. Eventually her grandnephew Johnny caught up to her—the rest of the family had turned back for shelter when it started to rain. Gracie wrote in her notepad, reflecting on this particular hike, "Breathe on me breath of God. Fill me with life anew that I may love what Thou dost love…and do what Thou wouldst do."

But her doctor, whom she saw the following week, was appalled when she asked him whether she might be fit enough to hike the full five miles to the lodge and back down again. He insisted the exertion would be too dangerous for her. But he also understood what hiking the mountain meant to Gracie, and agreed that she could go if she rode a horse both ways.

And so Gracie made her triumphant return to Le Conte on the back of Ben, a twenty-two year old gelding. Pete McCarter, whose family owned the horse stables that led the Le Conte hikes, got to know Gracie well over the course of many rides. "She was a grand person," he remembers. "A tough one, and she knew what she liked." Gracie would prepare carefully for the horseback ride, using nitro-glycerin cream to boost circulation in her legs, wearing three layers of clothes, and finally, using rubber bands to secure plastic bread bags around her boots and gloves as a final strategy for trapping heat. She always rode next to the horseback guide, in part because the guides liked her company, and in part so they could keep an eye on her. "She could be a little shaky," Pete remembers, "but she was completely fearless." She confessed that she knew it would be a hardship for others if she were to die on the mountain, but there was honestly no place on earth she'd rather be when the Lord called her home.

On her first horseback ride up Le Conte in 1967, the riders wound their way upward via the Rainbow Falls trail, and Gracie rewarded Ben with an apple for his help. "It was just like coming home to see all the staff again," she remembered. She found that she needed a day to rest before continuing down the mountain—two nights at the lodge instead of one—so her trips became more expensive, and therefore less frequent from 1968 to 1972. But she discovered the joys of spending an entire day on Le Conte's summit and was able to explore the top of the mountain in a completely different way than she had before. During her "rest day," she began seeking out and identifying flowers along the mountain top, which she called "gardens," sometimes venturing off-trail to do so. Her favorite garden was about half a mile down the Boulevard trail from where it crests the mountaintop. In summer the trail was lined with Turk's cap lilies, purple monkshoods, coneflowers, cohosh and bee balm. In fall, she took special delight in the goldenrod and asters in bloom.

All her life Gracie felt that God brought people together when they needed each other, often at unexpected times. This belief was reinforced in October 1972 as she was walking down to where the Bullhead and Rainbow Falls trails intersect to see the aftereffects of a landslide. A petite middle-aged woman with neither a pack nor a sweater despite the morning chill, was briskly heading up the mountain. Her name was Anita Crabtree, and she stopped to chat with Gracie about the wildflowers. She would have been happy to talk more, she explained, but she had to keep moving because she didn't have reservations at the lodge and needed to make it back to her car before dark (and her husband was expecting her home for dinner). Gracie had taken an instant liking to Anita and suggested they could bunk together for the night, if the lodge staff did not object. It was the fortuitous beginning of a long, close friendship, extended to Anita's husband John when Gracie eventually met him.

"Anita and John are perfect company," Gracie said to Emilie, "they're interested in the wildflowers too...and we all keep our eyes open. They don't distract me from enjoying nature." She was able to relax on the trail as well, her vulnerability when hiking alone no longer a concern. During 1974, their first season hiking together, Gracie, Anita, and John arrived so often the staff nicknamed them the "Gracie Three." The trio's arrival was a happy occasion for the staff not just because of their company, but because John, a strong, tall man, would bring up treats like fresh avocados and limes, or ice cream (in a cooler packed with dry ice). Since the lodge staff took such good care of them, Gracie Three said, they wanted to give something in return.

While Gracie was struggling to regain hiking health after her stroke, her competitor Rev. Rufus Morgan was steadily gaining on her record of "Most Hikes to Le Conte." On his fifth trip up Le Conte in June 1973, he listed his overall total as 141 hikes. This was verified and recorded in the register: "A total of 141 hikes up the mountain by each competitor." Gracie listed her trips on horseback separately—they didn't count toward her total— but she was getting closer to not needing the horse. On June 2nd she had ridden up, but walked all the way down. Her doctor still worried that the steep climb would be too much for her, but the trip back down was more gentle. By March 1977, Gracie had made 199 trips on foot up the mountain. At that time, only lodge personnel had hiked Le Conte as much as she had.

Her record-making 200th hike took place on July 12 and coincided with the 52nd anniversary of the lodge. John and Anita hiked up with her and presented her with a trophy that read "Champion Hiker;" the lodge staff gave her a leather plaque to commemorate the occasion. The weather gods of the Smokies, fickle at best, also granted Gracie a spectacularly beautiful sunset from Cliff Top that evening. As she sat on the worn shale outcropping, surrounded by friends and the beauty of God's creation, Gracie thought of all her blessings. 1977 was a poignant year: it was also the year that Reverend Morgan stopped hiking, when he was 92. Gracie vowed that she too would be hiking the mountain when she was 92; she wanted as many more years to enjoy the magic of Mount Le Conte as God would grant her. "Gracie enjoyed her slice of notoriety, telling people how old she was," Lisa Line remembered. "And she would happily launch into storytelling for a willing audience."

On October 1, 1981, Gracie rode up the mountain to celebrate her ninetieth birthday. The lodge was festive—full of balloons, a cake decorated with mountain ash berries, songs and presents, including new, warm hiking gear for Gracie. "I like excitement and there was excitement to spare," she remembered. But the party was only the beginning of the adventure.

On the way back down, another woman in the caravan of riders and hikers fell off her horse twice. One of the leaders asked Gracie to ride ahead and get help, knowing Gracie's familiarity with the trail. Gracie later reminisced to her friend Emilie Powell, "I thought what a fine way to start my 91st year, riding high and free on the mountain. I was alone and so happy, riding fast on a good horse." It wasn't quite rafting down a wild river, but permission to dig her heels in and urge the horse faster was a thrill. After two and a half miles, she met up with the other stable manager and relayed that the horse train was waiting for him, delayed by an inexperienced rider. The man took Gracie's horse, and she joined John and Anita who'd been waiting for her in the trailhead parking lot. She gave thanks to the Lord for her friends and Le Conte as they drove her home.

The same year Gracie turned ninety, her friend Emilie Powell published a biography about her called *Gracie and the Mountain*. After a chance meeting at the Sugarlands Visitor Center in 1977, they had become great friends. Emilie braved her fear of horses to ride up to Le Conte with Gracie, where she "showed me more on Mount Le Conte than I had ever imagined possible on my previous eight visits there." Emilie taped long interviews with Gracie, and spent hours with her on the phone to write the book. After its publication, Emilie received letters from readers all over the country that exclaimed how inspirational Gracie's story was.

Gracie's ninety-second birthday, October 1, 1983, was her final hike to the top of Le Conte, nearly thirty years after she first climbed off the bus on that auspicious day in 1954. As she had vowed to do, she matched Reverend Morgan's age at his final hike. It was her 244th official visit to the lodge. The staff, and other hikers as well, had come to anticipate October 1 as a day for celebration. Nine couples from Spartanburg, South Carolina serenaded her with kazoos, and friends brought presents and baked a cake. Gracie was overwhelmed. Someone asked her if she needed help, perhaps opening a present, but she said, "Yes, you can help me cry."

No one, not even Gracie, knew that would be her last hike. But over the winter of 1983 into early 1984, she began to have frequent, unpredictable spells of vertigo. Her doctor no longer felt it was safe for her even to ride a horse up the mountain. She could still go out with friends on shorter hikes, but Le Conte always loomed in the distance, so much a part of her life and yet now too high, too remote. When she was ninety-six, she hurt her hip and moved from Shady Grove into a retirement community in Knoxville. Friends from her Le Conte days would stop by to visit and share news of flower blooms, animal sightings, and other happenings at the lodge.

In 1991, Emilie Powell visited her at Oak Ridge Hospital. "I'm climbing Mount Le Conte in my mind this year," Gracie said to her. "I can almost see the red bee balm and turtleheads blooming beside the Bullhead Trail." She had gotten weaker since her hip injury, but she always remained lucid. And on September 10, 1991, Gracie passed away of pneumonia, twenty-two days shy of her 100th birthday.

Her legacy on the mountain remains, through stories and records in the lodge office, and also on the Alum Cave Trail itself. At the halfway point between the trailhead and the top of Mount Le Conte, a sizable outcropping of stone marks the spot where tired hikers get their first glimpse of Le Conte's western peak, Cliff Top. It's known as Gracie's Pulpit, a nod to her strong faith in the Lord, and her enjoyment of His creations in the Smokies. "I always stop there and thank God for creating all this beauty for us humans to enjoy," Gracie once said. "'Peace that passeth all understanding' is possible for me when I sit there viewing the peak, which is sometimes wrapped in wisps of pink to violet mist."

Gracie's ninety-second birthday at Le Conte, her last hike to the top of the mountain, might in retrospect also have been a passing of the torch to Margaret Stevenson. It was Gracie's 244th and final trip, and it was Margaret's 183rd. Margaret's time with the mountain was just beginning. Just under three years later, Margaret tied Gracie's record of 244 trips on March 28, 1986. By July 1987, she had reached the even mark of 300, but didn't slow down.

Nearly ten years and over 400 hikes later, however, Margaret wrote her last entry in her Le Conte hiking journal:

May 28, 1997: Wednesday, rain then clearing 3.0 miles. Bob and Ann Bird, Annabelle Libby, and Lois Costanza canceled our hike on the Middle Prong because of the weather forecast. By 8:30 the rain had stopped. I walked my usual circuit. Wrote letters to Ed Wright, John and Donna Mansfield, the Line family and Judy to say that I have decided that it is too risky for me to take any more trips to Le Conte Lodge. I have no trouble going up the Alum Cave Bluff Trail, but the downhill, even with help, is more difficult..."

She had made 718 official trips to the top of Mount Le Conte, as well as a handful of hikes that weren't recorded in the logbook. Her record-breaking hiking tally was so inspiring that her boots were bronzed and placed in a prominent display shelf in the lodge's main office, along with her hiking journal. Tired day hikers resting before continuing down the mountain can find inspiration in her accomplishment; more frequent visitors to the lodge, some of whom knew Margaret, find comfort in the objects that remind them of her vivacious presence.

After she retired from Le Conte, Margaret could still hike, but not as quickly or as far as she was accustomed to going. Debbie Way began to take charge of organizing the Wednesday Hiking Group, the most popular of Margaret's weekly group hikes. Even though Margaret couldn't walk with them the whole way, she and companion Lois Costanza often tried to meet the groups via shorter trails that intersected with their planned hikes.

After her hip replacement surgery in 1999, even easy mountain terrain began to be challenging. Margaret began to enjoy the mountains by going for drives with friends. She also continued to walk on the gently winding, paved Maryville Greenway a short distance from the center of town. Members of her old hiking group joined her every day of the week, happy to walk with her.

As she began to experience episodes of dementia, she moved to the Asbury Retirement Center in Maryville, but her warm, funny personality from her days as a trail leader never faded. She was always happy to visit with hiking friends, and never tired of hearing about changes, delights, and adventures in the mountains she knew so well.

When Margaret passed away in 2006, many of the people who had hiked with her gave memorial donations to the Friends of the Smokies, a nonprofit that provides support to Great Smoky Mountains National Park. They generously established a fund in Margaret's name worth over $40,000. In 2008, the fund became part of the endowment for Great Smoky Mountains National Park's "Trails Forever" campaign. The fund, now over $80,000, supports trail maintenance—bolstering hiking surfaces to prevent erosion, repairing bridges, removing trees felled by storms, including, most recently, on the Alum Cave Trail to Mount Le Conte. It is a fitting legacy for the first woman to hike all 900 miles of trail in the national park.

Although Gracie and Margaret approached hiking very differently—Margaret, the social counselor; Gracie, the quiet nature enthusiast with a few close friends—Mount Le Conte rejuvenated and inspired them in similar ways. It was part of a life-giving force, a chance to honor God, and a refuge from the monotony of old age. They knew every root, every turn, every view—in every kind of weather, in every season. Mount Le Conte's distinctive peaks, ecology, and views draw thousands of hikers each year. But as with many natural wonders, the beauty can be overwhelming, too much to assimilate in a single hike. This is perhaps what Gracie and Margaret felt more keenly than anyone, understanding John Muir's exhortation, "Climb the mountains and get their good tidings. Nature's peace will flow into you as sunshine flows into trees. The winds will blow their own freshness into you, and the storms their energy, while cares will drop away from you like the leaves of Autumn."

After dinner at the lodge, guests make one final evening pilgrimage to Cliff Top, the mountain's western peak, to watch the sun set behind the countless mountains that stretch to the horizon, all lower than the rocky vantage point on Le Conte. The chill in the air expands rapidly as the sun glows red, turning the mountains purple-grey before it disappears. Some people leave Cliff Top as soon as the sun dips below the highest peaks in the distance, eager to get back to their cabins, take off their hiking boots and relax. But a few linger, waiting for darkness and the vastness of the starry sky above them. Looking out over the mountains as the stars begin to speckle the heavens, tired, aching hikers sit where Margaret and Gracie sat hundreds of times, and feel alive, connected to something larger and more infinite than themselves.

Margaret Stevenson

Gracie McNicol with Marvin McCarter.

Chapter 17

Karen Wade

MY HEART IS FULL OF MEMORIES OF THE PEOPLE I MET IN THE SMOKIES... I'VE SHARED MANY A CUP OF COFFEE WITH OLD-TIMERS, AND THEY ALWAYS MADE ME FEEL LIKE FAMILY.

KAREN WADE · 1942 - PRESENT

—Karen Wade, reflecting on her leadership of Great Smoky Mountains National Park

Karen Wade

When Karen Wade remembers her time as superintendent of Great Smoky Mountains National Park—she was the first woman appointed to lead the park—she describes it as "the highest highs and lowest lows" of her career. Although she is quick to acknowledge collaboration with talented coworkers and community partners for achievements during her tenure from July 1994 to October 1999, it's often said that a national park takes on the style of the superintendent in charge. Her leadership style encouraged creative thinking and initiative which led to significant turning points and accomplishments in the park's long history.

Being superintendent is "like building a wall," says Phil Francis, who served as her deputy superintendent. "At any one park, you see the bricks others have put down before you, and you add your brick to the wall. Well I'd say Karen put a couple of bricks on the wall in the Smokies." From invigorating the park's role in scientific research to asking hard questions about threats to natural resources, she made significant changes to park policies, even when doing so put her at the center of controversy.

Managing Great Smoky Mountains National Park is not for the faint of heart or those without strong convictions. The land itself is one of the most complex, biologically diverse ecosystems in the country—and it is also a recreational resource for over nine million visitors a year. It is an economic driver for twenty-two different border communities, including a Native American reservation. Because it was once privately owned land, resentments and issues like loss of access are still felt keenly by some families—the decades haven't lessened the tensions. And the national park itself is no island—it is vulnerable to impacts from air pollution and non-native forest pests that originate outside its borders.

The Smokies were Karen's fourth superintendent position, and her most highly visible one. She was the first superintendent at Guadalupe National Park, a land of deserts and salt flats punctuated by stark limestone mountains about ninety miles east of El Paso, Texas. From there, she transferred north to be the third superintendent in Alaska's Wrangell-St. Elias National Park, the largest national park in America, a 13 million acre preserve of glaciers, rivers, and soaring peaks in south-central Alaska. She then traded breathtaking open space for Baltimore's Fort McHenry National Monument and Historic Site and Hampton National Historic Site in the mid 1980s. When she was offered the position in the Smokies, she was working as the acting deputy regional director based in Philadelphia—overseeing eighty national parks in thirteen states. In that role, she got to know Roger Kennedy, the Director of the National Park Service, as a friend and mentor. And when Director Kennedy was looking for a new superintendent for Great Smoky Mountains National Park—someone he knew had to be community-oriented and able to handle the pressures that would come with managing the nation's most visited national park—he chose her.

Karen had lived in the Smokies before, in the late 1970s, when she was married to the assistant chief ranger, Bill Wade. He'd been the love of her life but their marriage didn't work, and she had spent the intervening decades raising their two children while building her own park service career. Coming back to the Smokies as superintendent in 1994, she immediately noticed that the park was operating with the same staff numbers and resources as she'd seen in 1978. Her first goal was to better communicate the park's financial stress to the public—"people outside the [Park Service] didn't understand the challenges we had," she recalled.

Unlike most superintendents, Karen had studied business—not resource management—in school. "I had plenty of people around me who understood natural resources," she recalls. But she had managerial skills, wanted to build a rapport with her staff, and knew that it would take a concerted effort on her part to turn the Smokies into a well-maintained, financially stable, flourishing park.

Good processes and procedures were left alone, but nothing was taken as a given—particularly as Karen and her staff began looking to improve the fiscal health of the park. Unlike many Western national parks, the Smokies doesn't have an entrance fee, for a variety of reasons. But even at a time of relative economic prosperity in America, the budget of Great Smoky Mountains National Park was weak. She and Deputy Superintendent Phil Francis knew that if they couldn't find more money, the park would have to start cutting back on its services—maybe some trails wouldn't be maintained, restrooms might be closed, staff reduced—as the number of annual visitors crested towards an all-time high.

Karen had grown up in Cortez, Colorado, the little "gateway town" to Mesa Verde National Park, so she felt at home in Gatlinburg, Tennessee, one of the gateway towns to the national park in the Smokies—she remembers it felt like she was "coming full circle." And she was familiar with the unusual dynamics in such a place, a sense of the symbiotic relationship between national park and gateway city. Her sense was that the financially shaky position she'd found the national park in when she arrived was related to economic and planning woes in the surrounding towns. She began to reach out to community leaders to talk about how this could be improved.

Shortly after she arrived in the Smokies, she set up a meeting with community leader Wilma Maples. Karen had been told that Wilma Maples was "someone to know,"—someone who could help her get things done. So they met at The Gatlinburg Inn, the historic hotel downtown that Wilma ran, and had a great conversation, the first of many. And just before Karen left, Wilma, who'd been a secretary at the national park in her younger years, said, "Karen, I was prepared not to like you. I'm not sure about women taking men's jobs"—but she had reserved judgment until meeting Karen. Once Wilma had taken a shine to Karen, in spite of her earlier misgivings, she became a great, loyal supporter of Karen's outreach efforts. "She made sure I stood up to scrutiny," Karen later remembered. "Male, female—in this position, you just hope you measure up. She made sure I measured up."

The Friends of the Smokies, a nonprofit organization focused on raising money for the park, had been formed in 1993 under previous superintendent Randall Pope. Gary Wade (no relation to Karen) was Chair of the Friends at the time and recalled in a newsletter for the Friends in December 2009, "Upon [Karen's] arrival in Gatlinburg, I asked for her best estimate of what the Park really needed. She answered "about $3 million," which I thought might be doable in time, but she quickly added, "annually!" That got my attention."

The Friends began adding board members to help with fundraising and outreach, and worked hard to get Karen her millions. A couple of years later, they initiated a "Friends of the Smokies" license plate, to date the most popular specialty plate in Tennessee—which helped their fundraising efforts immensely. In addition, the Great Smoky Mountains Natural History Association, a nonprofit partner founded in 1953, stepped up its efforts to improve revenue from bookstores and memberships and to increase its fiscal support of the park.

But fundraising wasn't the only aid Karen had in mind for the park—she wanted to ask more from "all stakeholders." She turned her attention to Gatlinburg, the most visible gateway city to the park. At her request, in 1998, the Sonoran Institute was hired to do a study of community dynamics in Gatlinburg. Researchers concluded that the town was "at a crossroads. Residents and visitors alike frequently express concern over the appearance of the community. Many businesses have experienced flat years, and others have seen declines." The report made several recommendations for strengthening Gatlinburg's reputation as a vacation destination and its partnership with the national park. To implement the change, community leaders started the Gatlinburg Gateway Foundation in 2000, to give momentum to making changes and articulating a clear vision for the town. Through this study and in more subtle ways as well, Karen was instrumental in urging local leaders in Gatlinburg and other towns to think differently about their relationship with the park.

She also created a volunteer coordinator position at the park so that groups who wanted to help the park could be managed efficiently and areas of greatest need could be addressed promptly. One of the more influential groups of recreational users in the national park is the horseback riding enthusiasts. About 530 miles of the park's 800 total miles of trail are open to horseback riding, but along many trails, horse hooves dislodge soft surfaces and accelerate erosion. Horse travel creates more maintenance work for park staff, and impacts the area's ecology in measurable ways. Horseback riders weren't happy when Karen pointed out their intensive use of the trails—but eventually began to see that she had a point, and many became invested in giving either time or money to maintaining their favorite riding trails. Hikers too leave impacts, and Karen met with the leadership of the Smoky Mountain Hiking Club to invigorate their volunteer and trail maintenance commitments. Eight hundred miles is too much for park staff to keep in good shape alone; she made it clear that people for whom the park was a treasured "backyard" would need to help, and that they might even enjoy doing so.

She also worked to bolster the park's relationship with nearby colleges and universities; partnerships between scientific research and national parks were an important part of her vision for the Smokies. She made appointments to speak with department heads and additional faculty, and brought park scientists with her to the University of Tennessee and Western Carolina University. There had always been university-sponsored research in the park, but "the scale changed under Karen," park service biologist Keith Langdon explains. Bolstered by the longtime research partnership fostered by Karen's outreach, the University of Tennessee won a multimillion dollar grant from the National Science Foundation in 2006 to create the National Institute for Mathematical and Biological Synthesis. This innovative center is focused on figuring out how mathematical modeling can enhance biological understanding of species ranges, threats, and the ecology of the national park in a new way.

But Karen's time in the Smokies wasn't all friendly cooperation— the national park is too big, with too many competing interests for even the most talented superintendent to maintain constant peace and tranquility. Shortly after Karen settled into her office in the stone park headquarters building a few miles outside of Gatlinburg, she received a letter from the Eastern Band of the Cherokee Indians about a casino planned for the Qualla Reservation in North Carolina. The reservation borders national park land, and is accessed from the west by Highway 441, which runs through the middle of the national park. Therefore, casino patrons were expected to affect park resources in various ways, and it was up to Karen to ensure the issue was treated carefully and thoughtfully. The tribe wanted a response in two weeks.

Karen responded that it wouldn't be possible to conduct an environmental impact statement (an "EIS" in the jargon), as she was required to do by law, in that short a timespan. This heightened the already tense relationship between the tribe and the National Park Service—in fact, the tribal council accused Karen of deliberately undermining the financial stability of the reservation and demanded her resignation. But Karen's interest was in protecting park resources, and she wanted to understand realistically how they might be affected by a major casino a couple miles from the park boundary. Compared to other EIS reports that can take decades to complete, this one wrapped up in time for the Harrah's Cherokee Casino to open in 1997, only three years after the first request.

Flooding rains during the winter of 1994 triggered another management question that spiraled into a fraught public issue. Rampaging creeks washed out Parson Branch Road, an eight-mile, one-way gravel road that leads from Cades Cove to Highway 129 in Blount County. Under the national park's general management plan, Karen was given the opportunity to consider permanently closing the road to motorized vehicles instead of spending money to reopen and continue to maintain it. The road provides a slow, scenic, backroads experience for motorists, and many county residents were bitterly opposed to closing the route. On the other hand, conservationists saw an opportunity to turn the road into a hiking trail and reduce vehicle impact. Karen at first hoped the discussions around the decision would be thoughtful and polite. She was wrong.

On her way to a public hearing being held at Great Smoky Mountains Institute at Tremont, a small environmental education center nestled into a remote valley in the national park, she turned onto the Institute access road and discovered car after car lining both sides of the roadway. "We had intended to get public input through a structured workshop," Karen remembered. "I just remember thinking, 'so much for that idea. Looks like someone has been stirring the pot.'" The forum attendees were tightly wound and angry, but Karen kept thinking, "Even as stirred up as they were, I still knew it was because they cared and that was the ground we could stand on together. And the solution to keep the road open but maintain its character was that outcome."

This trial by fire in the first year of her superintendency was only the beginning. She soon found herself directing four different EIS reports at the same time—a nearly unheard-of undertaking. In addition to the casino issue, there was the question of what to do about Elkmont, the resort community nestled along the mossy banks of Jakes Creek and the Little River. Through political lobbying, some owners of Elkmont cabins had managed to extend their leases until 1992. The same year that Karen became superintendent, the "Elkmont District"—forty-nine of the seventy-five remaining homes, plus the Appalachian Clubhouse—was listed on the National Register of Historic Places. The designation conferred no legal protection, but added a layer of political wrangling to the already controversial management decisions surrounding the summer cabins. Rather than merely follow the general management plan, Karen asked for an EIS to evaluate seven different alternatives, ranging from no action to complete restoration and preservation. This was still going on when she left in 1999—and would take another decade, under two other superintendents and an interim super, to complete. In 2009, the NPS would commit to restoring the Appalachian Clubhouse and 18 cottages and outbuildings in the Appalachian Club area (which were older and more historically significant) and remove all other structures.

The third EIS took place in Swain County, North Carolina, a remote section of the park where light breezes occasionally ripple the surface of Fontana Lake, which borders the national park on its northern shore. The lake was created by the Tennessee Valley Authority's construction of Fontana Dam in the 1930s. Entire communities were relocated and the main road, Highway 288, disappeared under the water. The county government and people who were relocated were promised (contingent upon funding availability), the construction of a road which would help develop that edge of the park economically, and provide access to the old home sites and cemeteries. A few miles of the promised road were completed, and then construction stopped—earning it the name "The Road to Nowhere." Emotions ran high, with accusations of "broken promises" and repeated lawsuits, but Karen once again asked for options of action to be evaluated. This EIS was resolved long after her term ended, in February 2010, with a monetary settlement to Swain County, in lieu of a road.

Roads and traffic—connected to the worsening air quality in the area—were at the heart of her request for the fourth EIS. She and her deputy superintendent, Phil Francis, decided to consider a regional transportation plan with the national park as the hub of spokes on a wheel. They reached out to metropolitan planning offices as well as state departments of transportation in Tennessee, Georgia, and North Carolina for input on ways to manage the traffic in the national park, specifically on the popular eleven-mile, one-way loop through Cades Cove. Traffic congestion was increasing by 3-4 percent each year, meaning that during the peak of summer and fall leaf color displays in the mountains, the eleven mile loop through Cades Cove would become a parking lot, more congested than rush hour in many metropolitan regions. It could take hours to drive the loop—not because families were enjoying watching deer grazing in open fields or a black bear snoozing in a tree—but simply because the one-way road was gridlocked. The air pollution generated by so many idling automobiles was a concern as well. But to amend the general management plan to accommodate more modern, updated traffic management, Karen needed an EIS. "To look seriously into this problem, we need to consider how the park's traffic problems fit into the transportation system in the two state region," she explained.

Throughout her time running the park, she remained committed to exploring options for long-term management of resources, rather than giving in to pressure from people with vested interest in certain kinds of change or maintaining the status quo. She was also willing to make sure everyone had an opportunity to express their concerns over management of park resources—from Elkmont preservation to the closure of various roads. Instead of deciding herself who should be invited to a meeting, she made sure community forums encouraged a wider range of input, even if what resulted from those meetings ended up making her decisions more difficult and complicated.

Early on in her career, she'd worked for a superintendent who insisted his staff always sit in the same seat at meetings, who color-coded his notes—who, in short, personified a rigid top-down management style that commonly passed for leadership. Karen chose to implement a different kind of approach, informed by Peter Senge's idea of a "learning organization," which is very loosely characterized by teamwork, personal development at all employee levels, and thinking that encourages innovation and creativity to address problems. She concerned herself with high level, high-risk problems, and encouraged subordinates to take problem-solving responsibility for less fraught issues.

She was also committed to good communication, and she and Phil spent long hours in her office agonizing over just the right word choice for a particular letter or memo. Whether she was working on sensitive political issues like the casino in Cherokee or reviewing internal documents, Karen brought an almost obsessive level of attention to the craft of writing. She had an ear for poetry and brought her love of words, of clear and compelling language, to her government memos, policy statements, and speeches. Most government documents will never be page-turners, but why not try to make sure they're at least well-written for the people who have to read and implement them?

Karen also treated both her staff and local community groups as valued team members and friends. On most days, she would take time to write a short, thoughtful note in a birthday card for one of the park staff—everyone received one from her, each year, without fail. "She cared deeply about her staff, but held them accountable," her Deputy Superintendent Phil Francis remembered. She had an open door policy—anyone was welcome to come to her with suggestions, good ideas, or different approaches. What was *not* acceptable was resisting change because "it was the way things had always been done."

Perhaps this was the secret to her success—that even with the moments of argument, harsh words directed at her, petty misunderstandings, and longstanding grudges and hostilities that she'd had no part in creating—she focused on making the most informed decisions about what was best for the national park under her care. She loved the people, culture, music, and beauty of the mountains: "My heart is full of memories of the people I met in the Smokies," she remembers. She shared "many a cup of coffee" with old-timers and always "felt like family." This conviction that she herself was dedicated to what was best for the national park kept her strong and resolved.

Even with the frustrations of slowly turning bureaucratic wheels, with certain groups of people who saw her with a target on her back, and with a handful of hot button issues all bubbling to the surface at the same time, Karen had energy for bold new projects and exciting new programs for the national park.

One of her most joyful moments was beyond her control, beautiful in its simplicity, and a symbol of what she was working to protect for future generations. A razor thin ridge rises up across the valley from Mount Le Conte, so narrow that a circular hole has formed at one end, resembling an eye of a needle. It's called Duck Hawk Ridge, a nod to the local vernacular for peregrine falcon; the hole in the rock was once a favored nesting area. But no nesting falcons had been recorded in the park since the 1940s, despite attempts in the '80s to fledge thirteen captive-raised chicks in the park—a process known as "hacking." And then, in 1997, the unexpected happened: a nesting pair of peregrines was reported at Duck Hawk Ridge. "It was like we were all parents-to-be," Karen remembered—nervous, excited, waiting hopefully.

Every so often, Karen would hike several miles up the steep, rocky Alum Cave Trail to watch the falcons swooping and gliding across the sky. Each time, she'd hope to be there when the hatchlings took their first flight. And she was. "I still keep a photograph taken that day hanging at home," she explains. "The photographer who was there had his photo framed, and it hung in my office the entire time I was in the Smokies." The hope that a lost species could return to the park and thrive resonated deeply with Karen. In 1996, she'd asked for a feasibility study regarding reintroducing Wapiti elk to the park, after more than 170 years of local extinction. The first elk herd wouldn't be reintroduced until a misty morning in the fields of Cataloochee Valley in 2001, but she had set the wheels in motion five years earlier.

1997 was also the beginning of another exciting development in Karen's tenure in the Smokies. Keith Langdon, one of the park biologists, stopped in to see Deputy Superintendent Phil Francis after learning about fascinating research being done in Costa Rica—an inventory of the diversity of life in the tropical rainforest. Keith proposed to do the same thing in the Smokies: a systematic search to catalogue existing species and to search for new ones, with the ultimate goal of indentifying all the species in the park, from bacteria to plants to birds and mammals. This would be a particularly significant undertaking since the national park was already known as one of the most biodiverse places in the United States; it had escaped glaciation during the last Ice Age, becoming a haven for species moving south. Its highest peaks are home to plants also found in Canada; its lower valleys host hundreds of Southern species, some unique to the mountains.

Once Phil was convinced that such a large-scale biological inventory was actually possible, he explained the idea to Karen. She was immediately interested. One of her great friends and mentors, Boyd Evison, who had been superintendent of the Smokies in the late '70s, had instilled in her the conviction that the national parks should contribute to advancement of science. She decided the biodiversity inventory "would be the most perfect thing, thinking back to Boyd's great enthusiasm for science." So she, Phil, and Keith began sending out feelers for support of the project. "We didn't know what would happen if we convened scientists," she remembered. But around Christmas 1997, about 120 scientists from universities and other research institutions and government agencies gathered together in Gatlinburg to discuss undertaking the country's first "All-Taxa Biodiversity Inventory" (ATBI). The inventory's mission was to catalog all of the tens of thousands of species of plants and animals in the national park and expand understanding of ecosystems and genetic diversity. Keith remembers that Karen "gave a welcoming speech, and after that she was bubbling with ideas about how [we] could make things work."

Although Karen had fully given her support, the project wasn't officially sanctioned by the National Park Service until Earth Day 1998. Ultimately, the park service leadership at a national level concluded that the inventory could be seen as an exemplary project that showed changing approaches to managing national parks. For her role in developing the ATBI, considered a model project for how managers of national parks should encourage participation from the outside scientific and educational communities, Karen was awarded the "Superintendent of the Year for Natural Resource Stewardship" in 1998.

Karen immediately knew that they needed to start a nonprofit organization to get the funding they needed for the effort so she helped organize "Discover Life in America," the umbrella organization that facilitated the inventory. And then Karen stepped back and let it grow and flourish. Leadership is also knowing when you've left something in capable hands. "Keith is a magician," Karen remembers, describing how he turned an idea into a significant, successful scientific undertaking. To date, the ATBI has resulted in the discovery of over 950 species "new to science" and over 8,000 species that hadn't been observed in the national park before.

Although groups of scientists regularly take part in formal collecting expeditions throughout the park, citizen involvement is encouraged too. Discoveries sometimes came from unlikely places: a work crew clearing the Appalachian Trail after heavy rains found an eighteen-inch earthworm in the high elevations of the Smokies. They'd seen worms like it before, but this time decided to capture it and bring it down for the scientists to look at. As it turned out, they'd found a species never before recorded—officially "new to science." The worm was passed around the offices, and eventually Phil Francis brought it in to Karen and explained the story. "So I saw that worm as a great thing," Karen remembers. "It made my day."

Stream ecology was another of Karen's priorities—the delicate native brook trout, known as "brookies," had been disappearing from national park streams for decades, displaced by both stream destruction during the logging in the early 1900s and the larger, more aggressive rainbow trout that had been released to enhance recreational fishing. Brook trout restoration work had been going on since 1986, but it was slow, difficult work. It also required partnerships, which pleased Karen—park fisheries staff worked closely with members of other agencies and staff from Trout Unlimited. In particular, she admired the willingness of Trout Unlimited to participate in restoration work without any guarantee that the ban on fishing for brookies—in place since 1976—would ever be lifted. "The importance of science to restoration management is really what was driving them," she remembered. Karen joined one restoration expedition into the North

Carolina backcountry, hiking with a group of fisheries biologists and a couple of Trout Unlimited volunteers. One of the volunteers was a local man who was one of the group designated to haul the fish—essentially wearing a backpack with water and brook trout in it. It was clearly a heavy load, and the hike was long and arduous since brookies prefer high elevation streams.

"I offered to take the guy's pack for a little while," Karen remembered. And he politely refused, explaining that his grandfather had logged these slopes and been partly responsible for the disappearance of the brook trout. He wanted to atone by bringing the fish back to park land, on his back.

Most of Karen's work in the Smokies was rewarding, if occasionally tense and challenging. But her darkest professional times came in the Southern mountains as well. On June 21, 1998, a young ranger named Joseph Kolodski was the first responder to reports of a man with a rifle threatening visitors at Big Witch Gap on the Blue Ridge Parkway. He was ambushed and shot as he stood beside his patrol car. His death weighed heavily on her, and she will never forget the pain and sorrow of his murder, nor the murder of one of the young Student Conservation Association summer employees, who joined the park service after graduating from college, encouraged by Karen and others in the Smokies. He was killed during his first posting at Organ Pipe National Park along the Mexico-Texas border, by drug runners fleeing into the U.S. She still grieves for them. National parks are dangerous places—hikers get lost, animals attack, fierce storms occur unexpectedly—but murders, particularly of park rangers, are rare. Karen's strong friendships with other rangers and citizens in the surrounding community brought her comfort and strength, and helped her continue to guide the national park.

On a seemingly ordinary day in 1999, Karen drove from Gatlinburg through the mountains to North Carolina to give a talk to the Asheville chapter of the Garden Club of America. Finding that the slide projector didn't work, she was forced to talk off the cuff, and found herself inspired to tell the Garden Club members about her grandmother, one of the most influential people in her life. She loved to garden and delighted in thinking about Karen's position in the national parks as being a steward of enormous, wild gardens—and she was very proud. Karen's audience was enchanted by her personal, heartfelt presentation. And when Karen arrived home that evening, she was told that her grandmother had passed away. She found comfort in "having that connection on that day"—a special memory of something inexplicable shared with her grandmother. She tried to always be aware of those kinds of moments of serendipity and inspiration, whether they came as she was writing a memo, giving a speech, or hiking a trail.

One of her most poignant moments of her time in the Smokies took place during a quick hike in the Greenbrier area of the national park, a short drive from her house. As she walked, she noticed an elderly man sitting quietly beside the trail. She smiled at him, as was her friendly way, and he asked if she was interested in seeing something special. "He had no idea who I was," she remembers. "Why would he?" She said, yes, she was interested in seeing something special. He gently pushed away some dried leaves to reveal a little orchid. He explained to her that he'd lived near the park his entire life and found the orchid many years earlier. Every season he hiked the trail to make sure it was still there, and he showed her the index cards he'd been keeping, jotting down bloom dates. "It's the best example of what we want people to feel about a national park and stewardship," she remembers.

Leaving the Smokies was a difficult decision, but when she was offered the Denver-based position of Intermountain Regional Director in 1999, she couldn't say no to the opportunity to return to the West and be closer to her family in Colorado. She would oversee national parks in the eight-state region that runs from the Canadian border to Mexico, and includes Colorado, Utah, Arizona, Montana, New Mexico, Oklahoma, Texas and Wyoming. The region is home to some of the nation's oldest and best-known national parks, including Yellowstone, the Grand Canyon and Mesa Verde. As someone who had always been drawn to the concept of things coming full circle, she thought back to her first job as a radio dispatcher at Mesa Verde and decided it was time to go back to the West. And so, on October 22, 1999, she addressed her friends and coworkers, reading a beautifully crafted reminiscence of all her time in the Smokies, and the past five years of joys and sorrows as superintendent of the park. "Bid me no sad farewells," she said, "Give me no laments or regrets. Just be keepers forever of the shapes and hues and shades and stories that brought me back, have hold of me, and will bring me back once again. In grateful thanks for these times, this day, these years..."

Karen's work in the Smokies built on the projects of superintendents before her, and are part of the complex web of decisions that future superintendents would make. She would be the first to admit that she accomplished nothing by herself, that it was teamwork and partnership that made her time in the Smokies as productive as it was: a time of outreach, inclusion, and new thinking, meant to guide the park toward a more vibrant future—a future that continues to strengthen protection for the park's plants and animals, preserves scenic views and pure mountain streams—and ultimately provides the opportunity for future generations of photographers, writers, singers, hikers, and others to come to the Smokies and experience the mountains in all their glory.

Sources

Chapter 1: Lydia Whaley

Thornborough, Laura. *The Great Smoky Mountains*. University of Tennessee Press, printed with special arrangements with Thomas Y. Crowell Company: NY, 1956.

Spring, Agnes Wright. "Rough Outline of Visit with Aunt Lydia Whaley, May 31, 1924." Whaley Family folder, Archives of Great Smoky Mountains National Park.

Spring, Agnes Wright. "Thirty Years on Little Pigeon," *The Arrow of Pi Beta Phi, December 1941. www.lib.utk.edu/arrowmont*

"Lydia Kear Whaley by Simeon Husky (a grandson)" Whaley Family folder, Archives of Great Smoky Mountains National Park.

News clipping unidentified publication. "Aunt Lydia," Living in Shadow of Le Conte, Typifies Mountains Woman of Earlier Days; Is Bible Student." Whaley Family folder, Archives of Great Smoky Mountains National Park.

Caseantiques.com/2008/05/highlights-and-prices-realized-from-april-19th-2008-auction-in-knoxville

Chapter 2: Lizzie Caldwell

Davis, Hattie Caldwell, *Reflections of Cataloochee Valley and Its Vanished People in the Great Smoky Mountains*, 1999. Used with permission.

Dykeman, Wilma and James Stokely. *Highland Homeland: The People of the Great Smokies*. Division of Publications, The National Park Service, Dept. of the Interior, 1978.

Hattie Caldwell Davis, in discussion with the author, August 2014.

"Cataloochee Valley, Great Smoky Mountains National Park" *youtube.com/user/GreatSmokyMountains*. Published May 30, 2012.

Sources

Chapter 3: Dora Cope

Bush, Florence Cope. *Dorie: Woman of the Mountains*. University of Tennessee Press: Knoxville, 1992.

Walker, Melissa, editor. *Country Women Cope with Hard Times: A Collection of Oral Histories*. Chapter 3: Wilma Katherine Cope Williamson. University of South Carolina Press: Columbia, SC, 2004.

Weals, Vic. *Last Train to Elkmont*. Olden Press: Knoxville, 1991.

Chapter 4: Ella Costner

Costner, Ella. *Barefoot in the Smokies*. Self-published, 1969.

Costner, Ella. *Lamp in the Cabin*. Self-published, 1967.

Costner, Ella. *Love Affair Around the World: Volume 1*. Self-published, 1979.

Costner, Ella. *Love Affair Around the World: Volume 2*. Self-published, 1979.

Costner, Ella. *Song of the Smokies*. Self-published, 1971.

Costner, Ella. *Poems of Paradise*. New York: Carlton Press, 1968.

Ella Costner, interview by Jean and Lee Schilling, National Park Archives, April 15, 1972.

"Poet Laureate of Smokies Dies," *Kingsport Times-News*, July 16, 1982.

Chapter 5: Phyllis Higginbotham and Marjorie Chalmers

Chalmers, Marjorie. *Better I Stay*. Gatlinburg, TN: Crescent Color Printing Company, 1975.

"From Pi Beta Phi to Arrowmont" historical essays. University of Tennessee library. *www.lib.utk.edu/arrowmont/history.htm* Accessed October 2013.

Higginbotham, Phyllis. "Nursing in the Mountains," *The Arrow of Pi Beta Phi*, June 1923. *www.lib.utk.edu/arrowmont*

Higginbotham, Phyllis. "The Jennie Nichol Memorial," *The Arrow of Pi Beta Phi*, June 1922. *www.lib.utk.edu/arrowmont*

Konker, Claudia. "Interpretive outline of Gatlinburg History," unpublished, Archives, Great Smoky Mountains National Park.

McMahon, Carroll. "Evelyn Bishop dedicated her life to Pi Beta Phi School," *The Mountain Press*, November 25, 2012.

Miller, Kate B. "Report of the Chairman of the Settlement School Committee," *The Arrow of Pi Beta Phi*, October 1923. *www.lib.utk.edu/arrowmont*

Sources

"News from Little Pigeon: Nurse Higginbotham," *The Arrow of Pi Beta Phi*, June 1922. *www.lib.utk.edu/arrowmont*

Rugg, Sarah Pomeroy. "Report of the Settlement School Committee," *The Arrow of Pi Beta Phi*, October 1922. *www.lib.utk.edu/arrowmont*

Russell, Helen Moffett. "Settlement School Report," *The Arrow of Pi Beta Phi*, Fall 1960. *www.lib.utk.edu/arrowmont*

Spring, Agnes Wright. "The Settlement School on Little Pigeon," *The Arrow of Pi Beta Phi*, February 1936. www.lib.utk.edu/arrowmont/

Spring, Agnes Wright. "Word Pictures of the Health Center Service," *The Arrow of Pi Beta Phi*, March 1944. *www.lib.utk.edu/arrowmont*

Williams, Theresa. "Chalmers drawn to mountains for teaching," *The Mountain Press*, June 5, 1920

Chapter 6: Hattie Ogle McGiffin

Thomas, Lois Reagan, "A heritage of hard work, property purchase," *Knoxville News Sentinel*, April 29, 2001.

Mary Alice Cox in discussion with the author, May 2014.

Sandy Ogle McKown in discussion with the author, May 2014.

Jim Ogle in discussion with the author, May 2014.

Chapter 7: Ila Hatter

Dickey, Bronwen. "Into the Forest." *Our State Magazine, North Carolina* October 2011. Online at: *www.ourstate.com/joyce-kilmer-memorial-forest/*, accessed December 2014.

Kays, Holly. "Beyond blueberries: Backyard cornucopia revealed at native plants conference." *Smoky Mountain News*, July 30, 2014.

Nordahl, Darrin. *Eating Appalachia*. Chicago: Chicago Review Press, 2015.

"Marie Mellinger." January 14, 2007, posted by fauxtaographer. *thecelebration.blogspot.com/2007/01/marie-mellinger.html*

Ila Hatter in discussion with the author, March 2014, August 2014.

Eileen Wilson, email message to author, June 8, 2014.

www.wildcrafting.com, accessed, October 2014.

Smoky Mountain Field School website: *smfs.utk.edu*, accessed October 2014.

Profile of Ed Clebsch. *www.naeppc.org/08conference/plenary/Clebsch.html*, accessed June 2014.

Sources

Chapter 8: Mayna Avent

Mayna Avent Nance, in discussion with the author, February 2013.

Walter Nance, in discussion with the author, February 2013.

Jim Hoobler, in discussion with the author, March 2013.

Avent, Mayna Treanor, "Poems," unpublished.

Wedding Announcement: "Avent-Treanor" *Nashville American*, 1891.

"Mayna Treanor Avent," *The Nashville Banner*, January 1959.

"Mrs. Frank Avent Dies at Sewanee," *The Tennessean*, January 3, 1959.

National Register of Historic Places, Mayna Treanor Avent Studio, Elkmont, Sevier County, Tennessee. Reference number 93001575.

Ramsay, Paul. "Drifted Morning," unpublished. Used with permission.

Chapter 9: Olive Tilford Dargan

Ackerman, Kathy Cantley. *The Heart of Revolution: The Radical Life and Novels of Olive Dargan*. University of Tennessee Press: Knoxville, 2004.

Dargan, Olive Tilford. *Highland Annals*. Charles Scribner: New York, 1925; republished as *From My Highest Hill*. University of Tennessee Press: Knoxville, 1998.

"Olive Tilford Dargan Letters to William Crary Brownell. 7 January 1909; 19 December 1909; 21 July 1919," in William Crary Brownell Papers (Box 1, Folder 6), Archives and Special Collections, Amherst College Library.

Olive Tilford Dargan. Letters to Alice Stone Blackwell. N.d. May 1906; 30 July 1907; 28 April 1908. Olive Tilford Dargan Papers. bMS Am 1807.4 (26). Houghton Library, Harvard University, Cambridge.

Olive Tilford Dargan. Letters to Alice Stone Blackwell. 7 April 1916. Records of the National Woman Suffrage Association. Library of Congress, Washington.

Olive Tilford Dargan. Letters to Grant C. Knight. 10 June 1955. Knight papers, 1924-1955, 1M50M9, 1M64M77, 1M73M26, AAM7600LM, Special Collections, University of Kentucky.

Olive Tilford Dargan. Letters to Rose Pastor Stokes. 16 April 1929. Olive Tilford Dargan Letters (Tamiment Coll. #110). Tamiment Institute Library, New York University.

Dargan, Olive Tilford. *Highland Annals*. Charles Scribner's Sons: New York, 1925.

Johnson, E.D. *Dargan, Olive Tilford*. Dictionary of North Carolina Biography, 6 volumes, edited by William S. Powell. Copyright ©1979-1996 by the *University of North Carolina Press*, ncpedia.org/biography/dargan-olive, accessed September 2014.

Sources

Powell, William S., ed. Dictionary of North Carolina Biography, 6 volumes. University of North Carolina Press: Durham, 1979-1996.

Stewart, Gaither. When the revolution comes: The historic Gastonia textile mill strikes are not forgotten. Posted August 17, 2011; *www.intrepidreport.com/archives/2909#sthash.rT4Kh1c1.dpuf*, accessed October 2014.

Dargan, Olive Tilford. North Carolina Literary Hall of Fame: *www.nclhof.org/inductees/2000-2/olive-tilford-dargan/*, accessed October 2013.

"'Call Home the Heart' and other works of Fiction" Book Review, *The New York Times*, February 28, 1932.

Chapter 10: Lottie Stamper

Blankenship, Mollie and Stephen Richmond, Contemporary Artists and Craftsmen of the Eastern Band of Cherokee Indians: Promotional Exhibits, 1969-1985 (Cherokee, NC: Qualla Arts and Crafts Mutual, Inc.) 1987; quoted at *www.wcu.edu/library/DigitalCollections/CherokeeTraditions*

Bookout, Tommy Jo. *Traditional Basketmakers in the Southeastern and South Central United States* (Ann Arbor: UMI, 1987); quoted at *www.wcu.edu/library/DigitalCollections/CherokeeTraditions/People/Baskets_LottieStamper.html*

Braund, Kathryn E. Holland, editor; James Adair, author; *The History of the American Indians. Tuscaloosa*: The University of Alabama Press, 2009.

Cherokee Traditions: A project of Hunter Library Digital Initiatives at Western Carolina University, Qualla Arts and Crafts Mutual, and the Museum of the Cherokee Indian: *www.wcu.edu/library/DigitalCollections/CherokeeTraditions*

www.wcu.edu/library/digitalcollections/cherokeetraditions/People/Baskets_LottieStamper.html and *http://www.wcu.edu/library/digitalcollections/cherokeetraditions/People/Baskets_Youngbirds.html*

Dupuy, Edward and Clifford Hotchkiss interview with Lottie Stamper, 1965. Quoted with permission of Hunter Library Digital Collections at Western Carolina University.

Dupuy, Edward and Emma Weaver, Artisans of the Appalachians. Asheville: The Miller Printing Company, 1967.

French, Laurence and Jim Hornbuckle, editors. *The Cherokee Perspective*. Boone, NC: The Appalachian Consortium Press, 1981.

Hill, Sarah H. *Weaving New Worlds: Southeastern Cherokee Women and their Basketry*. Raleigh: The University of North Carolina Press, 1997.

Hill, Sarah H., "Chapter 7: Marketing Traditions: Cherokee Basketry and Tourist Economies" in *Selling the Indian: Commercializing & Appropriating American Indian Cultures* edited by Carter Jones Meyer, Diana Royer. Tucson: The University of Arizona Press, 2001.

Sources

Mooney, James. *Myths of the Cherokee*. Fairview, North Carolina: Bright Mountain Books, 1992.

Power, Susan. *Art of the Cherokee: Prehistory to the Present*. Athens: The University of Georgia Press, 2007.

Chapter 11: Wilma Dykeman

Ballard, Sandra. "Wilma Dykeman: An Interview." *Now and Then*; v6 n2 sum 1989: 18-23. *http://files.eric.ed.gov/fulltext/ED313194.pdf* Accessed March 2014.

Dykeman, Wilma. *The French Broad*. New York: Rinehart: 1955, 1974; Knoxville: University of Tennessee Press, 1955, 1965; Newport, TN: Wakestone, 1992.

Dykeman, Wilma and James Stokely. *Neither Black Nor White*. New York: Rinehart, 1957.

Dykeman, Wilma. *The Tall Woman*. New York: Holt, Rinehart, and Winston, 1962.

-. *The Far Family*. New York: Holt, Rinehart, and Winston, 1966; New York: Avon, 1967; Newport, TN: Wakestone, 1988.

-. *Look to this Day*. Newport, TN: Wakestone Books, 1968.

-. *Explorations*. Newport, TN: Wakestone Books,1984.

-. "The Rooted Heart and the Raging Intellect: A Conversation." The Iron Mountain Review 5.1 (Spring 2007): 8-13. Interview conducted by Richard Marius at the Wilma Dykeman Literary Festival, Emory and Henry College. 10 Mar. 1989.

James Stokely, email message to author, February 27, 2014.

Wilma Dykeman entry, *www.SmokyKin.com www.smokykin.com/tng/getperson. php?personID=191751*

"Dykeman Honored For Literary Contribution" *The Newport Plain Talk*, 16 Nov 2006. Accessed online: *www.newportplaintalk.com*

"Renowned Appalachian author Wilma Dykeman dies," *The Daily Times (Blount County, Tennessee)*, 24 Dec 2006. Accessed online: *www.thedailytimes.com*

"Dykeman lived her life for 'mighty' purposes," *Citizen-Times (Asheville)*, 24 Dec 2006.

"Appalachian writer Dykeman dies," *The Newport Plain Talk*, 26 Dec 2006.

"Wilma Dykeman Eulogized," *The Newport Plain Talk*, 31 Dec 2006.

"Southerner on the Grow: Wilma Dykeman—She Casts A Tall Shadow." *Southern Living* 1.5 (June 1966): 74

Sources

Chapter 12: Amanda Swimmer

Collins, Kaye Carver, Angie Cheek, and former Foxfire Students, eds. *Foxfire 12: War Stories, Cherokee Traditions, Summer Camps, Square Dancing, Crafts, and More Affairs of Plain Living*. New York: Anchor Books, 2004.

Fariello, M. Anna. *Cherokee Pottery: From the Hands of Our Elders*. Charleston, SC: The History Press, 2011.

Three Cultures of Appalachia: Women of these Hills/ a living documentary. T.Hop/Suttlefilm. 2002. Posted at: *nativeheritageproject.com/2013/05/20/women-of-these-hills-amanda-swimmer-cherokee* Accessed October 2014.

"Mandy Swimmer," The Heartland Series WBIR-TV, Volume XVI. Episode 5.

Amanda Swimmer, in discussion with the author, Ila Hatter, and Jerry Coleman, June 2011.

Amanda Swimmer, interviewed by Jerry Coleman and Ila Hatter, October 23, 1992.

"Swimmer, Amanda." *Traditional Artist Directory, Blue Ridge National Heritage Area*. 2011. Posted at: *www.blueridgeheritage.com/traditional-artist-directory/amanda-swimmer* Accessed October 2014.

Chapter 13: Dolly Parton

Parton, Dolly. *Dolly: My Life and Other Unfinished Business*. New York: Harper-Collins, 1994.

-. *Dream More*. New York: GP Putnams Sons, 2012.

Oermann, Robert K. *From America's Music: The Roots of Country*. Nashville: Turner Publishing, 1996.

Nash, Alanna. *Dolly: The Biography (Updated Edition)*. New York: Cooper Square Press, 2002.

McClatchy, Debby. "Appalachian Traditional Music." *The Magazine for Traditional Music*. June 27, 2000. Posted at: *www.mustrad.org.uk/articles/appalach.htm* accessed November 2014.

Olson, Ted. "Music: Overview". *Encyclopedia of Appalachia*. Posted online *encyclopediaofappalachia.com/category.php?rec=53* Accessed April 2014.

Dolly Parton, in discussion with the author, May 2014.

Ted Miller, in discussion with the author, May 2014.

American Eagle Foundation *www.eagles.org*

Dollywood Foundation and Imagination Library *www.imaginationlibrary.com*

"Park Announces Dolly Parton as 75th Anniversary Ambassador" NPS press release, October 2, 2008.

Sources

Chapter 14: Laura Thornburgh

Thornborough, Laura, *The Great Smoky Mountains*. The University of Tennessee Press, via special arrangement with Thomas Y. Crowell Company, New York, 1956.

Thornburgh, Laura, diary 1902-1917, unpublished. Used with permission from James Thornburgh.

Thornburgh, Laura. "Smoky Trails Work Goes On; Two Now Open," *Sunday Journal January 22, 1933*. Laura Thornburgh Collection, MS.0195. University of Tennessee Libraries, Knoxville, Special Collections.

Thornburgh, Laura. "Mountain Folk Read Eagerly in Tiny Gatlinburg Library," *Maryville Journal*, November 6, 1932. Laura Thornburgh Collection, MS.0195. University of Tennessee Libraries, Knoxville, Special Collections.

"Favorite Recipes: Guest is always right is rule for seasoning at Thornburgh Cottage." *Knoxville News-Sentinel*. April 15, 1938. Laura Thornburgh Collection, MS.0195. University of Tennessee Libraries, Knoxville, Special Collections.

"The Great Smoky Mountains by Laura Thornborough," *The New York Times Book Review*, April 18, 1937. Laura Thornburgh Collection, MS.0195. University of Tennessee Libraries, Knoxville, Special Collections.

Govan, Christine Noble. "The Voice of the Great Smokies," *The Chattanooga News*, April 6, 1938. Laura Thornburgh Collection, MS.0195. University of Tennessee Libraries, Knoxville, Special Collections.

Thornburgh, Laura. "Books that have influenced me." *Knoxville News-Sentinel*, April 21, 1940. Laura Thornburgh Collection, MS.0195. University of Tennessee Libraries, Knoxville, Special Collections.

Smoky Mountain Hiking Club History. Posted online: *www.smhclub.org/Diamond/diamond1.htm*. Accessed March 2014.

James Thornburgh, in discussion with the author, March 2011.

Chapter 15: Anne Broome

Brill, David. "The Save Our Smokies Hike" *Smokies Life Magazine #9*. 2011.

Bill and Marian Broome in discussion with the author, April 2013.

Bill and Alice Hart in discussion with the author, March 2014.

Anne Broome Memorial Service transcript, October 16, 1983.

Dan MacDonald, email messages to author, February 2013.

William Skelton, email messages to author, March 2013.

Anne Broome letter to Woody Brinegar, June 16, 1975. Harvey Broome Papers, C.M. McClung Historical Collection, Knoxville (H.C. Brinegar file).

Scot Danforth, email messages to author, February 2013.

Sources

Chapter 16: Margaret Stevenson and Gracie McNicol

Brewer, Carson. *A Wonderment of Mountains*. Knoxville: University of Tennessee Press, 2003, updated.

Powell, Emilie Ervin. *Gracie and the Mountain*. The Overmountain Press: Johnson City, TN 1996, revised edition.

Lisa Line in discussion with the author, August 2014.

Pete McCarter in discussion with the author, November 2014.

Annette Hartigan in discussion with the author, August 2011.

Margaret Ribble in discussion with the author, August 2013.

Ellie Doughty in discussion with the author, August 2013.

Lois Costanza in discussion with the author, August 2013.

Diana Eriksson in discussion with the author, August 2013.

Emily Anderson, pastor of New Providence Church, Meditation, Margaret Stevenson funeral service, October 9, 2006.

Stevenson, Margaret, personal recollections, unpublished. Used with permission from Margie Ribble.

Margaret Stevenson, interviewed by Nancy Cain. Unpublished transcripts, used with permission.

Margaret Stevenson's hiking journal, posted online by Ed Wright: *www.mtleconte. com/msleconte.htm* Accessed October 2013.

For information on Trails Forever Margaret Stevenson Fund: *smokiestrailsforever. org/Pathfinders.aspx*

Albert, Linda Braden. "Jenkins pens second book on hiking adventures in Smokies." *The Daily Times* January 22, 2011. Accessed online *www.thedailytimes. com/community/jenkins-pens-second-book-on-hiking-adventures-in-smokies/article_60c-5be59-bb20-5b5a-91a4-fb9d6e9f7657.html?mode=jqm* Accessed December 2014.

Chapter 17: Karen Wade

Karen Wade in discussion with the author, January 2014.

Phil Francis in discussion with the author, January 2014.

Keith Langdon in discussion with the author, January 2014.

"Smokies Superintendent Karen Wade Named to Head National Park Service's Intermountain Region," NPS press release, October 5, 1999.

Sonoran Institute report, November 1998.

Sources

Schell, Carroll J. and Karen P. Wade. "A New Perspective in Strategic Planning: The Great Smoky Mountains Experience." Accessed online: *www.georgewright. org/134schell.pdf* March 2014.

Wade, Gary. "Original Perspectives: Friends of the Smokies News & Views," Winter 2009. Accessed online: *www.friendsofthesmokies.org/pdf/97656_MiniNews.pdf*

Wade, Karen "A Superintendent Speaks Out on the Value of Inventory and Monitoring," Park Science, February 1999, Volume 19, No. Accessed online: *archive.org/ stream/parkscience1921nati/parkscience1921nati_djvu.txt* November 2014.

Oakley, Christopher Arris. "Indian Gaming and the Eastern Band of Cherokee Indians" *North Carolina Historical Review*, Volume LXXVIII, Number 2, April 2001. Accessed online: *nehsouthernindians.web.unc.edu/files/2011/05/6665316.pdf*, March 2014.

Acknowledgments

This book wouldn't exist without the support of my editor, Steve Kemp, who saw the potential in a couple of disconnected magazine articles to become something more. My great thanks to you for sticking with me even as the chapters and pages multiplied far beyond what either of us initially envisioned. Your encouragement and advice were always helpful—even when (especially when) it was to step away from the computer and go for a walk.

Thank you to Lisa Horstman for her beautiful illustrations in each chapter. Her art enlivens the text and celebrates the spirit of each woman, giving the book a depth of character that words alone cannot.

Some parts of this book were incredibly research-heavy, with chapters knit together from obscure sources that likely only reside in one place: the Great Smoky Mountains National Park archives, a treasure-trove in the basement of the Sugarlands Visitor Center. For advice, and guidance navigating myriad resources, I am indebted to the GSMNP librarian-archivists Annette Hartigan and Michael Aday.

I also can't say enough good things about the University of Tennessee-Knoxville's digitization of the Pi Beta Phi newsletters and other information about the early days of the settlement school, "From Pi Beta Phi to Arrowmont." I despaired of writing anything about Phyllis Higginbotham until I found the digital collections online. The same can be said for Anna Fariello's work at Western Carolina University—the resources about Lottie Stamper and other Cherokee artists are unparalleled. Thanks also to Kent Cave, who has a breadth of knowledge about local people and places that is, as best I know, unmatched. Bill and Alice Hart also offered research help, suggestions, and support whenever I asked for it. You are both truly Smoky Mountain scholars, and I enjoy every conversation.

Florence Cope Bush, author of *Dorie: Woman of the Mountains* wrote a perfect book about her mother's life as logging changed the Smokies. It's rare to find a book that's both wonderful research material and a very enjoyable read. My great thanks to Hattie Caldwell Davis as well, for so thoroughly recording life in Cataloochee when

Acknowledgments

the old timers were still alive. My copy of *Reflections of Cataloochee Valley and Its Vanished People in the Great Smoky Mountains* is dog-eared, underlined, and well loved. I'm one of many writers who has benefitted from your foresight. A third, critically important book to my work was written by Emilie Ervin Powell. *Gracie and the Mountain* is a tribute to Grace McNicol, and inspired me to add her to my own anthology of women of the Smokies. Lisa Line and Pete McCarter also told wonderful stories of Gracie and Mount Le Conte.

Thank you to Ted Miller for completely stunning me by working me into the lineup of international journalists scheduled to interview Dolly, and offering helpful comments and corrections. I owe Dolly Parton herself great thanks for being so friendly and gracious—and patient with my surface-level understanding of Appalachian music. I can't say enough good things about everyone at the Dollywood Foundation, in fact, particularly Mary Lyda Wellons for being so supportive, thoughtful, and generous at every point in my research.

I would also like to thank all the family members and friends of the women in this book who generously shared their time, photographs, and memories with me. Detail is the trick to making nonfiction come alive, and few institutional sources can shed light on a person like family members can.

Many thanks to Jim Dykeman Stokely for gamely answering my questions and for offering wonderful suggestions for the chapter. You have your mother's sense of storytelling and eye for detail. Wilma felt like a kindred spirit to me. Thank you to Mary Alice Cox, Jim Ogle, and Sandy McKown for a lovely evening of reminiscing. I look at Gatlinburg differently now that I know more about Hattie Ogle McGiffin. And many thanks to Lee Shilling, for his generous permission to quote from Ella Costner's books, and insight into her larger-than-life personality.

My correspondence with Walter and Mayna Avent Nance began from an email address scrawled on a guest book in the Avent Cabin, and has turned into a long-standing friendship. Thanks for making me always feel welcome in Sewanee, and your generosity with Mayna's scrapbooks, art, and photographs. I look forward to the year we finally get to hike to the cabin together.

James Thornburgh, too, welcomed me into his Aunt Laura's wonderful cabin in Gatlinburg, and has provided unending enthusiasm for my writing since the *Smokies Life* article in 2011. I am honored that you shared Laura's diary with me, and many other special memories.

Ila Hatter has been a friend and inspiration for many years. It was delightful to have an excuse to find out more about you—and thank you for being so honest about your life. Thank you to Jerry Coleman also for constant encouragement and enthusiasm.

Acknowledgments

Writing about Margaret Stevenson was also a wonderful reason to be back in touch with Margie Ribble, who was incredibly generous and honest with information about her mother. Thank you also for your unconditional support of the book, and my writing. To Nancy Cain as well, who entrusted me with her priceless, detailed interviews with Margaret.

Thanks to Bill and Marian Broome for stories and coffee cake, and generously sharing Anne's journals with me. Anne was one of the more elusive women to research, but Dan MacDonald, Will Skelton, and others of the Smoky Mountain Hiking Club—which seemed to be an extension of Anne and Harvey's family at times—helped fill in important details.

I confess that when it was suggested that I write about the first female superintendent of GSMNP, I was concerned I'd end up with a string of bureaucratic checklists. Karen Wade is exactly the opposite: inspiring, thoughtful, poetic, and truly a woman whose great vision and convictions have been a boon to the national park. My thanks to her for taking the time to speak with me, as well to Phil Francis, Keith Langdon and other National Park Service and Gatlinburg friends for sharing stories about Karen.

And finally, many hugs and thanks to my own family and friends. As with any multi-year undertaking, momentum ebbs and flows. I give thanks for everyone who listened supportively to my stories about writing triumphs and travails. Thank you to Chris, for patience and understanding when it seemed like I was spending more time with my computer than anyone or anything else, and for making space on our bookshelves for my ever-growing library on Smoky Mountain people, places, and things. You may not have realized what you were getting into when you agreed to offer comments on the manuscript, but the book is much better for your thoughtfulness, and refusal to let me be lazy with my prose.

Most of all, thank you to my parents, who introduced me to great books and fully expected that I would write one myself, and who moved me to the mountains. I couldn't have written this book without you both, and I love you very much.

Recommended Reading

For more detailed accounts of women profiled in this book:

Bush, Florence Cope. *Dorie: Woman of the Mountains.* University of Tennessee Press: Knoxville. 1992.

Powell, Emilie Ervin. *Gracie and the Mountain.* The Overmountain Press: Johnson City, TN. 1996, revised edition.

Chalmers, Marjorie. *Better I Stay.* Gatlinburg, TN: Crescent Color Printing Company, 1975.

Ackerman, Kathy Cantley. *The Heart of Revolution: The Radical Life and Novels of Olive Dargan.* University of Tennessee Press: Knoxville, 2004.

Parton, Dolly. *Dolly: My Life and Other Unfinished Business.* New York: Harper-Collins, 1994.

For first-hand writing by authors profiled in this book:

Costner, Ella. Several selections of poetry about the mountains: *Barefoot in the Smokies.* Self-published, 1969; *Lamp in the Cabin.* Self-published, 1967; *Song of the Smokies.* Self-published, 1971.

Dargan, Olive Tilford. *From My Highest Hill: Carolina Mountain Folks.* University of Tennessee Press, subsequent edition: Knoxville. 1998. (Originally titled *Highland Annals,* published by C. Scribner, 1925.)

Dykeman, Wilma. Any of her books are wonderful, but I particularly recommend these two: *The Tall Woman.* New York: Holt, Rinehart, and Winston, 1962; *Look to this Day.* Newport, TN: Wakestone Books, 1968.

Thornborough, Laura. *The Great Smoky Mountains.* University of Tennessee Press, printed with special arrangements with Thomas Y. Crowell Company: NY, 1956.

For more about the Smokies, with a particular connection to women profiled in this book:

Fariello, M. Anna, *Cherokee Basketry: From the Hands of Our Elders.* Charleston, SC: The History Press, 2009; *Cherokee Pottery: From the Hands of Our Elders.* Charleston, SC: The History Press, 2011.

Gillespie, Michele and Sally G. McMillen. *North Carolina Women: Their Lives and Times (Southern Women: Their Lives and Times Series)*. University of Georgia Press, 2015.

Davis, Hattie Caldwell, *Reflections of Cataloochee Valley and Its Vanished People in the Great Smoky Mountains*. Self-published, 1999.

Broome, Harvey. *Out Under the Sky of the Great Smokies: A Personal Journal*. Knoxville: University of Tennessee Press, 2001.

Maddox, Marie. *A Lifetime in Gatlinburg: Martha Cole Whaley Remembers*. Charleston, SC: The History Press, 2014.

Recommended Listening

Butterfly Rose, "Women of the Smokies": 10 delightful songs about Smokies women, many of whom are included in this book.

Dolly Parton, "Little Sparrow": showcases Dolly's love of traditional Appalachian music.

A Note to the Reader: Some of these books were self-published, and some are out of print. I've found third party vendors on amazon.com and libraries to be helpful resources in tracking them down. Rest assured that they are worth the effort! Additionally, the "Sources" section contains a more complete list of books and other resources about these women. Happy Reading!

Index

Index

Index

Index

Index

Index

Index

About the Author

Courtney Lix grew up in the Great Smoky Mountains. She is the author of Frequently Asked Questions about Smoky Mountain Black Bears, *and is a regular contributor to* Smokies Life Magazine. *Her writing awards include the Ferris Prize for Journalism from Princeton University, the Gregory T. Pope Prize for Science Writing, and recognition of* FAQ Bears *as the best general interest publication by the Association of Partners for Public Lands in 2011. She lives in Washington, D.C., but returns to the Smokies as often as possible.*